Brooklyn!

In the series
Critical Perspectives on the Past
edited by Susan Porter Benson,
Stephen Brier, and Roy Rosenzweig

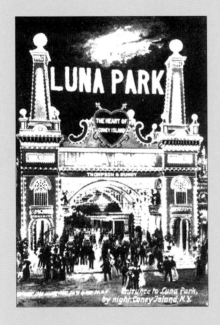

Brooklyn!

An Illustrated History

by
Ellen M. Snyder-Grenier
for The Brooklyn Historical Society

TEMPLE UNIVERSITY PRESS
Philadelphia

Temple University Press, Philadelphia 19122

Copyright © 1996 by Temple University

All rights reserved

Published 1996

Printed in Canada

This book is printed on acid-free paper for greater longevity

Text design by Eliz. Anne O'Donnell

Library of Congress Cataloging-in-Publication Data

Snyder-Grenier, Ellen M.
    Brooklyn! : an illustrated history / by Ellen M. Snyder-Grenier for
The Brooklyn Historical Society.
      p. cm.
    Includes bibliographical references and index.
    ISBN 1-56639-408-2 (cloth : alk. paper)
    1. Brooklyn (New York, N.Y.)—History—Pictorial works. 2. New
York (N.Y.)—History—Pictorial works.   I. Brooklyn Historical
Society (Brooklyn, New York, N.Y.)   II. Title.
F129.B7S69   1996
974.7'23—dc20   96–10169

Contents

Foreword

Brooklyn looms large in the imagination, but its long history seems difficult to capture. Until now. Through images and words, *Brooklyn! An Illustrated History* presents over 300 years of the community's history—from the time when it was occupied by Native Americans to today, when it is home to 2.3 million people from all over the world. But this is not one of those dry accounts of impersonal historical forces. Much of Brooklyn's story is told in terms of the people who shaped the neighborhoods, ran the homes and businesses, worked in the factories, and made things happen by pursuing a better life for themselves and their families.

Page after page of wonderful illustrations show the people, places, and events that made Brooklyn what it is: a painting of an old Dutch home in Gravesend and a portrait of an eighteenth-century colonist; photos of Jewish and Italian immigrants who arrived at the turn of the century and African Americans who migrated north a few decades later; a rendering of a grand fireworks display on the evening of the Brooklyn Bridge's dedication in 1883; a base from Ebbets Field; photos of the West Indian Carnival on Eastern Parkway. There are personal accounts from Navy Yard workers during World War II and recent arrivals like a Puerto Rican family building a new life in Brooklyn. Some of these things are familiar but, brought together in this comprehensive history, they help me to understand how Brooklyn has changed and what various groups and individuals have contributed toward its development.

Only The Brooklyn Historical Society could have woven together these compelling stories and wonderfully varied illustrations. The Society not only houses what is indisputably the finest collection of Brooklyn-related material, but it also is now recognized as one of the preeminent history institutions in the United States. This book, as well as ongoing research for exhibitions and public programs, reflects the Society's commitment to helping Brooklyn's residents connect at many levels with their history. It is because the Society never loses sight of that important connection between people and history that this story is so compelling; there is something for everyone here, for real Brooklynites and for more distant admirers.

My connection is personal. My family roots are deep in Brooklyn's past. In the 1860s one of my ancestors, Father Joseph Fransioli, established St. Peter's Hospital on Henry Street and the organization that today is known as the Brooklyn Bureau of Community Service, among other institutions. My grandfather, Charles M. Higgins, was born in Ireland in 1856 and came to Brooklyn as a child. Once he had invented Higgins India Ink, he started his business in South Brooklyn; his ink-producing plant made his fortune. *Brooklyn! An Illustrated History* doesn't tell the stories of these men in my family, but it tells about others like them and helps me to understand how my family's history is intertwined with Brooklyn's. In a similar way it describes the community in which Independence Savings Bank, where today I am president, was founded in 1850. Chartered as the South Brooklyn Savings Institute, it has grown and flourished along with its community. Just as we outgrew our South Brooklyn corporate headquarters and moved downtown to Montague Street in 1994, other institutions have moved, neighborhoods have changed, and new groups of people have become part of our community. If there is a lesson in *Brooklyn! An Illustrated History,* it might be that Brooklyn stays vibrant because it embraces such change.

And so it is with great pride that Independence Savings Bank supports the publication of this fine book. Whether you are a current or a former resident, or someone who has just been intrigued by this wonderful place, *Brooklyn! An Illustrated History* will revive old memories and delight you again and again.

Charles J. Hamm
President
Independence Savings Bank
Brooklyn, New York

Acknowledgments

The idea for this book evolved from an innovative and highly popular exhibition on view at The Brooklyn Historical Society through December 1996. We chose the title "Brooklyn's History Museum" for the exhibition because of the breadth of the subject matter covered and the incredibly rich array of historical artifacts included in the show. Ellen Marie Snyder-Grenier is the creative individual who organized and developed "Brooklyn's History Museum." Though no longer on our staff, she generously agreed to write this book so that the Society's rich collections might be shared with a wider audience. We are deeply indebted to her.

Since its founding in 1863, The Brooklyn Historical Society has assembled the largest and most comprehensive array of Brooklyn-related artifacts and research materials in existence. This book features important selections from our collections, most published here for the first time. Represented are photographs, paintings, drawings, and prints that reflect generations of attempts to portray Brooklyn's changing landscape and the faces of its sons and daughters in celebration and conflict. There are also wide-ranging artifacts—a delicate porcelain pitcher made in a nineteenth-century Greenpoint factory; a *cuatro* (guitar) fashioned by the artisan son of a Puerto Rican instrument maker in his Atlantic Avenue shop; a Dutch *kast,* or wardrobe, owned by an eighteenth-century Flatlands farmer's family; the christening gown worn by the children of Italian immigrants who settled in Williamsburg in 1900. And there are unusual "relics" of a sort, such as the piece of Brooklyn Bridge cable saved by its chief engineer. Unless otherwise noted, all materials illustrated in this book are from the Society's collections.

Along with these very tangible remnants of Brooklyn's past, the book captures first-hand accounts of days long gone, from visitors like Jasper Danckaerts, who described the area briefly in 1679; to residents like Gabriel Furman, who lived in Brooklyn and wrote a detailed diary of everyday life in the 1820s; to Francisco Pratts, who tried to find work on the Brooklyn waterfront in the 1920s and speaks movingly of discrimination against Puerto Ricans. The book also draws upon the words of writers, journalists, and modern-day historians who have recalled and interpreted Brooklyn's history for present-day and future readers.

We are very much indebted to The J.M. Kaplan Fund and its former president, Joan K. Davidson, for their generosity in underwriting the extensive research required to assemble the manuscript for this book. A major grant from Indepen-

View in "Brooklyn's History Museum."

The borough's first long-term exhibition on its history opened in 1989 at The Brooklyn Historical Society. Photograph by Helga Photo Studio, 1990.

dence Savings Bank and its president, Charles J. Hamm, enabled us to actually publish the book and to include many more illustrations, and more color, than would have otherwise been possible.

We would like to thank various people who have contributed their efforts to this book and/or the exhibition that inspired it: staff members (past and present) Irene Tichenor, Clara Lamers, Margo Williams, Judith M. Giuriceo, Dwandalyn Reece King, Laura Miller, Jessica Stolzberg, Roger Mohovich, Elizabeth Reich Rawson, Sarah Weatherwax, Anne Marie Barba Palone, Herman Eberhardt, Robert S. Grumet, Jill Vexler, Benjamin Filene, and Rose Garvin; volunteers Manning Field, Ronald Wogaman, Joseph Henehan, Dominick DeRubbio, and David Demeritt; scholarly advisory board members Kenneth T. Jackson, Ronald J. Grele, Margaret Latimer, and Thomas J. Schlereth; and scholarly consultants Michael J. Ettema, Joshua B. Freeman, Barbara Kirshenblatt-Gimblett, Kathy L. Peiss, Steven Allen Riess, Robert W. Snyder, and Michael Wallace. Many thanks also to those who have undertaken Society exhibition and research projects; they are listed in the bibliographical essay. Our sincere gratitude also goes to the many generous people who donated items now illustrated in this book, and to those who contributed their reminiscences: Martin Adler, Solomon Brodsky, Grace Chan, Virginia Grant Cobb, Jack Daly, Peter DeConza, Michael Faiella, Tessie Gordon, Frances Haber, Charles F. Hummel, Daniel King, Anne Marie Barba Palone, Elliott Rogel, Lilly Santangelo, Catherine Hennings Sarnowski, Leslie Sachs Sherman, Leo Skolnick, Eugenie Miller Sternfield, Henry Tatowicz, Vonceil Turner, and John Yulo.

Many thanks to those who reviewed the manuscript of the book: Joshua Brown, Fath Ruffins, David Schuyler, and Melvin Adelman. While many institutions and organizations provided information and/or images, we would especially like to thank the Brooklyn Public Library, the Borough President's office, Brooklyn's community boards, and the Brooklyn Dodgers Baseball Hall of Fame. And, of course, many thanks to David Bartlett and Janet Francendese at Temple University Press and series editor Roy Rosenzweig.

David M. Kahn
Executive Director
The Brooklyn Historical Society

Introduction

"It may not be generally known that our city is getting to have quite a world-wide reputation," wrote Walt Whitman, Brooklynite and poet, in 1862. Today, the whole world knows about Brooklyn. From Sicily to Singapore, from Bangor to Berkeley, mention Brooklyn and almost everyone will have a memory or an image of that sometimes venerated, sometimes beleaguered, ever changing borough. Mention a few of Brooklyn's claims to fame and watch people's eyes light up. Who hasn't heard of the Brooklyn Bridge or Coney Island or Jackie Robinson?

In *Brooklyn!,* five of Brooklyn's most famous features—its people, the Brooklyn Bridge, the Brooklyn Navy Yard, Coney Island, and the Brooklyn Dodgers—serve as points of entry to the borough's rich history and everyday life.

The first chapter chronicles the stories of Brooklynites who came in search of new opportunities. They arrived in successive waves: some by boat across the Atlantic, then others by train (like the African Americans from the rural South in the early twentieth century), and still others in the 1940s and later by plane from Puerto Rico and the world. Here are the stories of the early Brooklynites, among them accounts of the Native American families who once made their camps on Brooklyn shores, Captain Thomas Dring's tale of the horrors aboard the prison ships moored in Wallabout Bay during the Revolutionary War, Democratic Party boss Hugh McLaughlin's maneuverings, and Walt Whitman's song of the poor districts that housed early immigrants. Seventeenth-century Dutch landowner Simon Aertsen de Hart has a story here, and so do nineteenth-century African American doctor Susan Smith McKinney Steward, Italian newcomer Rocco Yulo, and the Mexican congregants of All Saints Church.

The Brooklyn Bridge dominates the next chapter, as it for many decades dominated the borough's landscape and connected Brooklynites with all those people not fortunate enough to live in their neighborhoods. "And if you believe that," goes a classic American punch line, "I've got a bridge to sell you." Its source is the apocryphal story of a shyster offering naive New York newcomers a piece of the Brooklyn Bridge, a bit of Americana that this chapter explores along with the growth of the borough and of its transportation system, from the small wooden boats that once ferried Native Americans and colonists across the East River to the speeding subways that hurtle through Brooklyn's tunnels today. The chapter is peopled by characters like Hezekiah Pierpont, who spearheaded the

Brooklyn Heights real estate boom in the nineteenth century; Sylvanus Smith, an early African American landowner in Weeksville; and Brooklyn artist John Mackie Falconer, who chronicled Brooklyn's changing landscape.

The mammoth Brooklyn Navy Yard once churned out U.S. battleships, and at its peak during World War II employed some 70,000 men and women who worked around the clock in three shifts. Its development from tiny shipyard to massive industrial complex, its decline and subsequent revitalization as an industrial center for small businesses, in many ways mirrors Brooklyn's industrial history. The third chapter tells its story and chronicles all the goods made in Brooklyn, from shoes to beer. It recalls the worlds of the German and Irish laborers who clashed at the Atlantic Docks in 1846, and the nighttime excitement of Sands Street, where sailors on leave once swaggered down the sidewalks. And it remembers people like World War II Navy Yard worker Hazel Licouri and Puerto Rican newcomer Lucila Padrón, a Williamsburg garment factory worker, as well as movers and shakers of the time—factory and refinery owners like Freeman Murrow and Charles Pratt.

On the subject of movers and shakers, many people with only a passing knowledge of New York geography are surprised to learn that Brooklyn is home to Coney Island. Probably the most famous amusement park in the country before Disney's advent, Coney competed with other forms of entertainment in the rapidly expanding city. From leisurely walks through nineteenth-century Gowanus to a visit to Lilly Santangelo's wax museum, the fourth chapter evokes Brooklyn's lighter side.

The last chapter, on those beloved "bums," the Brooklyn Dodgers, combines the history of the baseball team and a story about community pride. Rich with colorful characters like nineteenth-century star of the diamond James Creighton, Superbas manager Ned Hanlon, and base stealer par excellence Jackie Robinson, here's the whole story, from triumph and victory to that dismal day in 1957 when the Dodgers walked out of Ebbets Field for the last time. In the Epilogue, find out about Brooklyn's subsequent rebirth.

Brooklyn's Beginnings

Located at the far western end of Long Island, Brooklyn is one of New York City's five boroughs and home to 2.3 million. Native American life flourished here until the seventeenth century. While explorers like Giovanni de Verrazano and Henry Hudson visited the New York Bay area in the sixteenth and early seventeenth centuries, European settlers did not arrive until the Dutch established a trading post in New Netherland (now New York) in the early 1600s. Europeans began to buy land in what is now Brooklyn only in 1636.

Over the next thirty years the Dutch created five towns in what is today the borough of Brooklyn: Breuckelen (Brooklyn), New Amersfoort (Flatlands), Midwout or Vlacke Bosch (Flatbush), New Utrecht, and Boswick (Bushwick). A sixth, Gravesend, was settled by the English in 1643, when Lady Deborah Moody, fleeing religious persecution in England and then in the Massachusetts Bay Colony, settled there with her followers.

For ten years, the English and Dutch tossed the colony back and forth. In 1664 the English took over New Netherland and renamed the colony New York after James, Duke of York. The Dutch recaptured it in 1673; in 1674, the English

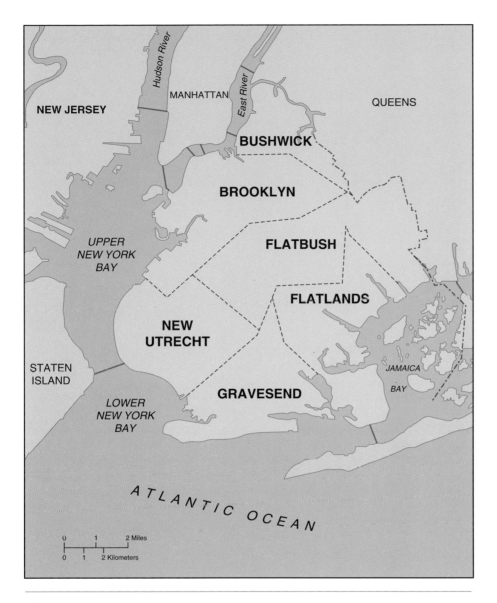

Six Towns.

The six towns of seventeenth-century Kings County—today, Brooklyn.

again, this time for a century. In 1683 the six towns were united under one jurisdiction: Kings County in the English colony of New York. One year later, the last of the Native American lands in Brooklyn were "sold" to European new-comers. By 1698, when the first census of Kings County was taken, the six towns had a combined population of 2,017. Roughly 15 percent (296) were people of African descent, forcibly brought from their homelands as slaves and indentured servants.

Most early Brooklynites made their living on farms, often an isolated way to live, and they established various social institutions. Church on Sunday might well be at the Flatbush Dutch Reformed Church; legal disagreements were re-

Hooker's New Pocket Plan of the Village of Brooklyn. *Engraved and printed by William Hooker, 1827.* **Bird's Eye View of the Borough of Brooklyn, Showing Parks, Cemeteries, Principal Buildings, and Suburbs. Specially Prepared for the *Brooklyn Daily Eagle* Consolidation Number, 1897.**

Brooklyn mushroomed from its origins as a small settlement, until by 1897, on the eve of consolidation as part of Greater New York, its southernmost boundary was the Atlantic Ocean.

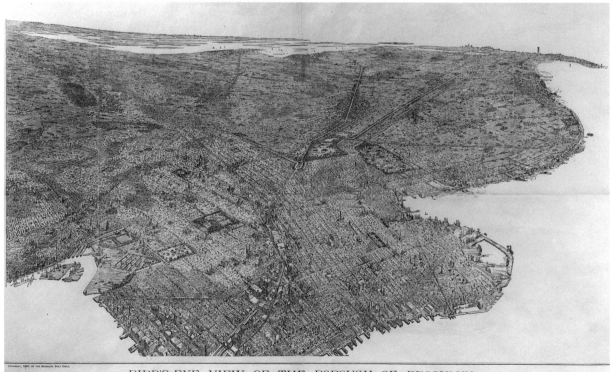

BIRD'S-EYE VIEW OF THE BOROUGH OF BROOKLYN
SHOWING PARKS, CEMETERIES, PRINCIPAL BUILDINGS, AND SUBURBS.
SPECIALLY PREPARED FOR THE BROOKLYN DAILY EAGLE CONSOLIDATION NUMBER.

solved at local courts. Over the course of the eighteenth century, the population grew slowly—more slowly in fact, than in any New York county. French visitor Moreau de St. Méry attributed this lag to the fact that newcomers could not afford to buy Brooklyn farmland; he suggested that it was "high-priced, because the nearness of New York assures a market for all farm products, and because the Dutch families who form such a large part of the population refuse to sell their holdings."

In 1772, residents founded a volunteer fire department, then paused for the Battle of Long Island in 1776, one of the major conflicts of the war, fought on Brooklyn soil from Gravesend to Gowanus. In a move that showed just how strong a Dutch presence remained even after seven years of British occupation, in 1786 the Flatbush Reformed Dutch Church opened Erasmus Hall Academy as a private school for Dutch farmers' children. The academy still stands. It is in the courtyard of Erasmus Hall High School, a public school, the alma mater of such luminaries as singer Barbra Streisand and chess great Bobby Fischer.

In 1790, the first official U.S. census showed that the population of Kings County had more than doubled in less than a century—to almost 4,500; as today, almost one-third of the population was African American. Most of Kings County's growth occurred in the Town of Brooklyn; directly across the East River from Manhattan, the town profited from its neighbor's emergence as one of the world's greatest ports. Still, Brooklyn's population was so small that everyone probably knew everyone else. In 1794, Moreau de St. Méry wrote that "Brooklyn has almost one hundred houses, most of them only one story high . . . most are chiefly along the shore."

As Brooklyn moved into the nineteenth century, people like Joshua Sands, a speculator and merchant, bought up land and started manufacturing businesses.

Using machinery imported from England and British workers, Sands established an important early Brooklyn industry, rope making, on the waterfront. As the area grew, and word of mouth no longer served as an informal news carrier, Brooklyn's first newspaper was founded in 1799, the *Long Island Courier*. The U.S. Navy opened a yard on Wallabout Bay in 1801, which became a hive of activity during the War of 1812. And in 1814, the advent of the first steam-ferry service between Brooklyn and Manhattan further cemented a long, although not always harmonious, relationship. It was also the catalyst that made Brooklyn Heights emerge as an early suburb.

In 1816, the Village of Brooklyn was incorporated within the Town of Brooklyn and had grown beyond the few scattered homes of the previous generation. In 1822, lawyer and amateur historian Gabriel Furman listed these structures there (among others): 493 dwelling houses, 48 taverns, 48 groceries, 10 boot and shoe manufactories, 12 tar sheds, 26 store houses, 92 stables, 6 bakeries, 7 confectionary shops, 5 butcher's stalls, 5 tailor's shops, 5 blacksmith's shops, 8 schoolhouses, 5 rope walks, 1 windmill, and 6 house-carpenter's shops. By 1816, Brooklyn also had three churches, and in 1818 the town's first Black church, today's Bridge Street African Methodist Wesleyan Episcopal Church, was founded.

Brooklyn mushroomed during the 1830s and 1840s, in part because the Erie Canal was completed in 1825, which dramatically spurred the growth of the Port of New York. By the 1830s, Manhattan's main residential areas reached farther and farther uptown; as the area below Canal Street was converted to commercial and business use, Brooklyn became increasingly attractive as a place to live—commuting across the river seemed almost as easy as traveling uptown. Where once artists had carried their canvases and sketch pads across the river to contrast its rural landscape with Manhattan's densely packed waterfront, by the 1840s, printmakers were portraying Brooklyn's own bustling waterfront.

Brooklyn assumed the status of a city in 1834, and over the next fifteen years a rapid succession of changes boosted the young city's pride. Green-Wood Cemetery opened, one of the first rural cemeteries in the United States; a city plan was

View of Brooklyn, Long Island from the U.S. Hotel, New York **by E. Whitefield, color lithograph, 1846.**

By the mid–nineteenth century, almost any view of the East River was a crowded one. In the Manhattan foreground, an omnibus lets off a passenger. Beyond the ferry steaming toward Fulton Street lies the Brooklyn waterfront, lined with industrial buildings, docks, and warehouses.

VIEW OF BROOKLYN, L. I.

FROM U.S. HOTEL, NEW YORK.

Brooklyn! *An Illustrated History*

adopted; the Brooklyn Board of Education was established; gas lights were introduced; and the long-delayed Brooklyn City Hall was finally completed and became—with its distinctive rotunda and cupola—a crowning glory.

The Nation's Third-Largest City

From the 1840s into the early twentieth century, Brooklyn saw massive European immigration. By 1855, almost half of Kings County's population was foreign-born. By 1860, Brooklyn ranked as the third-largest city in the United States
(after New York and Philadelphia), a result of this massive immigration as well as
the merging in 1855 of the City of Williamsburgh and Town of Bushwick with
the City of Brooklyn. (The final "h" in Williamsburgh dropped out of usage by
the late nineteenth century.) The industrial landscape continued to evolve as
manufacturing grew. The city's built environment changed not just by the
pulling down and putting up that accompanies growth but also by great fires that
were a fact of nineteenth-century urban life, like the devastating blaze that tore
through downtown Brooklyn in 1848. The rural landscape, itself shaped by the
farmers who cut down trees and tilled the soil, increasingly gave way to the features of the city. One-time rural retreats like Brooklyn Heights gave way to the
seaside lures of Bay Ridge.

New York Bay from Bay Ridge, L.I.
by F.F. Palmer; Currier and Ives, New York, printers and publishers, color lithograph, 1860.

By the turn of the twentieth century, wealthy Brooklynites and New Yorkers had discovered the views from Bay Ridge, and summer mansions like this one lined the bluffs overlooking the entrance to New York Harbor.

Judge John Courtney, president, Brooklyn Veteran Fireman's Association, ca. 1890.

The portrait of this former volunteer fireman gains stature and status from its elaborate frame adorned with firefighting imagery. Although Brooklyn switched to a paid fire department in 1869, many fire companies reorganized as verterans' organizations, honoring their tradition with parades, fancy balls, and story-swapping conventions.

Services developed to address the changing needs of an expanding city. In 1869, the fire department professionalized, changing from a volunteer to a municipal paid force. A new water-supply system was introduced in 1858, when the Ridgewood Reservoir began providing water to the city. And cultural institutions like The Brooklyn Historical Society emerged on the landscape, odes to a growing city.

Two years after General Robert E. Lee surrendered to General Ulysses S. Grant at Appomattox in 1865, marking the end of the Civil War, a group of civic-minded men formed the New York Bridge Company to build a bridge between Brooklyn and Manhattan. Completed in 1883, the Brooklyn Bridge was a monument to nineteenth-century technology. It reoriented downtown Brooklyn,

The Brooklyn Historical Society, ca. 1883.

This engraving views the Society from the corner of Pierrepont and Clinton Streets, with Holy Trinity Church in the background. Founded in 1863, the Society commissioned this handsome building with its fashionable terra-cotta ornamentation; it was completed in 1880.

Brooklyn Daily Eagle building, ca. 1892.

From the portal of this building in downtown Brooklyn, an enormous, cast-copper eagle glared down at all who passed through the doors of the paper, for a time edited by Walt Whitman. In business for 114 years, until 1955, the *Eagle* was one of Brooklyn's trappings of citydom.

rerouting traffic farther up Fulton Street and away from the traditional waterfront hub. Theaters, stores, hotels, and business offices sprang up in the burgeoning downtown area.

In the meantime, industry continued to expand, so that by 1880, the manufacturing census showed Brooklyn with five thousand factories employing 49,000 people. With a population of 566,663 it was still the third-largest city in the nation, and growing, as it continued to annex outlying towns—in the decade from 1886 to 1896 it annexed the towns of New Lots, Flatbush, Gravesend, New Utrecht, and Flatlands. Then Brooklyn itself was annexed, becoming a borough of Greater New York in 1898. With the end of the century came some of Brooklyn's most enduring treasures: the Brooklyn Public Library was founded, the Brooklyn Museum began to build its present home on Eastern Parkway, and The Brooklyn Children's Museum opened its doors. By 1900, the population of the Borough of Brooklyn topped one million.

The first decade of the twentieth century was marked by major additions to Brooklyn's transportation network, as the Williamsburg Bridge opened in 1903, and the Manhattan Bridge in 1909. In the interim, the subway finally reached from Manhattan to Brooklyn and eventually helped kill ferry service.

Like other industrial centers across the country, over the years Brooklyn has geared up to serve the country in war. During World War I Brooklynites worked long shifts in defense industries; many went to battle. Between the world wars,

Brooklyn! *An Illustrated History*

thousands of Brooklynites lost their jobs in the Great Depression. When they could afford it, they flocked to the magnificent Loew's Kings theater just opened in Flatbush to lose themselves in celluloid fantasies or to Coney Island for some fun. As Japanese warplanes over Hawaii signaled the entry of the United States into World War II, Brooklyn once again geared up, as companies like Mergenthaler Linotype were converted into defense plants. With rumors of nighttime German air attacks, Brooklynites pulled down the blackout shades in their homes and doused the lights that might serve as guides to bombers. Employment soared as workers toiled in round-the-clock defense work. In the 1950s, the pulse quickened again with the Korean War.

Cake-eating contest, Coney Island, September 1941.

"Underprivileged" children of the metropolitan area were invited to the ninth annual three-day Kiddy Party at Coney Island's Luna Park by Drake Bakeries, Inc. Radio singers Diane Courtney and Bradford Reynolds judged the cake eating.

By the 1950s, however, Brooklyn's population and status as an industrial center had peaked. Hard times lay ahead. Industry seeking cheaper locales and veterans' families eager to apply low-interest G.I. loans to suburban dream houses were forsaking the city. Government policies that backed new highway construction and automobile use encouraged the exodus of both businesses and people. Technological advances meant fewer or less skilled jobs. And in 1957, the Dodgers left for Los Angeles.

But Brooklyn's story doesn't end there. Among the dynamic people and institutions rooted in the community were leaders such as Reverend Milton Galamison and the Siloam Presbyterian Church. Continuing in the activist tradition of the Black church, Galamison, an outspoken advocate of school integration, and Siloam were the focus of national attention in the late 1950s and 1960s; in 1964 he and parents organized a school boycott aimed at instituting educational reform. During the Vietnam War, students at Brooklyn College protested U.S. activities in Asia; in 1968, a public school strike centered in the Ocean Hill-Brownsville area put the largely Jewish United Federation of Teachers against African American advocates of community control in a bitter fight; in 1969, Medgar Evers College opened in Crown Heights, a memorial to the slain civil-rights leader.

Hollywood captured Brooklyn in the 1970s with its portrayal of teenage life in Bay Ridge in the film *Saturday Night Fever*, but for residents the drama of the decade lay also in concrete. One of the city's best known schools, Boys High School, moved to a new building on Fulton Street and became Boys and Girls

Milton Galamison, 1951.

The Reverend Milton Galamison led Siloam Presbyterian Church in Brooklyn's annual Sunday School Parade in 1951. Siloam, which joined the historic Black church movement of Brooklyn in 1849, named this worker for social justice its pastor in 1949. Photograph courtesy of the Society for the Preservation of Weeksville and Bedford-Stuyvesant History.

Brooklyn! *An Illustrated History*

Eighth Avenue, Sunset Park, 1994.

If anything remains the same about Brooklyn, it's its diversity. Each of the borough's neighborhoods has its own special flavor. Along Eighth Avenue, the bustling, main commercial thoroughfare of Sunset Park's Chinese community, shoppers crowd the streets and crates of fish and produce vie for space on the sidewalks. Once largely Norwegian, the area still boasts Scandinavian businesses alongside more recent Chinese ones and the even newer Middle Eastern shops. Photograph by Rex Chen.

High, the Bedford-Stuyvesant Restoration Plaza was built, and the massive new Fulton Mall, New York City's first pedestrian and transit way shopping mall, opened. There was more to come: One Pierrepont Plaza, Brooklyn's first skyscraper since 1929, opened in 1988 and soared above Brooklyn Heights, and in the mid 1990s, MetroTech, an enormous office and research complex, brought new energy and thousands of workers to downtown Brooklyn.

The easing of U.S. immigration restrictions in 1965 brought an influx from the Caribbean, Latin America, and Asia, and by 1990, 2.3 million residents made Brooklyn the most populous borough in New York City. With more people than eighteen of the states, it would be the fourth-largest city in the United States if it were still independent. Its economic base has turned from manufacturing to service, but many industries still thrive in Williamsburg and other older industrial areas, as entrepreneurs adapt the old to new needs. And Brooklyn's population—as always, diverse—remains central to the borough's ongoing revitalization. While media attention has focused on such incidents as the Crown Heights riots of 1991, the stories about how well so many different people get along go largely untold.

This brief introduction only hints at the richness of a complete history of Brooklyn. This entire book can tell only part of it. As Thomas Wolfe summed it up in *Death to Morning*, "It'd take a guy a lifetime to know Brooklyn t'roo an' t'roo. An' even den, yuh wouldn't know it all."

Portraits of Brooklynites.

Credits (*left to right, top to bottom*): © Roberta Grobel Intrater; Brooklyn Public Library–Brooklyn Collection; Long Island College Hospital; Brooklyn Public Library–Brooklyn Collection; the Jackie Gleason Estate and CBS; The Brooklyn Historical Society; Barney Stein; The Brooklyn Historical Society; Dinanda Nooney; The Brooklyn Historical Society; The Brooklyn Historical Society; Hayden Roger Celestin.

Brooklynites, Real and Imagined

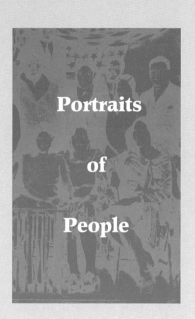

Portraits

of

People

"Yo, Ralphie boy!" So Ed Norton greeted Ralph Kramden as he sauntered through his buddy's front door, while millions of TV viewers in the 1950s settled in for thirty hilarious minutes. *The Honeymooners* was set in a sparsely furnished apartment on Chauncey Street in Brooklyn, and the characters were intended as pure Brooklyn archetypes. Particularly Ralph. Created by consummate comedian (and born Brooklynite) Jackie Gleason, Ralph, was the bus driver with a heart of gold, forever trying to scheme his way out of the working class but forever fated to fail, the quintessential common man. Most people could relate to Ralph, but they didn't always like him. He could be blustery, opinionated, and loud-mouthed, and viewers may well have imagined that he and the others on the show were typical Brooklynites. Gleason's portrayal of the type—like those featured in countless 1940s comedy and war movies before him—was a firmly established American image, a symbol of Brooklyn equal to the Brooklyn Bridge, the Dodgers, or Coney Island.

Even today, Hollywood's portrayal of the Brooklynite is hardly ever glamorous. Characters like hardware store clerk and discoer Tony in *Saturday Night Fever* (1977), aspiring writer Eugene in *Brighton Beach Memoirs* (1986), or Mookie in Spike Lee's film *Do the Right Thing* (1989) are all everyday people who live in Brooklyn's ethnic communities and yearn for something better. In the end, though, they are fictional characters, and real life is more complex than fiction. Brooklynites have always been a diverse lot. "That is one of the things I love best about Brooklyn," wrote Carson McCullers. "Everyone is not expected to be exactly like everyone else."

Since the displacement of its original inhabitants, Brooklyn's people have come from everywhere. During the seventeenth century, Netherlanders came to farm land in Flatbush, and African American artisans were forcibly brought to colonial Brooklyn. New Englanders sought their fortunes in the burgeoning port of New York in the 1820s. Italian immigrants came to Carroll Gardens (then called South Brooklyn) at the turn of the century in search of work on the industrial waterfront. Puerto Ricans migrated to Brooklyn in the 1920s and found homes on Columbia Street. Orthodox Jews fled Poland as World War II erupted and sought refuge in Crown Heights. The Haitian bakery owner on Church Avenue who immigrated a decade ago, the store owner from Manhattan's China-

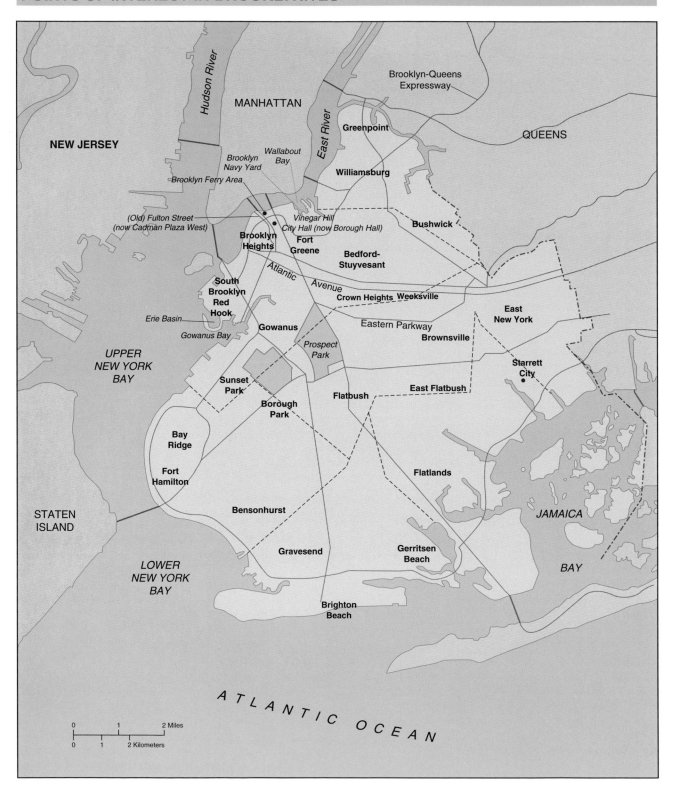

New Jersey

Hudson River

MANHATTAN

East River

Brooklyn-Queens
Expressway

Greenpoint

QUEENS

Wallabout
Bay

Brooklyn
Navy Yard

Williamsburg

Brooklyn Ferry Area

(Old) Fulton Street
(now Cadman Plaza West)

Vinegar Hill
City Hall (now Borough Hall)

Bushwick

Brooklyn
Heights

Fort
Greene

Bedford-
Stuyvesant

Atlantic

Avenue

South
Brooklyn
Red
Hook

Crown Heights Weeksville

East
New York

Erie Basin

Eastern Parkway

Gowanus

Brownsville

Gowanus Bay

Prospect
Park

Starrett
City

UPPER
NEW YORK
BAY

Sunset
Park

Borough
Park

Flatbush

East Flatbush

Bay
Ridge

Flatlands

Fort
Hamilton

Flatlands

JAMAICA

STATEN
ISLAND

Bensonhurst

BAY

LOWER
NEW YORK
BAY

Gravesend

Gerritsen
Beach

Brighton
Beach

ATLANTIC OCEAN

0   1   2 Miles

0   1   2 Kilometers

The Honeymooners, 1955.

Ralph, Ed, Alice, and Trixie, imaginary Brooklynites whose lives on Chauncey Street endeared them to millions of TV viewers. *Left to right:* Jackie Gleason, Art Carney, Audrey Meadows, and Joyce Randolph. Photograph courtesy of the Jackie Gleason Estate and CBS.

town who was drawn to the burgeoning Chinese community along Brooklyn's Eighth Avenue in Sunset Park, the Salvadoran refugee who arrived only yesterday and now calls Williamsburg home: all have come in search of a new life. Today, as *New York* magazine noted in an April 21, 1986 feature story, "In Brooklyn, you can find the dishes of the Old Country, whether that means jerk chicken, gefilte fish, or stuffed cabbage."

Newcomers pass through Brooklyn's neighborhoods of brick and brownstone homes, of apartments, condos, and Victorian mansions, of rowhouses and

It Happened in Brooklyn, 1947.

In this MGM musical, a returning vet, played by Frank Sinatra, moves into New Utrecht High School's basement. He falls in love with a teacher, and then recalls a nurse he met overseas—from where else, but Brooklyn. Poster, used by permission of Turner Entertainment Co.

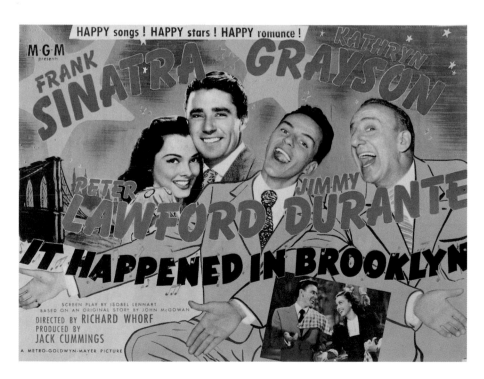

suburban tract housing. Many put down roots; others move on or return home. All leave their mark.

"The Noblest of All Lands": Brooklyn in the Years Before the Revolution

The first people on the land that would become Brooklyn, Native Americans, called themselves by the places where they lived: they were Nayacks while living at the village at Nayack, Canarsies when living in Canarsie. To designate the whole group they used Lenape or People. They hunted deer, fished for bass and sturgeon, and planted corn and tobacco in Marechkawieck (today's Brooklyn Heights) and Nayack (now Fort Hamilton). The Europeans who arrived in the early 1600s called them and their neighbors River Indians, Manhattans, or *wilden* ("wild or natural people").

"They are intense in everything they do," wrote Jasper Danckaerts of the Native Americans he met in the seventeenth century. "They penetrate matters thoroughly and speak only when appropriate." A member of a communal Protestant sect in Holland, the Labadists, Danckaerts came to New York in 1679 in search of land for a religious colony. He created a rare portrait of Native American life in Brooklyn through words and tiny, detailed pen-and-ink drawings, including what is probably the only known rendering of a Brooklyn Native American woman. Their rich culture was irrevocably changed by contact with Europeans, whom, Danckaerts felt, looked upon the Lenape with contempt and cheated and

Brooklyn Native American woman, from Jasper Danckaerts, *Journal of a Voyage to New York,* **pen and ink, 1679.**

Jasper Danckaerts sketched the sights and people of Brooklyn, including a Native American woman. She wears a typical skirt of tanned deer or elk hide. Since she is bare-chested, it is probably summer, when neither men nor women wore shirts.

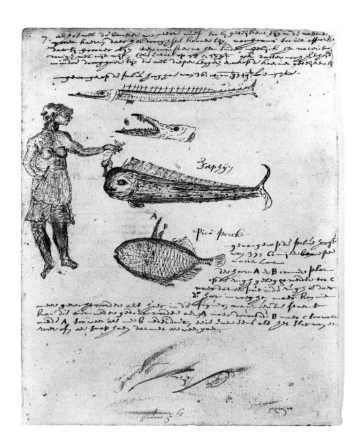

exploited them whenever possible. Already devastated by disease, war, and dispossession, Native Americans watched, powerless, as colonists moved onto their lands in growing numbers. Danckaerts wrote that "there are not even 1/10th of the Indians left (not even 1/20th or 1/30th) times as many." Yet these early Brooklynites were tenacious survivors.

Danckaerts wrote that Native American hunters in Brooklyn relied on a "gun and pouch for powder and lead" to hunt deer and other game, which reveals one way they had adapted European technology to their own uses. When he visited the Gowanus fishing camp (the waterfront area roughly south of Carroll Gardens and north of Sunset Park), he watched Native Americans harvest foot-long oysters and catch fish with traps, nets, and spears. Traveling south along the shoreline to Fort Hamilton, Danckaerts and a companion came upon the home of the Nayack Indians in an area "planted with maize," beans, squash, gourds, and peaches. Danckaerts observed "dogs, fowls, and hogs," which, he noted, the Native Americans "learn by degrees from the Europeans to manage better."

The village of Nayack was most likely a summer settlement with one large longhouse. Danckaerts described it as "low and long, about sixty feet long and fourteen or fifteen feet wide," with a "bottom of earth" and sides and roof "made of reed and the bark of chestnut trees," adding that it sheltered "seven or eight families, and twenty or twenty-two persons." He observed that "they build their fire in the middle of the floor, according to the number of families which live in it, so that from one end to the other each of them boils its own pot, and eats when it likes. . . . By each fire are the cooking utensils, consisting of a pot, or calabash [gourd], and a spoon also made of a calabash."

Through pages upon pages written in a tiny, neat hand, Danckaerts described traditions and religious practices among Brooklyn's Native Americans as their days of living on their own land drew to a close. With the arrival of increasing numbers of colonists, conflicts arose over land ownership. Europeans saw land purchases as final sales. Native Americans, on the other hand, saw deeds as treaties of alliance and looked upon trade goods exchanged at treaty signings as gifts that sealed agreements. In 1684, the last tract of Native American land in Brooklyn was "sold." Forced from their homes, Brooklyn's Native Americans camped in small temporary settlements at Gowanus, Canarsie, and Nayack, essentially homeless upon their own land. Many moved east to Long Island; others decamped for Staten Island, New Jersey, and Native American towns in the Hudson and Delaware River Valleys. Epidemics of smallpox, a disease brought to the New World by Europeans, swept across the area between 1679 and 1703, killing most remaining Native Americans.

The Europeans who ultimately destroyed the Native American presence in Brooklyn were primarily from the Netherlands, attracted to the New World by inducements from the Dutch West India Company (WIC). The company had a government-chartered monopoly on trade and colonization in New Netherland, the name given the series of settlements between the Connecticut and Delaware Rivers, and attempted to increase settlement and growth by offering free one-way passage, as much land as a person could farm, and generous tax exemptions. With New Amsterdam (Manhattan) as its administrative and commercial center, WIC began to spread out to neighboring land after 1630, "the better to people their lands, and to bring their country to produce more abundantly," in the words of an early chronicler. In 1636, Dutch settlers established the first European colonies in what is today Brooklyn, at Flatlands and Flatbush. WIC's venture never really prospered, despite grandiose praise from settlers like poet Jacob Steendam, who purchased a Flatlands farm in 1652 and wrote that "New Netherland is the flower, the noblest of all lands, a rich blessed region, where milk and honey flows."

Drawn for the Dutch WIC in 1639, and later copied, what is today known as the Manatus (Manhattan) map includes much of present-day Brooklyn and shows Native American longhouses near Dutch-owned homes. By the 1660s, just under 50 percent of these early European settlers were Netherlanders. The rest had come from Germany, England, France, Scandinavia, Flanders, Belgium, and elsewhere—among them African Americans forcibly brought to the country as slave labor or as indentured servants. Although most were farmers, among the settlers were soldiers and artisans, as well as servants, farm workers, laborers, and fishers.

These early arrivals created a farming society of free, indentured, and slave workers, where work was governed by the seasons and days were ruled by the

De Manatus. Gelegen op de Noot Riuier (**Manhattan Lying on the North River**), **1670 after 1639 original.**

This bird's-eye view of Manhattan includes Brooklyn and depicts its early diversity: Dutch homes, a farm owned by a Norwegian, Claes Carstensen (#39), in present-day Williamsburg, and Native American longhouses near Conyné Eylant (Coney Island) at left. Courtesy of the Library of Congress.

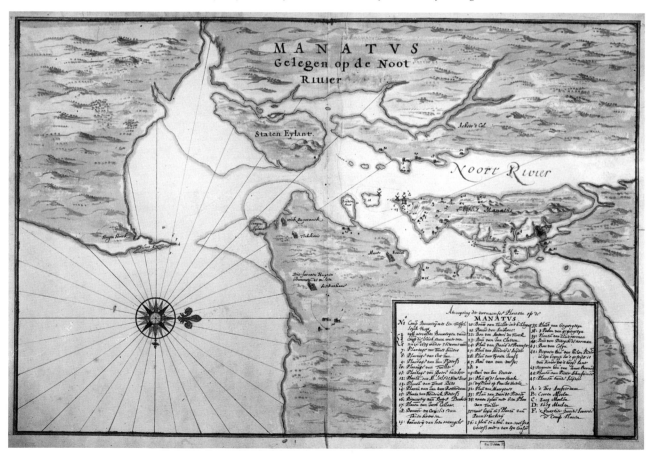

Brooklyn! *An Illustrated History*

rising and setting of the sun. Like the Native Americans, the newcomers relished the bounty of the sea. Simon Aertsen de Hart, whom Danckaerts met on one of his countryside jaunts, offered the traveler "a pail-full of Gouanes oysters, which are the best in the country." So plentiful were these local delicacies that locals pickled them "in small casks, and sent them to Barbados and the other islands" to sell, noted Danckaerts. The land too produced rich harvests: Danckaerts wrote of peach trees "as full as they could bear" and "a whole hill of watermelons, which were as large as pumpkins, and which Symon was going to take to the city to sell." Though painted almost two centuries later, James Ryder Van Brunt's portrayal of a Dutch farm provides a sense of Brooklyn's seventeenth-century landscape and farmhouses.

Van Brunt's idyllic rendering fails to capture one of the harsh realities of Brooklyn farm life: slave labor. While the Dutch West India Company hired some workers, even recruiting many in the Netherlands to work on Brooklyn farms, the company regarded African American indentured servants and slaves as necessities because of the difficulties they had in attracting a free labor force to the settlement. The earliest record of an African American slave in Brooklyn shows a Gowanus landowner conveying a slave, cruelly relegated to the status of property, to Richard Lord in 1646.

Slavery flourished, particularly in the more rural areas of Kings County. By 1698, 15 percent of Kings County was African American; in 1737, 24 percent; and by 1771, one-third. By 1790, 60 percent of all Kings County families owned slaves, a portion unmatched in any New York State county. Among slave-holding families, most owned two to four, although others had as many as nineteen.

Brooklynites, Real and Imagined

In Brooklyn as elsewhere, African Americans trapped in a brutal slave system revolted—usually unsuccessfully. Lieutenant Colonel Henry Pilkin of the Kings County Militia issued a warrant written in Dutch on August 2, 1706, commanding Captain Joost Van Brunt of the New Utrecht Company to arrest those deemed riotous. "Since I have learned that various blacks, mainly from all parts of this county, gathered together on the Sabbath in a rebellious manner near the house of Dirck Van Sutphen in the village of New Utrecht's yellow corner, in order to break the Sabbath against the peace, etc., this [warrant] is thus sworn out in his Majesty's name in order that you be commanded on this Sabbath or any

Sabbath hereafter when occasion should arise, to send a troop of musketeers . . . and that if any such blacks be thus found as forenoted, to capture them . . . but if the aforesaid blacks dare do any harm of the aforesaid musketeers or refuse to submit, then shoot them dead."

Even though most African Americans during this period were enslaved, historians have found evidence of free African Americans living in Kings County as early as the mid–seventeenth century. For example, records refer to "black Hans" in the Village of Brooklyn and to Janse Van Luane/Lowaanen, a free Black man who emigrated to New Netherland in 1654 and soon after bought land in New Utrecht.

Since Kings County continued to be at least half Dutch through the late eighteenth century, Dutch traditions had a strong influence on life there even after the British takeover in 1664. Nicasius de Sille, who immigrated in 1653, lived his later life in a house made of stone and Dutch-style terra-cotta roof tiles that were either imports from the Netherlands or Brooklyn-made imitations. In 1699, thirty-five years into English rule, Nicholas Vechte incorporated into his new home (at what is now Third Avenue near Fifth Street) the steeply pitched roof and stepped gable popular in the Netherlands. When the Lott family built a house in New Lots (in an area that would one day become Brownsville) in the eighteenth century, they imported the fireplace decoration—tin-glazed earthenware tiles depicting biblical scenes—from the Netherlands. In their seventeenth- and eighteenth-century homes, well-to-do-Dutch decorated their fireplaces with this sort of tile, in imitation of courtly European styles. And at the Bergen homestead in Flatlands, owners commissioned a local artisan to create an object with clear ties to home: a kast. Introduced to New York by the Dutch, the kast, a massive wardrobe, was used to store some of the most expensive items a family owned, such as clothing, linens, and other textiles (no houses had closets). While the expensive piece was also intended to indicate high social status, by the time this kast was made the form no longer carried much cachet among the upper classes in the Netherlands and was popular only in more isolated areas of New York.

Tin-glazed earthenware tile from the Lott House, ca. 1750.

Biblical scenes rendered on eighteenth-century decorative tiles—in this case the story of the Good Samaritan—offered one way to learn about the Bible when books were scarce.

Late eighteenth-century kast.

Standing more than six and a half feet high, with its heavily molded cornice and bold detailing, this kast, or wardrobe, would have occupied an important place in the Bergen farmhouse in Flatlands. Crafted by a Brooklyn artisan, it was made of all local woods: pine, poplar, cedar, and sweetgum.

Brooklyn's Dutch colonists retained ties with the Netherlands not only through material goods but spiritually as well. Into the mid-eighteenth century, ministers were sent directly from Amsterdam to Brooklyn. Flatland's Reverend Ulpianus Van Sinderen (or Zinderen), who arrived in 1746, is described in the memoirs of a contemporary, Colonel Alexander Graydon. "The principal person in a Low Dutch village appears to be the *Domine,* or minister. . . . At Flatlands there was . . . a Domine Van Zinderen . . . a lean and shrivelled little man," with a "triangular sharp–pointed hat," and "silver flowing locks, which streamed like a meteor to the troubled air, as he whisked along with great velocity in his chaise through Flatbush." During the Revolutionary War, Van Sinderen led his Flatlands congregation in prayers in Dutch for an American victory while British officers looked on unaware.

Strategically, Brooklyn was enormously important in the war. General George Washington, commander of the American troops, hoped to prevent the British from occupying Brooklyn Heights and the ferry to New York, thus denying them the port, a foothold they desperately needed. In March 1776, work began on Fort Putnam on the site of what is today Fort Greene Park, and went forward at speed when Washington called on all male inhabitants of Kings County to aid in the cause.

In August 1776, as British forces prepared to land at Gravesend Bay, the Provincial Convention of New York State ordered Kings County farms destroyed. It was rumored that the predominantly Dutch residents would side with the British, and the Americans' aim was to bar them from offering assistance to the enemy. The rumor probably had some truth in it, for some Dutch sided with the Crown. But many had chosen neutrality and many were patriots–among them Isaac Boerum of Flatbush, Peter Miller of Bushwick, and Joseph Smith of Brooklyn.

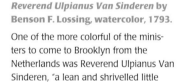

Reverend Ulpianus Van Sinderen **by Benson F. Lossing, watercolor, 1793.**

One of the more colorful of the ministers to come to Brooklyn from the Netherlands was Reverend Ulpianus Van Sinderen, "a lean and shrivelled little man."

Brooklyn! *An Illustrated History*

The Battle of Long Island by Alonzo Chappel, oil on canvas, ca. 1850.

British troops pursue a group of American soldiers at Gowanus Creek, filled with men trying to escape. A battle-scarred mill, Yellow Mills, stands at the water's edge.

In his 1842 *History of Flatbush,* Thomas M. Strong describes the scene that August, as terrified farmers and their families fled. "The inhabitants had reason to apprehend that should they remain at home they would be cruelly treated, and perhaps massacred. They were regarded as rebels, to whom but little quarter would be shown. Hence as expeditiously as possible after the landing of the British troops, the inhabitants of the village either sent or carried off the females and children with what little furniture and conveniences they could. . . . It was a scene of great confusion, and of no ordinary distress. . . . Some had not gone far before they saw smoke ascending from the neighborhood of the farms, and knew not but their dwellings were already in flames."

Flatbush, Flatlands, Gravesend, and New Utrecht sustained the worst of it, first at the hands of the Americans as rebels torched their fields and seized their livestock in order to starve out the British, and later under the British during the Battle of Long Island, the first major battle of the Revolution. In the mid-nineteenth century, artist Alonzo Chappel painted the scene at Gowanus Creek on August 27, 1776, when American troops were surrounded by the British. Having suffered major losses, Washington determined that the only way to salvage the remains of his army was to flee, and the American troops escaped across the East River. Ultimately, neither the skirmishes throughout Brooklyn nor the fortifications at Fort Putnam kept the British from taking over Kings County and the Port of New York.

For the duration of the war, the British made themselves at home in Kings County, where they found friends among Americans loyal to King George. Two Loyalists, Charles Loosely and Thomas Elms, gave up their tavern in Manhattan to convert the Corporation House, a two-story building on the Ferry Road (later Fulton Street), into the King's Head Tavern. On September 20, 1780, they announced that "the anniversary of the coronation of our ever good and gracious king will be celebrated at Loosley's 22 inst. It is expected that no rebels will approach nearer than Flatbush wood."

Brooklynites, Real and Imagined

Prison Ship Jersey **by James Ryder Van Brunt, watercolor on paper, 1876.**

The rotting hulk of a one-time British warship housed rebel prisoners, most taken captive at sea during the Revolutionary War. After the war, the ship was left to sink in the mud.

While the British and the fashionable Loyalist set frolicked at the King's Head, the groans of American and foreign prisoners of war carried across Wallabout Bay on still nights from the old hulks that the British used as floating prisons. The prison ship *Jersey*, the biggest and longest lived, held up to 1,200 prisoners at a time from the winter of 1779/1780 to the end of the war. Among them was Captain Thomas Dring, who described conditions aboard the *Jersey*, beginning with his arrival under the "charge of the notorious David Sproat," Commissary of Prisoners. "We at length doubled a point . . . and came in view of the Wallabout, where lay before us the black hulk of the OLD JERSEY . . . to which Sproat pointed in an exulting manner, and said 'There, rebels, *there* is the *cage* for you!'"

The water was foul, disease ran rampant, and prisoners were kept below deck at night, where the air was stale and suffocating. The images never left Dring's memory, which "still brings before me those emaciated beings, moving from the galley with their wretched pittance of meat; each creeping to the spot where his mess were assembled, to divide it with a group of haggard and sickly creatures, their garments hanging in tatters around their meager limbs, and the hue of death upon their careworn faces. By these it was consumed with their scanty remnants of bread, which was often mouldy and filled with worms. And, even from this vile fare they would rise up in torments from the cravings of unsatisfied hunger and thirst."

The thousands who died aboard the *Jersey* and its fellow prison ships were quickly buried along the Brooklyn shore. From 1807 on, when much of that shoreline was filled in to create more dry land for the Navy Yard, these burial sites were covered over, leaving enormous unmarked graveyards holding almost 11,000 war dead. Years later, the Martyrs' Memorial Association, established to commemorate them, proposed a burial site in Brooklyn's new Washington Park (now Fort Greene Park). In 1908, the Prison Ship's Martyrs' Monument was built, an imposing column designed by architects McKim, Mead, and White that stands almost 150 feet tall at the park's summit, overlooking Brooklyn and the harbor.

For years after the British army left Brooklyn on November 15, 1783, Evacuation Day was observed in Brooklyn as a holiday. Brooklyn also bore physical reminders of the war, skulls and cannonballs that turned up by the sides of roads and in farmers' tilled soil for many years, and miles of useless fortifications.

"A Casual Collection from All Quarters": The Nineteenth Century Is Ushered In

A little more than a decade after British occupation ended, the West Indies born French traveler Moreau de St. Méry, who journeyed through the colonies between 1793 and 1798, visited the area. "The air of Brooklyn is unusually healthy," he noted in 1794. "Its water is not too good, but is better than that of New York." Describing the small community around the ferry landing, he wrote that its approximately one hundred mostly one-story houses were located "chiefly along the shore, or scattered without regular plan" and found "the streets in Brooklyn, or rather the highway which forms its principal street . . . bad, heavy and unpaved, so that the smallest amount of rain makes Brooklyn muddy."

Five years later, that cluster of taverns, stores, and dwellings huddled near the ferry landing had begun to acquire the trappings of a village. In 1799, its first newspaper, the *Long Island Courier,* was published. In 1801, the U.S. Navy bought land on Wallabout Bay for a navy yard, which became a bustling enterprise during the War of 1812, occupied with outfitting ships. In 1814, steam-ferry service began between Manhattan and Brooklyn. In 1816, the Village of Brooklyn was incorporated within the Town of Brooklyn.

Yale president Timothy Dwight, visiting Brooklyn in the early 1810s, found "extensively, descendants from the original Dutch settlers . . . the rest are a casual collection from all quarters." This "casual collection" included African Americans—many descendants of early slaves, indentured servants, and free Black people; English; new arrivals from the New England states; Irish fleeing rebellion at home, and many others. Native Americans were almost completely gone. Jim de Wilt, reportedly the last "full-blooded" Native American in Brooklyn, died at Canarsie in 1832. It was a time of great change.

In the decade after 1825, Brooklyn's rural demeanor began to slip away, as warehouses and factories sprang up along the waterfront. Tremendous economic forces were at play: a new canal system, the development of domestic commerce, and increased industrial growth. Merchants, manufacturers, and mechanics poured into the growing village, alert to the new opportunities it promised.

Many came from New England, drawn south after the Revolution either to expand already prosperous businesses to New York or to seek work in the booming commercial world of that city's great port, particularly if they were from coastal areas. So many settled in Brooklyn that by the 1820s the growing village was dominated by Yankee "immigrants."

Bold, entrepreneurial, and civic minded, Vermont-born Alden Spooner represented this new breed of Yankee, dedicated to establishing Brooklyn as a city in every sense of the word. Some called him politically "too independent . . . too self-opinionated, to succeed." About 1832, shortly after they were married, Hubbard Latham Fordham painted portraits of Spooner and his second wife, Mary Ann Wetmore Spooner, who shared his devotion to civic affairs and cultural activities.

Colonel Alden Spooner by Hubbard Latham Fordham, oil on canvas, ca. 1832–33.

Mary Ann Wetmore Spooner by Hubbard Latham Fordham, oil on canvas, ca. 1832–33.

Descended from journalists and printers, Alden Spooner ran the *Long Island Star* for almost three decades; beneath his right hand is probably a copy of the newspaper. The book in the companion portrait of Mary Ann Wetmore Spooner may symbolize her talents as a writer.

Born in New York City in 1794 and married to Spooner at the age of thirty-seven, she wrote prose and poetry, conducted a girl's school in Brooklyn, and frequented such events as concerts at Erasmus Hall Academy and lectures at the Brooklyn Lyceum. Spooner published her work in the *Long Island Star* before they married and printed her volume of poems, *Gathered Leaves,* for Putnam in 1840.

By the time Alden Spooner died in 1848, he had lobbied for a village charter for Brooklyn in 1816; begun publishing the *Long Island Star;* worked for the village's incorporation as a city in 1834; founded a library; and helped establish Fort Greene Park, the Brooklyn Gas Light Company, the Female Seminary of Brooklyn, the Lyceum of Natural History, and the Apprentices Library Association, the forerunner of The Brooklyn Museum. On the state and national front, he was an early Erie Canal advocate. Fittingly, he was buried in Green-Wood Cemetery, one of Brooklyn's modern innovations.

Other New Englanders also immersed themselves in the commerce of the port and led community efforts to found Brooklyn's first banks, newspapers, schools, and cultural institutions. Cultural differences separated New Englanders and Brooklyn's Dutch residents and sometimes resulted in unneighborly derision. Alden Spooner's satirical editorial "The Last of the Leather Breeches," in the May 11th, 1826 issue of the *Long Island Star,* poked fun at local butcher Jacob Patchen and through him the "old fashioned ways" of the Dutch. Spooner derided him for his backwardness. "Every observer of 'men and things,' has doubtless noticed in the village of Brooklyn a thickset little gentleman in a broad brimmed hat, brown bob-tail coat, vest half way down his thighs, and leather breeches. . . . He might often be seen before a small Dutch built house, of antiquated appearance, seated on a stoop . . . surveying with a philosophic visage the passing milk-carts and inhaling the dust from their wheels."

The cultural differences were embedded in geography. By the 1810s residents of the ferry district and those along the shoreline were predominantly non-Dutch (like Spooner), whereas the surrounding farms were still largely owned and occupied by descendants of the earliest Dutch immigrants, such as John Gerritsen, born in Gravesend in 1771 on the eve of the American Revolution. When he sat for his portrait around 1830, the artist used a common portrait convention. He incorporated objects or scenes that reveal information about the sitter, in this case Gerritsen's extensive land holdings, home, and tidal mill, built on the Gravesend/Flatlands border before the middle of the eighteenth century. Located at what is now Avenue V between Kimball and Ryder Streets (a short distance from Kings Plaza Shopping Center), the mill was powered by the waters of the tidal creek that indented the shore of Gerritsen's property. Typical of the mills for grinding grain that had once dotted the rural landscape, it was in 1830 the last remaining tidal mill in Kings County. Included in the portrait, it symbolizes the continuous and tenacious Dutch presence in Brooklyn—as well as its waning years.

By the time Gerritsen posed for his portrait, a system of gradual emancipation of slaves who had provided labor for farms like his and countless others had changed the economy drastically. It began in 1799, and by 1827 all African Americans in New York State were free. On July 19 of that year, *The Long Island Star,* Brooklyn's leading newspaper, described the huge celebration that brought together Brooklyn and Manhattan "societies" of African Americans to mark the end of slavery. The day, the reporter wrote, "was very fine, and the assemblage was indeed numerous. The societies repaired to the African church [probably Bridge Street A.W.M.E. Church, Brooklyn's oldest], where in addition to the religious exercises, an address was delivered. . . . The societies, forming a very long and handsome procession, bearing banners, and accompanied by several bands of music,

John S. Gerritsen **by unknown artist, oil on canvas, ca. 1830.**

John S. Gerritsen was a descendant of one of Brooklyn's early Dutch families, from which today's Gerritsen Beach neighborhood takes its name.

proceeded throughout principal streets; and after which a large company partook of a splendid dinner provided for the occasion." At the time slavery officially ended in New York State, African Americans made up roughly 10 percent of the total Kings County population, a proportionate decrease from the eighteenth century. Even though the African American population had risen consistently, the white population had grown at a faster rate.

Legally free, African Americans nevertheless were not free of economic problems or the discrimination that affected every area of their lives. Determined to establish their own social, cultural, and educational institutions, they marshalled their meager material resources and their enormous resourcefulness. From the very beginning, the independent Black church was the backbone of the community.

Brooklyn's earliest Black church, located downtown, had its roots in Brooklyn's first Methodist Episcopal Church, incorporated in 1794 as the Sands Street Church and begun in 1766 as open-air meetings conducted by a British sea captain, Thomas Webb. The congregation that developed around Webb and later around Woolman Hickman included whites, free Black people, and slaves. By 1798 Black people constituted a third of the membership. Black membership grew so quickly that the church demanded that African American members pay ten dollars quarterly for the "privilege" of worshiping in restricted pews. In response, every Black person withdrew from Sands Street to form the first Brooklyn African Wesleyan Methodist Episcopal (A.W.M.E.) Church in 1818. A year later a building went up on High Street near Jay Street in downtown Brooklyn, where the church became known as the High Street A.W.M.E. Church.

From the beginning, education was a church focus. As early as 1815, Peter Croger, a High Street trustee, was conducting a school in his home. With the

The trustees of Bridge Street A.W.M.E. Church, 1911.

The deacons of Brooklyn's first independent Black church, with more than a century of history behind it by 1911. Courtesy of Bridge Street A.W.M.E. Church.

Brooklyn! *An Illustrated History*

complete abolition of slavery in New York State in 1827, the church established an African free school to educate Black children who were being neglected by the tax-supported system. This emphasis on education—as well as on political activism and social service—continues to this day, among Bridge Street Church and others that serve the African American community (the church, now located on Stuyvesant Avenue in Bedford-Stuyvesant, takes its name from 309 Bridge Street, its downtown location in 1854).

As African American workers made their homes in downtown Brooklyn at the turn of the nineteenth century, Irish newcomers were settling at the northern edge of Fort Greene near Williamsburg, fleeing British reprisals for a 1798 uprising at Enniscorthy in Ireland's County Wexford. Some bought small plots of land from shipyard-owner John Jackson, who was selling off his property—the navy purchased most of it for a shipyard in 1801. The area was dubbed Vinegar Hill after Enniscorthy's Vinegar Hill, the site of a tragic last stand in the 1798 rebellion—perhaps named by Jackson himself, who may have seen it as a clever way to make his real estate attractive to Irish newcomers. Many Irish found work in the small factories that sprang up along the waterfront; later they hired on at the new Navy Yard.

By the 1830s, Irish were also living in the area below Brooklyn Heights; in wood-frame dwellings and hotels along the waterfront; along Fulton Street, the city's main business and shopping thoroughfare that wended its way up from the water's edge; and along the lower part of Atlantic Avenue. It was a large enough community so that the Roman Catholic Society of Brooklyn, made up mostly of Irish families, was able to worship in its own building by 1823.

In Brooklyn, as elsewhere in the United States, some people became alarmed about the number of Irish arrivals. Many Protestants saw Catholicism as "strange." They harbored fear toward the Irish who practiced it—and they feared that the new arrivals might take their jobs. Nativism, an anti-Catholic, antiforeign movement of the mid 1800s whose major targets were Irish and German immigrants, found its ugly voice in Brooklyn. At an August 1835 meeting of Brooklyn nativists, members adopted resolutions, aimed largely at the Irish, that reflected their antagonism; for example: "Resolved, As a sense of this meeting, that all native born Americans are called upon, by the present situation of our affairs, to band themselves together, without distinction of [political] party, for the holy and patriotic purpose of rescuing our civil institutions and liberties from the hands of foreigners."

If nativists were uncomfortable with Brooklyn's increasing diversity, they would have been horrified had they glimpsed the future. Within a decade, Europeans would begin to pour into the city in unprecedented numbers, a healthy proportion of the thirty-five million who left their homelands to settle in America between 1820 and 1920. Between 1835 and 1850 alone, the population of the City of Brooklyn more than tripled, from fewer than 25,000 to almost 97,000, making it the seventh-largest city in the United States even before consolidation with the City of Williamsburgh and Town of Bushwick, which would come in 1855.

This huge immigration occurred in two distinct waves. At midcentury, northern and western Europeans, predominantly Irish and Germans, began to pour in. Beginning in the late 1880s, extraordinary numbers of eastern and southern Europeans, including Russian Jews, Italians, and Poles, flocked to the United States. They came to escape pogroms, revolutions, wars, famine, and land loss in search of the opportunity to make a better life.

The Irish who made Vinegar Hill home at the end of the eighteenth century were only a fraction of the massive numbers of Irish who, almost fifty years later, fled a variety of economic, agricultural-based problems crowned by the devastating potato famine of the 1840s. As hunger and disease spread across the countryside, hundreds of thousands of Irish—almost all from rural areas—left Ireland for England and the Continent. Many others came to America as part of the initial wave of mid-nineteenth-century immigration.

The majority were women, and in Brooklyn many entered domestic service, low-level work that was almost all that was available to them. Irish laborers helped build vast construction projects—the modern Atlantic Docks along the South Brooklyn waterfront in the 1840s, extensive housing in what is today Sunset Park and elsewhere, the Brooklyn Bridge in the 1870s and 1880s, and the subways in the early years of the twentieth century.

The Parish

It is a happy event: the christening of Michael Cagney at St. Brendan's in Flatbush on a fine summer's day in August 1945. Michael's godmother, Mary Burns, cradles the swaddled infant.

As for many other Irish Americans, religion was a centerpiece of community life for baby Michael Cagney's parents, Margaret and Michael. Both children of Irish immigrants, they lived at East Nineteenth Street near Avenue O, a community that had been home to a sizeable Irish population since the nineteenth century. Like many other Irish communities in New York City, it was closely identified with the Catholic church. To outsiders, the Cagneys lived in Flatbush, but the Cagneys would have told you they lived in St. Brendan's parish. Even today, in the Irish sections of Bay Ridge, Flatbush, and Gerritsen Beach, residents often identify themselves by their parish instead of their neighborhood, a legacy of Brooklyn's early Irish immigrants and their influence.

Brooklyn's early Irish community developed around the church, which in Ireland had traditionally stood as a bulwark against English hostility and in Brooklyn offered a refuge in the face of bigotry. Brooklyn's first Catholic church was organized in the early 1820s by a group of men that included Hugh McLaughlin, whose son and namesake would become Brooklyn's Democratic Party leader; William Purcell, who worked at the Navy Yard; dairy farmer George McCloskey; and County Wexford-born Peter Turned, who had come to Brooklyn around 1800. After extensive fundraising, they broke ground for a building in April 1822. A little over one year later, Gabriel Furman happily reported, "Morning early and clear and pleasant, but rather damp—. . . . This morning St. James Roman Catholic Church in this village, consecrated by the Rt. Rev. Bishop Conelly—It is the first Roman Catholic Church erected on Long Island."

Michael Cagney's christening, 1945.

Most Irish immigrants arrived in desperate circumstances, with almost no material resources and few urban skills. Faced with widespread discrimination, they were forced to take the lowest-paying jobs and to live in some of the poorest parts of Brooklyn. In the August 16, 1847 issue of the *Brooklyn Daily Eagle,* editor Walt Whitman described one of the worst areas, a shantytown near Clinton Avenue. "Descending Fort Greene," he wrote, "one comes amid a colony of squatters. . . . They are permitted by the owners here, until the ground shall be wanted, to live rent free, as far as the land is concerned."

The continuing anti-Irish sentiment inspired a group of Irishmen meeting in a small coffeehouse near Fulton Ferry in 1850 to organize the St. Patrick Society. As did other newcomers, they created the organization to address their community's needs. Their mandate was to preserve Irish tradition, help indigent members, and make business contacts. The society so prospered, by 1910 its annual March 17 banquet was held at Manhattan's grand Waldorf-Astoria hotel—no Brooklyn site was large enough to accommodate it. By this time, as well, discrimination against the Irish had largely eased.

In 1855, the Irish represented 59 percent of the total foreign-born population of Brooklyn. By the 1860s, Irish communities were concentrated in the area just south of the Navy Yard (the site of the initial late eighteenth-century settlement) and between City Hall and Red Hook, as well as in Sunset Park and Flatbush. Many Irish built lives around these neighborhoods and took such avenues as politics, the fire and police departments, and business to establish positions for themselves in city life. Hugh McLaughlin chose politics. The youngest of ten children of immigrant parents from County Donegal, he was born in a house at the foot of Columbia Street. An early interest in politics led to hard work on the

Medal, St. Patrick Society of Brooklyn, 1913.

This tiny medal with its green ribbon features St. Patrick, Ireland's patron saint, commemorating the sixty-fourth annual banquet of the society, founded in 1850 to promote ethnic cohesiveness among Irish newcomers, who faced intense discrimination.

Hugh McLaughlin, ca. 1875.

Even though the *New York Sun* claimed in an August 1875 article that Hugh McLaughlin's hat was "always last year's with the silk brushed the wrong way," the Brooklyn Democratic boss—who amassed a fortune in real estate—appears distinguished and fashionably dressed in this portrait.

Joseph Ignatz Miller by Herman Schmahl, oil on canvas, 1846.

Sophia Theresia Miller by Herman Schmahl, oil on canvas, 1846.

The Millers left Germany for East New York's German community in 1842. While we know Joseph Miller was trained as a gardener in France and then worked as a botanist in Germany (he is pictured performing a plant splice here), all we know about Sophia Miller comes from an inscription on the back of the canvas: She was born in Alzey, Germany, in May 1793 and was married on February 6, 1815. The German-language newspaper on the table beside Joseph is probably the *New-Yorker Staats-Demokrat,* included to indicate Miller's interest in current affairs.

presidential campaign of 1856; his reward was the title of "Boss Laborer" at the Brooklyn Navy Yard, where he was a master foreman and where many workers were Irish. McLaughlin gained a local following, and after holding several political positions, by the 1860s headed Brooklyn's Democratic Party. Describing his arrival at what was most likely Brooklyn's City Hall, a *New York Sun* reporter wrote in 1875: "As soon as he is within the rotunda, he is encompassed by politicians. He stands above them all, erect, uncompromising in his bearing and with a mild yet powerful dignity."

Along with the Irish, who arrived at mid-century, came Germans, fleeing the economic and political upheaval that followed the unsuccessful 1848 revolutions. In 1845, 2,229 people in all of Kings County were listed as German-born. Ten years later there were 19,119 in Brooklyn alone, including more than 7,000 in Williamsburg, often forced to live in the same squalid conditions the Irish faced. Many settled in the Eastern District, the communities of Greenpoint, Williamsburg, and Bushwick. Others, such as Joseph and Sophia Miller, opted for East New York. Along with their sons Francis, Theodore, and Anton, the Millers arrived from Germany in 1842, joining three children who had immigrated two years earlier. Francis quickly established himself as a doctor in the New York City medical community and bought his parents a house. Joseph Miller, trained as a botanist, eventually established a nursery with his son Henry.

Many newly arriving Germans found life difficult and, like the Irish, took jobs doing heavy, unskilled labor. But the Millers' modest success was not unusual. Other Germans (particularly German Jews, many of whom had owned small businesses or been skilled workers at home) had developed urban skills in the cities they had left, so they were better equipped than many other newcomers (notably the Irish) to adapt to life in Brooklyn's expanding urban industrial world. Some Germans took jobs in Brooklyn's furniture- and clothing-manufacturing concerns; others dominated the brewing industry, particularly in Bushwick. German-language schools, churches, and newspapers flourished there and in Williamsburg and East New York, where residents spoke German and read such papers as the Williamsburg-published *Long Island Anzeiger.* As had the *Forward* for the immigrant Jewish community and as does the *Irish Voice* for Irish newcomers today, the *Anzeiger* helped German immigrants adapt to their new home by offering the news and listings for jobs and housing in their native tongue. Places like the local *turn halle,* or gymnasium, also played an important role in community life. Gymnastic societies were popular among Germans both for their emphasis on physical culture and as outlets for socializing and discussing politics.

In communities from Red Hook to East New York, Irish and Germans settled in Brooklyn in increasing numbers. Native-born Brooklynites began to fear becoming a minority. Former New Englanders, who since the early nineteenth century had been major players in Brooklyn's economic and cultural life, banded together in the 1840s to form the New England Society. In that era of nativist sentiment, the society was at least in part founded in reaction to the newly arriving immigrants and their different ways and cultures. While it eventually disbanded, in 1880 seven influential Brooklyn men came together to incorporate a new group, the New England Society in the City of Brooklyn, to cater to the large number of New Englanders in the community. Founded to "commemorate the landing of the Pilgrims," its objective was to "encourage the study of New England history and for such purpose to establish a library, and also for social purposes, and to promote charity and good fellowship among its members." Using Plymouth Rock as their emblem, members identified themselves as "true Americans" by drawing on their heritage as descendants of the country's founders, the Pilgrims of Massachusetts Bay, holding tight to their own traditions as the tide of immigration continued to sweep across Brooklyn.

Following the example of Alden Spooner, a second generation of New Englanders pursued professions as merchants, lawyers, and businesspeople. Among

Turn Halle in Williamsburgh, L.I. **by F. Wogram; F. Schmidt, publisher; lithograph, ca. 1850.**

This gymnasium was typical of the gathering places that also served as German social and political clubs where community members could visit with friends and neighbors. Turners, as members were called, were known for their support of labor and abolition causes. Collection of the The New-York Historical Society.

them were Abiel Abbot Low, whose firm, A. A. Low and Brothers, established a profitable trade in tea and silk with China and Japan; Henry E. Pierrepont, who created a transportation and real-estate empire that built on the work of his father, New England-born Hezekiah B. Pierpont; and Connecticut-born Simeon B. Chittenden, who moved to Brooklyn in 1842 and established himself as a dry-goods merchant. This enterprising generation of merchants and entrepreneurs established, within roughly twenty years at midcentury, some of Brooklyn's most lasting and prominent institutions, including Packer Collegiate Institute (founded as The Brooklyn Female Academy in 1845) and the Brooklyn Academy of Music (chartered in 1859). In 1863 they formed The Long Island Historical Society (renamed The Brooklyn Historical Society in 1985) out of a desire to collect and preserve evidence of the area's history. All these institutions were originally located in the Brooklyn Heights/City Hall area, making that neighborhood a center of Brooklyn cultural life into the late nineteenth and early twentieth centuries.

And to assuage the consciences of Brooklyn's growing Protestant Anglo-American business population, there was Connecticut-born Henry Ward Beecher, pastor of Plymouth Church in Brooklyn Heights. The most prominent Protestant minister of his time assured his congregation—largely transplanted New Englanders—that success in Brooklyn's commercial world was neither sinful nor selfish.

A suffragist and abolitionist, Beecher preached to the nation as well, espousing themes central to middle-class Victorian America: fixed moral laws and

faith in education and high culture. Huge crowds were drawn to Plymouth Church, where Beecher's rich voice rang out as his long hair flowed behind him, his ruddy complexion deepening as he exhorted his flock. One Sunday, writer Mark Twain watched Beecher in action and observed how he "went marching up and down the stage, sawing his arms in the air . . . and exploding mines of eloquence, halting now and then to stamp his foot three times in succession to make a point." Not only sensationalist, but also charismatic and magnetic, he achieved enormous popularity. The public's desire for "Beecherania" generated masses of consumer goods, ranging from books to prints in popular magazines to souvenir spoons. The pastor even appeared in advertisements endorsing such products as Pear's Soap.

At the height of his popularity, Beecher was tried for adultery in 1875, in the most highly publicized social scandal of the time. Accused of adultery with

"The Tilton-Beecher Scandal Cast.– Scenes and Incidents of the Trial," ca. 1875.

Contemporary newspapers pandered to the demands of a Victorian public clamoring for details of the Henry Ward Beecher trial. This series of vignettes, pasted along with dozens of others in a nineteenth-century scrapbook devoted to the trial, pictures the judge, lawyers, courtroom spectators, and participants. Beecher, running the gauntlet, *top right*, third from right; Elizabeth Tilton at lower left.

congregant Elizabeth Tilton, his best friend's wife, Beecher had denied it. But when the husband came forward and said the accusation was true, uproar followed. While Beecher was exonerated at his trial, he was eased from his post in deference to widespread opinion that he was indeed guilty, although his influence and popularity remained high.

Summertime Violence, Bigotry, and Brownsville

Brooklynites supported the Northern cause in the Civil War, with Henry Ward Beecher, true to his reputation, dramatizing the horrors of slavery by staging auctions of slaves, "selling" them to buy their freedom from bondage. The auctions drew upon a tradition begun in independent Black churches, where congregants pooled their resources to purchase and free a member of the church, a relative, or, more rarely, a friend. The tradition was taken up by both Black and white antislavery activists to free people in what was a form of public theater.

Others—mostly members of the New England community in Brooklyn—supported Northern troops in the Civil War by mounting an event then popular in Northern cities, a sanitary fair—to which Beecher donated some items for sale. An outgrowth of the U.S. Sanitary Commission, a private organization created to help sick and wounded soldiers, sanitary fairs were huge bazaar-like events organized to raise money, collect food and clothing for the poor, and help wives and children of draftees. Brooklyn's fair was held in 1864 at the new Brooklyn Academy of Music on Montague Street and in several nearby buildings. War-related exhibitions, displays of manufactures, a restaurant, and a fancy-dress ball

Pinky, tintype, 1860.

One of the most famous slaves "auctioned" by Henry Ward Beecher was a nine-year-old girl, Pinky. Beecher called her to the pulpit after a Sunday sermon and appealed to churchgoers to buy her freedom. They responded with contributions of money and jewelry that far exceeded the required amount.

Brooklyn! *An Illustrated History*

Brooklyn Sanitary Fair, 1864. New England Kitchen, **lithograph by A. Brown & Co., N.Y., for** *Henry McCloskey's Manual of 1864.*

The combination of pails, spatulas, fireplace tools, tall case clock, spinning wheels, and drying herbs was intended to evoke the kitchen of an eighteenth-century colonial New England home.

drew huge crowds. One of the most popular attractions was a replica of "the old New England Kitchen, and faithfully was it carried out, to the unbounded mirth of the visitors, as well as to the great pecuniary profit of the Treasury," noted the *Brooklyn Long Island Sanitary Fair,* an account written in 1864. "A Special Committee was selected to take charge of the 'New England Kitchen,' comprising among its members the ladies and gentlemen who originated the plan. This committee took hold of the work *con amore,* their New England blood fired with the determination to make the 'Kitchen' a grand success."

Henry McCloskey's Manual for 1864, the official annual New York City publication, included a series of prints of the Brooklyn fair, including one of the kitchen that romanticizes eighteenth-century domestic life. Visitors to the kitchen could feast on "pork and beans, cider apple-sauce, Boston brown bread, pitchers of cider, pumpkin, mince, and apple pies, doughnuts, and all the savory and delicate wealth of the New England larder," according to the fair history—and pretend they were in colonial New England. Faced with two Brooklyn histories to re-create, the primarily New England organizers chose to re-create their own, bypassing the eighteenth-century Dutch heritage that was more truly Brooklyn's.

As the Civil War raged on, industry was booming; however, long-festering social and economic tensions exploded forth. In August 1862, angry mobs of Irish workers marched on several tobacco factories on Sedgwick Street in South Brooklyn. The factories were largely manned by African Americans, since tobacco was one of the few industries open to them. While the Irish were divided on abolition, they feared that a Union victory would bring freed Southern slaves north and saw cheap Black labor as a direct threat to their already low-paying jobs. Although the *Brooklyn Daily Times* account of the attack noted that it was

Brooklynites, Real and Imagined

motivated by "several local politicians," the paper, which served Brooklyn's heaviest industrialized area, did not attempt to identify the leaders.

> The first overt act was committed last Saturday night, when some colored women and children employed in the Sedgwick street tobacco factories were hooted and stoned by a party of Irishmen, but without doing any serious damage. Yesterday afternoon, however, a systematic attack was made by a party of Irishmen, upon Watson's tobacco factory, at the foot of Sedgwick street, with splendid success. . . . At the time all the employees present were colored persons—twenty in number—five men, and the balance women and children.
>
> Shortly after noon, some 50 persons collected together and making known their object, assembled a crowd numbering between 2000 and 3000 persons and proceeded to the factories, which are three story buildings, of brick, and in which between 300 and 400 persons are employed. The overseer or foreman of Watson's Factory is a colored man, and all the persons employed in the factory, consisting mostly of women and children, are colored to the number of 50 to 75. In Lorillard's Factory about 250 are employed, white and colored.

The attackers entered Watson's on the lower floor and tried to set a fire. The workers took refuge upstairs. A half dozen of the men stood at the top of the stairs, armed with whatever they could find, and finally drove back the rioters. The *Anglo-African*, a weekly newspaper published by Black people, ran an editorial on the attack on August 9, 1862. "Americans!" it beseeched, "We charge you before high Heaven and the whole civilized world with being the authors of this great wickedness. It was you who first taught them [the Irish] to hate us. . . . Why, our countrymen, will you not put away this great wickedness from you?"

In July 1863, the New York City draft riots—the bloodiest riots in U.S. history—broke out in Manhattan. The outbreak was sparked by the introduction of military conscription. Many working-class white men, already fearful that Black people would take their jobs while they served in the military, were further inflamed by a provision in the draft law that allowed affluent men to buy their way out of fighting. The violence spread to Brooklyn, where nearly every house occupied by an African American family in the Second Ward (the East River waterfront area north and east of Fulton Street) was sacked. Black people caught by frenzied rioters were viciously beaten; some were killed.

Some who escaped sought refuge in the Forty-First and Forty-Second Precinct station house, while crowds ransacked their homes and destroyed their furniture. When rioters attempted to organize in Gowanus, police dispersed a large crowd armed with sticks. Many African Americans assembled for safety in the German turn halle in the Eastern District, which must have appealed as a place of refuge because turn halle members often served as bodyguards at abolition speeches. Germans organized themselves into a militia for protection and prevented a riot from taking place in Williamsburg.

During the riots, many African Americans fled New York City for Brooklyn. Some found refuge in Weeksville, an African American community in Bedford. The Brooklyn correspondent for the *Christian Recorder* wrote in the July 25, 1863 issue of the courageous efforts of residents who helped those fleeing for their lives. "In Weeksville and Flatbush, the colored men who had manhood in them armed themselves and threw out their pickets every day and night, determined to die defending their homes. Hundreds fled there from New York. . . . Most of

the colored men of Brooklyn who remained in the city were armed daily for self-defense."

Founded in the 1830s, by the time of the draft riots Weeksville and neighboring Carrville had become places where residents could have some autonomy, create their own institutions and educate their children. In the years following the Civil War, residents established the *Freedman's Torchlight*, a newspaper published by the African Civilization Society in 1866; the Garnet Field Club; the Howard Colored Orphan Asylum, which housed orphans and served as a child-care center, offering trade skills for older children as well; and the Zion Home for Colored Aged.

The creation of the Zion Home for Colored Aged in particular reflects the important role women played in the community. The institution was in 1869 at Zion African Methodist Episcopal Church in Manhattan; several years later the church bought land in Brooklyn on Dean Street between Albany and Troy to provide housing for upwards of a dozen residents. In the 1890s, donations were sought to build a new home, and women's organizations were especially active fundraisers. The Willing Workers Circle of the Kings Daughters, an interdenominational and interracial church group, sponsored annual dramatic entertainments as part of its efforts to gain financial support for the home and with the Concord Baptist Church, under the direction of Rev. William T. Dixon, organized a mass meeting to raise funds. In 1900, a new home was built at St. John's Place and Kingston Avenue.

Downtown resident Sylvanus Smith, a Weeksville landowner who helped open land to African Americans, was listed in the 1850 census as a "hog butcher" and in the 1860 census as a "drover." His grandfather, Solomon Hubbs, had escaped an African slave ship and, according to family history, was an African prince. Smith also traced his lineage to the Montauk Indians of Long Island. He married Anne Springsteel and raised a large family that included Susan Smith McKinney Steward, the first Black woman doctor in New York State and an active suffragist, and Minsarah Smith Tompkins, a grammar-school principal who married prominent abolitionist and antislavery orator Henry Highland Garnet. Smith himself served as a trustee of Brooklyn's first Black school district.

Over time, as new roads cut through the Weeksville/Carrville area and increasing numbers of whites moved in, the area became integrated. By the 1870s it had lost its distinctive African American character.

Sylvanus Smith **by unknown artist, charcoal on paper, ca. 1870s.**

Sylvanus Smith was listed in the Census of 1860, when he was fifty-six, as owning $8,000 worth of real estate, most likely his land in Weeksville.

Brooklyn! *An Illustrated History*

Susan Smith McKinney Steward, ca. 1900.

A dynamic woman and a middle child in Anne and Sylvanus Smith's family, Susan Smith McKinney Steward became not just the first African American female doctor in New York State but the third in the entire country. She practiced in Brooklyn from 1870 to 1895.

Meanwhile, other settlements of free African Americans were thriving downtown, in a small portion of Williamsburg (later abandoned by the African American community for uptown areas toward Fort Greene and Bedford-Stuyvesant), and in the Fort Greene (Washington) Park area. In Fort Greene, a community of free Black people had prospered since the 1840s; many of them worked in the shipbuilding trades. The Black people who lived in these communities most often held jobs on the lowest rung of the economic ladder, forced to compete with cheap European labor as more and more newcomers arrived in Brooklyn looking for work. Most continued to be excluded by whites from manufacturing pursuits. In the late nineteenth and early twentieth centuries, many Black seamstresses, for instance, worked at home because they were largely banned from factories. Still, by the Civil War years, an upper class had emerged within the African American community. It absorbed many transplanted Manhattanites, drawn by Brooklyn's superior educational facilities for Black people and by the existence of this prosperous community.

As the *Brooklyn Eagle* published several articles in 1892 about the "Negro 400" and numerous African American literary societies that had emerged in Brooklyn, new waves of immigrants were streaming into the city. Following the Irish and German influx of the 1840s came Italians and Eastern European Jews in large numbers by the 1890s. Louisa and Michael Caiafo arrived in Brooklyn from Italy in 1900, when she was fifteen, and he was twenty-two. Both were from the province of Salerno, and Michael, who had been to Brooklyn a few years earlier, was now returning with his new bride. Their first home was on York Street, near the Brooklyn Navy Yard, in a small Italian community where friends of

theirs lived. A handmade christening dress saved by their daughter is one of a few reminders of their lives there, as well as a symbol of family continuity. Each of the children born to Louisa and Michael wore it—Louis, Anthony, Ralph, James, and Jennie.

The Italians who immigrated to the United States in vast numbers beginning in the late 1880s came largely from rural peasant communities, fleeing poverty and overpopulation. Quite a few moved to Brooklyn after a stay in Manhattan's Little Italy. The 1855 Census of the State of New York did not list any Italian na-

Jennie Caiafo, ca. 1914.

Jennie Caiafo poses for the camera. She and her brothers, the children of Italian immigrants Louisa and Michael Caiafo, were christened in this delicate silk dress (above), which became a treasured family heirloom.

tives in Brooklyn; by 1890 there were 9,563, and by 1900, the borough's Italian population was second only to that of Manhattan. Facing a language barrier and discrimination, life was often difficult. Italian women often worked in the needle trades, either in factories or doing piecework at home. The men frequently took jobs as laborers in construction or along the docks that lined Brooklyn's industrial waterfront, many of them recruited by labor bosses in Italy. Many found jobs and made their homes in Williamsburg with its numerous factories, and in the South Brooklyn/Red Hook area, where the huge Erie Basin had spawned a complex of great warehouses, plants, and piers that made it one of the busiest shipping centers in the country. Italians also settled in Sunset Park, with its rows of

The *Giglio*

The *capo*, or leader, takes his place in front of the giglio, an ornate, three-ton tower. As the band begins to play, 120 lifters take their places. On the last note of the tune, the capo pierces the air with his cane, the lifters hoist the enormous structure, spectators cheer, and the giglio is aloft!

"Dancing" the giglio—moving the tower through a series of elaborate lifts and turns—has been a summer tradition in the Williamsburg section of Brooklyn since 1903, when Italian immigrants from Nola (a small town near Naples) celebrated the feast day of their patron saint, Paulinus, for the first time in their new home. They made a giglio—a festively decorated platform and tower surmounted by the saint's image—and carried it through neighborhood streets lined with cheering celebrants. The festival has become an annual show of tradition and culture, both poignant and clamorous.

Immigrants from Southern Italy began to arrive in Brooklyn in great numbers in the late nineteenth century. In Williamsburg they made homes alongside the Irish, Germans, Jews, Poles, Lithuanians, and Russians already living there, built Our Lady of Mount Carmel Church in 1887, and formed societies to honor the patron saints of their hometowns in Italy.

As neighborhood men left for the front in World War II, the annual event was discontinued. The neighborhood was further devastated when the Brooklyn-Queens Expressway sliced it in two. Not until 1949 did the giglio feast and the neighborhood revive. While many left the neighborhood, those who stayed were joined by postwar arrivals from Italy in a neighborhood that today is a mix of single-family homes, walk-ups, businesses, factories, warehouses, and churches. Residents gather every July, welcoming visitors and former neighbors. As the lifters carry the giglio past the church and through the streets of Williamsburg, the procession grows from block to block, drawing onlookers into this vibrant celebration of shared heritage and community values.

Dancing the giglio, 1956. Photograph courtesy of Thomas Bello.

piers and the thriving Bush Terminal. In each of these neighborhoods, Italian newcomers brought old traditions—such as the 1,500-year-old Feast of St. Paulinus in Williamsburg—and created new community landmarks, such as St. Rocco's Chapel in Sunset Park.

Over time these early Italian immigrants often moved to outer parts of the borough, where the farmland and fields, the open, almost bucolic landscape, reminded them of the rural Italy they had left behind. Rocco Yulo, for example, had come to Brooklyn by cargo ship in 1895 from the village of La Ransonia. (The family name had been Iulla until immigration officials who did not understand its pronunciation changed it.) Like most Italian immigrants, Yulo came alone, got a job, and saved enough money to bring his family over to join him. Within two years they moved into a tiny apartment behind Yulo's cobbler shop on the fringe of Williamsburg and in 1912 left for a newly built home at Avenue U near East Third Street in rural Gravesend, in the southernmost part of Brooklyn. Of the three generations of Yulos that gathered for a group portrait in 1923, five members stayed in the neighborhood.

Like many of the Italian immigrants, Eastern European Jews fled to the United States to escape poverty at the least, and often to escape both economic hardship and persecution. Daniel Wolin left Russia for New York at the turn of the century, among tens of thousands of Eastern European Jews pouring into the country. Daniel came with an uncle, following his mother, and the family lived first on the Lower East Side's Hester Street, the hub of Manhattan's Jewish quarter, then in East New York. They changed their name from Vilensky to Wolin to sound more "American." Daniel went to work for the U.S. Navy at the Fleet Supply Base in Brooklyn and became engaged to seventeen-year-old Fannie Mondry

The Yulo family, 1923.

Italian immigrants Rocco and Maria Gracia Yulo surrounded by their children and grandchildren.

Brooklyn! *An Illustrated History*

Daniel Wolin on a bike in East New York, 1914.

Like many newly arrived Jews from eastern Europe, Russian-born Daniel Wolin lived on Hester Street in Manhattan and later moved to East New York.

The Mondry family, 1910s.

Fannie Mondry (who later married Daniel Wolin) stands at right next to her sister Rose. Seated, from left, are her father, Moses; her sister, Augusta; and her mother, Nadya. Leon, a future Brooklyn prizefighter, sits on a small stool in front next to his sister Pauline.

in 1919. Fannie, her parents' first child, was conceived in Russia and born on Hester Street. Since her parents and Daniel Wolin's were from the same Russian village, the marriage in 1920 helped maintain community ties in a new setting.

Like Daniel and Fannie Wolin, most Eastern European Jews who arrived in the United States between the late 1880s and World War I were from Russia, where poverty and persecution had intensified with a wave of pogroms that followed the assassination of Czar Alexander II and the installation of an intensely anti-Semitic government. Of the roughly 150,000 Jews who fled their homeland in the 1890s, 90 percent came to America, and a huge portion of these came to New York. Unlike other immigrants during the same period, the Russian Jews knew they could not return home.

Until about 1905, the first home for many Eastern European Jewish newcomers was Manhattan's Lower East Side, already a thriving immigrant community. With the opening of the Williamsburg Bridge in 1903 and the development of rapid transit, a large number left Manhattan's overcrowded streets and tenements for Brooklyn's lower rents and more plentiful housing. In Brooklyn, they first clustered around old German neighborhoods like Williamsburg, where property owners got busy converting single-family brownstones and wood-frame homes to multiple dwellings that would increase their rental income. Because in Russia clothing manufacture had employed one-third of the Jewish labor force, many Jews entered the German-dominated clothing industry. And as the clothing industry moved from Manhattan to Williamsburg and Brownsville in response to Manhattan's skyrocketing factory costs, the workers followed. Besides the needle trades, many Jews also found jobs in tobacco and construction, and as shopkeepers.

Brownsville in particular became largely a working-class Jewish community. The roughly 4,000 Jews in and near Brownsville in the early 1890s had by 1905 grown to around 50,000; many Jews now immigrated directly to Brownsville instead of to the Lower East Side. Not only did Brownsville's synagogues, settlement houses, and other institutions resemble those the newcomers had left behind in European shtetls (Jewish towns), but the immigrant residents lent their new community a distinctly radical cast with their political activism. Pitkin Avenue, the neighborhood's main thoroughfare, commonly hosted street rallies of Jewish socialists. One of Brownsville's only drawbacks, many newcomers felt, was its distance from Manhattan, the center of Jewish cultural life in New York.

But the cosmopolitan allure of the big city was to some degree offset by its bigotry, which struck Jews just as it had struck earlier immigrants. In 1896 the *New York Tribune* characterized Brownsville in terms that make clear the kinds of stereotyping and ignorance Jews faced. Essentially, their neighborhood was reported to be filthy and backward, "a land of sweatshops and whirring sewing machines, of strange Russian baths, of innumerable dirty and tiny shops, of cows which are milked directly into the pitchers and pails of customers at eventide, of anarchists, of Jew dancing school and of a peasant market." By the 1920s, the populations of Brownsville and its neighboring communities of East New York and New Lots had outstripped the Eastern European Jewish settlements of the Lower East Side or Williamsburg.

By the turn of the century, Irish, German, Italian, and Eastern European Jewish newcomers had created or enriched Brooklyn neighborhoods with new sounds, new flavors, new sights. Others who came to Brooklyn in much smaller numbers also left indelible imprints on the cityscape, such as Scandinavians, many of whom first lived in the area at the harbor end of Atlantic Avenue—in

1893, the *Standard-Union* called it the "Swedish Broadway." Norwegians often settled in Park Slope, Sunset Park, or Bay Ridge.

Most immigrant Swedes, Norwegians (who came in the greatest numbers), and Danes had been ships' carpenters, seamen, and longshoremen displaced by a dying shipbuilding trade in their homelands and were drawn to Brooklyn's waterfront and its maritime trades. Finns who arrived in the mass migration of the 1890s, however, were mainly tenant farmers and landless laborers from agricultural regions.

Although the rural roots of most Norwegian immigrants drew them to the Midwest, before long Brooklyn was home to the largest urban concentration of Norwegians in the United States. From just north of Sunset Park, settlement eventually moved south, into Bay Ridge, and found in its ocean view and hills a reminder of Norway. Because as non-English-speaking immigrants they had difficulty obtaining health care, in the 1880s they established the Norwegian Deaconesses' Home and Hospital, the forerunner of the Lutheran Medical Center, today located at Second Avenue and Fifty-fifth Street in the former American Machine and Foundry Company building. A keystone of the Sunset Park community, it continues to serve a diverse population (although now, residents are just as likely to be Latino or Chinese) and provides thousands of jobs. Finns in Sunset Park built Imatra Hall, founded in 1890 as an aid society for newly arriving immigrants, which remains active as a social center.

Along with the Scandinavian immigrants to Brooklyn in the late 1800s came the city's heaviest influx of Poles. With its thriving waterfront and jobs Sunset Park attracted many of these newcomers, just as it had the Irish and Italians before them. Around 1880, a small Polish community began to develop in the area near Third Avenue and Twentieth Street.

While Polish women often took domestic and service jobs, many cleaning Manhattan's new office buildings, Polish men generally found work at the Ansonia Clock Company in Park Slope and other factories, as dock hands or labor-

Ambulance, Norwegian Deaconesses' Home and Hospital, ca. 1895.

Ambulance service from the Sunset Park hospital founded by Norwegian immigrants began in the early 1890s. Shortly after, the first hospital building rose at Fourth Avenue and Forty-sixth Street. Photograph courtesy of Sunset Park Restoration.

ers, or as gardeners or workers at Green-Wood Cemetery at Fourth Avenue and Twenty-fifth Street. By 1890 a largely Catholic Polish community was thriving in Sunset Park. Alongside the stores of earlier immigrants, Poles established shops along Third Avenue, where locals could purchase foods that reminded them of home. Poles also settled in the rowhouses of Greenpoint and Williamsburg, drawn by factory jobs along Brooklyn's industrial waterfront, and built at the centers of their communities great churches. At St. Stanislaus Kostka Church on Humboldt Street in Greenpoint, founded in 1896, today's worshipers can choose on Sundays from the seven masses held in Polish or the five in English. In Sunset Park, Poles established Our Lady of Czestochowa, where parishioners—many second- and third-generation Poles—worship at the elaborately carved altar brought from Poland by the church's first pastor at the turn of the century.

"A Good Place to Land One's Feet"

By 1900 a borough of New York City, Brooklyn had changed dramatically from a century earlier. An enormous bridge spanned the East River. Huge factories lined the shores. Instead of two Dutch farmers discussing the market price of corn as they ferried their crops to Manhattan by sailboat, two lawyers strolling across the Brooklyn Bridge discussed the latest decrees of Democratic Party Boss Hugh McLaughlin. The old-stock Brooklyn family that visited Prospect Park with friends on Sunday now rubbed shoulders with Russian immigrants who had traveled there from Brownsville for a day outdoors. Newcomers continued to arrive, bringing their special cultural experiences to the borough and being altered themselves by the burgeoning metropolis. Brooklyn entered the twentieth century, once again poised on the brink of massive change.

Blatantly xenophobic legislation enacted in 1924, aimed largely at the southern and eastern Europeans of the second great wave of nineteenth-century immigrants, sharply reduced immigration for the next forty years and, combined with the worldwide depression in 1929, reduced the influx to little more than a trickle. Now, newcomers came largely from within the United States and its territories: African Americans from the rural South and Puerto Ricans.

Southern Blacks who listened to northern job recruiters heard stories of a better life and employment in the urban industrial North. Hundreds of thousands fled a failing rural economy, second-class status, and a minimal education system for their children. They came largely between World War I, when wartime labor shortages offered some employment opportunities, and the 1930s. People made "the Great Migration," as it has come to be known, by sometimes circuitous routes. Clyde Vernon Kiser, a sociologist who interviewed many of those who journeyed north from South Carolina, recounted the story of a man who left St. Helena Island in 1917. "I figured it this way," said the young man,

> I just wanted to travel. I could work and dig all day on the Island and the best I could do would be to make $100 and take a chance on making nothin'. So I decided I'd be a fool to stay there n' dig all my life at that rate.
> First place I went to was Savannah. Thought I'd soon save up enough to travel up North. I began writing my brothers who were up here. They said, "Yes, jobs are good up here."

Graduating class at Hampton Normal and Agricultural Institute, 1897, with Mary Susan Bailey Edwards second from left.

Mary Susan Bailey Edwards, posing with fellow nursing graduates of the Hampton Normal and Agricultural Institute in Virginia (now Hampton University, it is one of the many Black schools founded in the South in the late nineteenth century), came north to Brooklyn in the 1910s. Family treasures include her dues book and medal.

In 1923, some of my friends I was working with and I decided to catch the boat and travel up to Philly. We stopped there, worked one month. Didn't like it. Came on over to my brothers in Brooklyn.

By 1930, over 60 percent of Brooklyn's African Americans had been born outside the borough.

Most of those who made the journey and settled in Brooklyn came by train up the Atlantic seaboard from Virginia and North and South Carolina, bringing with them rich histories and filled with hopeful plans. Mary Susan Bailey Edwards arrived in the 1910s, a graduate of Virginia's prestigious Hampton University, the alma mater of Booker T. Washington. Trained as a nurse, she became a matron at the Home for Colored Aged People on St. John's Place and was an active mem-

Dues book and medal, Order of the Eastern Star, Queen Esther Chapter No. 9, belonging to Mary S. [Bailey] Edwards, ca. 1915.

Members of the Lewis family.

Henry Luther Lewis's family photos trace his roots from southern slavery to Bedford-Stuyvesant: his great-grandmother Amy Greer, a slave on a southern plantation, 1875 (*center*); her daughter Elizabeth (Greer) Lewis and her husband, around 1887 (*top left*); their daughter Adelaide Viola Lewis-Campbell (Henry Luther Lewis's mother), 1968 (*top right*); Lewis himself, 1932 (*bottom left*); and his daughter, Amy, in front of her brownstone home in Bedford-Stuyvesant (*bottom right*). Photographs courtesy of Henry Luther Lewis.

ber in the Order of the Eastern Star, a volunteer worker for the poor, and president of the Women's Missionary Society of the First Episcopal District of the A.M.E. Church in Brooklyn.

South Carolinian Henry Luther Lewis traces his ancestry back to great-grandmother Amy Greer and her husband James, slaves on a South Carolina plantation. When Lewis first came to Brooklyn on a vacation in 1927 after graduating from grammar school in Charleston, he stayed with relatives, and returned to South Carolina with tales of talking pictures, els, and other urban delights. In 1929, the whole family moved north to settle on Bedford-Stuyvesant's Gates Avenue, one of only six African American families on the block. During the Depression Henry helped his mother Adelaide, who worked as a laundress and a hand ironer. Although the family moved to Pitkin Avenue in East New York in 1936, Henry Lewis put down roots in Bedford-Stuyvesant after serving in World

War II; he bought a home on Madison Street, where his daughter Charlotte Amy was born. Today, both call the neighborhood home.

The African Americans who came north were joined by West Indians and Black people from other areas, drawn by the borough's cheaper, more available housing and its historic African American roots. But the kinds of opportunities available to European immigrants were denied these new migrants, who faced not only prejudice but de facto segregation. As more Black people moved into Bedford-Stuyvesant, for instance, some white residents responded with suspicion, fear, and even hatred. Hoping to discourage Black people from buying homes in the area, a group of whites formed the Gates Avenue Association in 1922 to establish restrictive covenants. The entry in the group's minute book for the October 29, 1924, meeting outlines a strategy for keeping housing in white hands: "The president's report of the year's activities mentioned . . . the 'widening spread of the black belt' all over Brooklyn. The president said that the only remedy that has been devised is found in neighborhood solidarity and disposing of property. Miss Claxon of the Downing St. Assn. [advised us] as a real estate dealer . . . not to list property with unknown or questionable dealers and not to sell to people one does not know."

African Americans continued to flock to Brooklyn in the years following the Depression, when the borough experienced a phenomenon linked directly to the evolution of mass transit. In 1936, the "A" train (the Independent Fulton Street line) was extended to Brooklyn, which encouraged thousands of African Americans to leave Harlem (by then losing some of its attractiveness) and cross the river in search of lower-priced, roomier housing, especially in the growing African American community in Bedford-Stuyvesant. "Take the A Train" sang Duke Ellington in 1941, and they did.

Like African Americans, Puerto Ricans who headed north in the 1910s found conditions less rosy than they had anticipated. "I suddenly realized that there was no future for a young man in Puerto Rico, but the future of the sugar cane field, with starvation wages," wrote a Brooklyn political activist, Jesús Colón. "I came to New York [in 1918] to poor pay, long hours, terrible working conditions, discrimination. . . . Somehow in New York I did not seem to find the pot of gold at the end of the rainbow that I was so sure I would find in my dreams while in Puerto Rico."

As U.S. citizens, Puerto Ricans were free to travel back and forth to the mainland, and many came to Brooklyn, a journey that took five days by steamship. Leaving a devastated agricultural-based economy in search of jobs, newcomers arrived via huge steamers that docked in Red Hook, where Columbia Street soon became the site of a Puerto Rican colony, as did the Borough Hall area; these rowhouse neighborhoods were mainly populated by Italian and Jewish families. Newcomers also settled in the Navy Yard area and Greenpoint.

While some Puerto Rican newcomers found jobs along the Brooklyn waterfront and in manufacturing, others, like Jesús Colón, found disappointment and discrimination. Francisco Pratts, an early Puerto Rican *pionero,* or pioneer, recalls that in Brooklyn in the 1920s "there were factories on Jay Street and in many places [where] they had signs [saying] 'No Puerto Ricans allowed.' If you got on line for a job, the minute they found out you were a Puerto Rican you got beaten up." Two industries requiring skilled labor that were open to Puerto Rican newcomers were the needle trades, which drew mainly women, and cigar making.

Cigar factories employed male and female Puerto Rican (as well as Cuban) artisans, called *tabaqueros* or *tabaqueras.* These highly skilled workers, often well educated, were made obsolete when cigar making declined in the 1920s in the face of increased mechanization and cigarette consumption, and were forced to compete with other ethnic groups for jobs as unskilled laborers. But Puerto Ricans drew on their rich tradition of political activism, creating numerous political clubs in the 1920s and 1930s to work toward important social changes such as political representation and education.

One of the people at the heart of the Puerto Rican social and political community was activist Antonia Denis, who came to Brooklyn in the World War I era from Vega Baja. Over the course of her life, she saved many photographs that reflect the emergence of a Latino political movement in Brooklyn, among them a rare 1930 portrait of members of the Betances Democratic Club 51. Denis was a founder of this club, named for Ramon Emetrio Betances, a leader in the Puerto Rican independence movement from Spain.

In 1929, the New York stock market crashed. During the Great Depression that followed, Brooklynites lost their jobs or could not find steady work. As bread lines lengthened and men sold apples on street corners, "the New York police began taking a census of the needy as the city made plans to feed 12,000 to 15,000 persons daily throughout the Winter," noted the October 24, 1930, edition of the *New York Times.* "The Salvation Army will open eight free food stations in Manhattan and Brooklyn today." Midwood's John Yulo, whose father Rocco had come to Brooklyn at the turn of the century, recalls that just as he finished an apprenticeship in the printing industry and was ready to get his journeyman's card, he was unable to find work. After a brief stint on a soda truck for $2.50 a day, he saw an ad for a job in Pennsylvania running a linotype machine on the night shift.

Members of the Betances Club, 1930.

Brooklynite and Puerto Rican political activist Carlos Tapia, center, with other Betances Club members, gained recognition for Puerto Ricans as part of New York's political base. The club was founded on Sackett Street in 1918, when Puerto Rican political action was centered in Brooklyn.

Brooklyn! *An Illustrated History*

He worked there for years, returning to Brooklyn on weekends, where he recalls being aware of "a feeling of desperation."

The Depression ended as the United States entered World War II, and by the time Brooklyn soldiers returned home, many immigrant neighborhoods had entirely changed, as second- and third-generation families moved farther out into the borough and beyond. For instance, many Italians moved to such neighborhoods as Bensonhurst and Gravesend. Jews created second-generation settlements in Flatbush, Borough Park, Eastern Parkway, and Brighton Beach, and spread down Flatbush Avenue to Canarsie and Sheepshead Bay, to suburban New Jersey and Long Island communities, and even to Miami.

The postwar years signaled another great migration to New York City, as hundreds of thousands of African Americans left the South and a new wave of Puerto Ricans boarded planes for the six-hour flight from San Juan to the New York area for fares of from thirty to fifty dollars. It was a new age: the Puerto Rican diaspora was the first by airplane. In the 1940s and 1950s, some of the original pionero settlements fell victim to urban renewal and to large-scale projects like the Brooklyn-Queens Expressway. New arrivals tried other neighborhoods, including Gowanus, Cobble Hill, Bushwick, East New York, Sunset Park, and Williamsburg.

In 1965, Congress amended U.S. immigration laws in force since 1924, making the United States more accessible; immigrants flowed into Brooklyn in unprecedented numbers. This time, the largest groups came not from Europe but from the Caribbean, Latin America, and Asia.

Author Paule Marshall was born in Brooklyn to immigrants from Barbados. In a November 3, 1985 *New York Times Magazine* article, she notes that "today whenever I visit my old neighborhood of Bedford-Stuyvesant and walk along Fulton Street or Nostrand Avenue, its twin commercial hubs, I have to remind myself that I'm in Brooklyn and not in the middle of a teeming outdoor market in St. George's, Grenada, or Kingston, Jamaica, or on some other West Indian island. Because there, suddenly, are all the sights and sounds, colors, smells and textures of the entire Caribbean archipelago, transplanted intact to the sidewalks of New York."

In a swath that cuts through parts of Bedford-Stuyvesant, Crown Heights, and East Flatbush, Haitians, Jamaicans, and other Caribbean Americans now make their homes, part of the largest West Indian population outside of the Caribbean. Although small numbers of people of West Indian heritage arrived in the first half of the twentieth century—among them Bertram Baker, the first Black person elected to the state assembly, and Shirley Chisholm, America's first Black congresswoman—most immigrated after 1965, largely from rural areas. Fleeing economic hardship and political oppression—such as the harsh dictatorship of Haiti's François Duvalier and his son Jean-Claude—many were drawn by the promise of a better life. "In Haiti," writes author Samuel Friedman, "people hear about the riches of 'Bouklin-lan'—the Creole word for Brooklyn."

Many new arrivals, particularly women, found jobs as domestic houseworkers or in nursing and other professions. Men often found work as security guards and laborers. A large number have pursued higher education and white-collar employment. In East Flatbush, for example, where an overwhelming percentage of the population is from Jamaica, Granada, Haiti, Guyana, and elsewhere in the Caribbean, many work in the health-care industry in places like Brooklyn Hospital, Long Island College Hospital, and SUNY Downstate. West Indian restau-

Carnival on Eastern Parkway, 1984.

Eastern Parkway is alive with the pulsating rhythms of Carnival on Labor Day, as spectators crowd brownstone-lined streets. This participant, dressed in a costume that is itself a work of art, moves gracefully down the center of the thoroughfare. © Roberta Grobel Intrater.

rants, businesses, bakeries, groceries, and discount shops flourish on Nostrand and Utica Avenues, some alongside stores of Korean and Arab merchants. Papers like the *Haïti-Observateur* provide news of home and a feeling of community. Brooklyn, with its supply of available housing, has proven particularly attractive to West Indians, to whom home ownership is very important.

Brooklyn's Caribbean Americans are active in the borough's commercial, business, religious, and cultural life. One of the most visible ways that newcomers have made Brooklyn more like home is through Carnival, which unites West Indian people from many different countries in one setting and has come to symbolize New York's Caribbean community. Before Brooklyn became the hub of New York City's West Indian population, Carnival was held in Harlem. But since 1969, each Labor Day revelers and enthusiastic onlookers have taken over Eastern Parkway, the broad boulevard that stretches from Ralph Avenue to Grand Army Plaza and cuts through neighborhoods that boast huge African American and Caribbean populations. Taking over Eastern Parkway, one of Brooklyn's busiest, most prominent thoroughfares, not incidentally symbolizes the community's political strength. Today, Brooklyn's Carnival, organized by the West Indian/American Day Carnival Association, ranks as one of the largest regularly scheduled street events in North America, annually attracting more than one million marchers, viewers, and vendors.

This annual celebration springs from ancient European, African, and Asian roots. Brought to the New World by Catholics, in the nineteenth century emancipated Black people in the islands made it their own, using the yearly pre-Lent celebration to criticize the social order and keep African traditions alive. In Trinidad, Carnival became, for many, a symbol of freedom. Brought to Brooklyn's

Crown Heights neighborhood—where West Indian/American Day Carnival Association president Carlos Lezama says the open spaces, neighborhood feeling and constant coming and going of friends resembles home—it is a way to claim and assert African and Caribbean roots and traditions in a new setting. But in the transplanting, Carnival is somewhat changed. In Trinidad, it takes place in February; in Brooklyn, it is held on Labor Day weekend, more suitable to an outdoor celebration in a cold northern climate. And, instead of a largely Trinidadian affair, Brooklyn's Carnival brings together the borough's diverse Caribbean population—simultaneously preserving a tradition for some New York West Indians and creating one for those who come from places where Carnival is not celebrated. And where staged competitions in Trinidad culminate on Port-of-Spain's Savannah Stage in Queen's Park, competitions in Brooklyn are staged at The Brooklyn Museum on Eastern Parkway.

Six months after Carnival, in another part of Brooklyn, other newcomers have sponsored a different kind of procession annually since 1974. This one is religious, and its participants are members of Williamsburg's All Saints Church. Most left Piaxtla, a small Mexican town in the state of Puebla, when several local textile plants closed. As in Mexico, the procession commemorates the appearance of the Virgin of Guadalupe to Juan Diego, a young Indian man, in Mexico in 1531. The Virgin then became the patron saint of Mexico. In place of Piaxtla's narrow village streets, celebrants in Brooklyn parade under the elevated tracks of Williamsburg, moving through commercial and residential neighborhoods,

Carnival

Organizing Carnival is a year-long effort. Months before Labor Day, individuals and "camps," or groups, fabricate elaborate costumes in storefronts and homes. Creativity, skill, and enthusiasm transform feathers, sequins, glue, metal armatures, and a host of other materials both extravagant and ordinary into fantastic costumes. Like ice sculptures meant to dazzle for a brief period and then dissipate, they are sometimes discarded after use. Often, though, parts are recycled for use in carnivals in places like Trinidad and Toronto.

As is true in Trinidad, the costumes are fashioned to express the theme selected for the year—1994's theme, for instance, was "Tribes," recalling the participants' roots. That year, in his Jefferson Avenue shop, Trinidad-born Francis "Jackie" Clavery fashioned an elaborate costume as part of the

work of his camp, "Culture of Black Creation." Drawing on the Caribbean tradition of fine metalwork, he holds one of his designs, a costume called "Quetzalcoatl."

Francis "Jackie" Clavery making a costume, 1994.
Photograph by Hayden Roger Celestin.

Procession of the Virgin of Guadalupe, 1988.

In a striking procession against the backdrop of the elevated tracks in Williamsburg, festival participants carry a banner bearing the image of the Virgin of Guadalupe. December weather forces the children in the procession to wear winter coats over their traditional clothing—a switch from Mexico's warmer climate. Photograph by Tony Velez.

through areas home to Latino and Italian families, temporarily transforming Brooklyn's streets into a religious pathway. They carry a processional banner that melds home and host country. The striking, multicolored embroidered image of the Virgin was made in a local Mexican workshop and added to a banner purchased in Brooklyn, reflecting the same aesthetic and care of a traditional Mexican banner.

Mexicans are just one piece of the mosaic of Brooklyn's emerging Latino communities. Today, grandchildren of the turn-of-the-century pioneros are joined by people from all over Latin America, most of whom arrived after 1965, and Brooklyn is now more than 20 percent Latino. Enriching the textures and traditions of the borough are residents from Puerto Rico, the Dominican Republic, Cuba, Mexico, Panama, Nicaragua, El Salvador, Guatemala, Ecuador, Colombia, and Peru. Here, their histories intersect. Latinos and Latinas share the Spanish language and a heritage nourished by Spanish, Indian, African, and Asian cultural roots—at least.

Newly arriving Latinos often move into neighborhoods established by earlier Puerto Rican and Cuban arrivals in Sunset Park, East New York, or Williamsburg's Los Sures. In Sunset Park, Fifth Avenue is lined with businesses that bring the tastes and feel of former homelands to this one—Puerto Rican, Dominican, Mexican, and Cuban restaurants; corner bodegas where residents can buy tropical fruits and vegetables; botánicas, or spiritual pharmacies, selling religious articles and herbs; and travel agencies with brightly colored signs advertising trips to the Caribbean and Central and South America. Walking along Fifth Avenue in Sunset Park on a hot summer day, one is likely to hear the call of Pablo Santos selling flavored ices from his *piragua* cart, a bit of Santo Domingo re-created in Brooklyn.

Latino residents now share Sunset Park with Chinese neighbors, who have created a community along Eighth Avenue and nearby streets several blocks from the Latino community's main commercial thoroughfare, Fifth Avenue. Many Chinese residents call their neighborhood Bat dai do or Ba da dao (Eighth Avenue), after its principal street. Grace Chan, who has lived in the neighborhood since 1985, opened a video store on Fifty-Second Street in Sunset Park when she realized that her neighbors were having to rent tapes in Manhattan's Chinatown. Standing in front of her shelves of Hong Kong-made videos, she reflects on what her new home means to her. "Sunset Park," she explains in her native Cantonese, "is 'luo guek diem'—a good place to land one's feet."

No wonder. While Brooklyn is home to Koreans, Vietnamese, Cambodians, and other Asians, the largest group, the Chinese, have made their mark on Sunset Park. A steady influx of newcomers to Bat dai do has made it New York City's "third Chinatown," after Manhattan and Flushing—the fastest growing, largest

Piragua (snow-cone) cart, 1989.

Pablo Santos came to Brooklyn from Santo Domingo, Dominican Republic, in 1985, bought a piragua cart, painted it, topped it with an umbrella from a liquor-distributing company, imported the best tropical flavors from Santo Domingo, added a block of ice, and opened for business in Sunset Park.

Chinese settlement in Brooklyn, surpassing communities in Bay Ridge, Sheepshead Bay, Bensonhurst, Flatbush, and Starrett City.

Throughout the late nineteenth century and most of the twentieth, U.S. restrictions limited Chinese immigrants to a few a year, even as Europeans arrived by the tens of thousands. With the lifting of quotas in 1965, the loosening of the People's Republic of China's emigration laws in the 1970s, and the impending end of Hong Kong's status as a British colony in 1997, Chinese have flocked to the United States. Persuaded in part by a long and widely held perception that jobs are plentiful in America, many were particularly drawn to New York, where they had family ties. Manhattan's Chinatown became their main destination. As its population mushroomed, a satellite community grew up in Flushing, Queens. When it, too, overflowed, new arrivals searched for more available housing at lower rents, and in the 1980s discovered Sunset Park. The neighborhood offers easy access via subway to Manhattan's Chinatown, where many Sunset Park residents work in garment factories; available housing; vacant stores; and comparatively low rents.

Today, Chinese businesses along Eighth Avenue include restaurants, video stores, groceries, and a pharmacy, which share space with earlier Scandinavian residents and Middle Eastern business owners. Here, modern and traditional often go hand in hand, as residents make connections with their former homes. Herbalist Zhang Zhong Oy practices a tradition he learned in Zhang Gang, China.

Zhang Zhong Oy, 1991.

Standing underneath the sign that announces his practice as an herbalist, Zhang Zhong Oy has brought to Sunset Park's fast-growing Chinese community a little bit of home.

Lantern from Master Tin Sun's office, ca. 1980s.

This lantern hung in front of the office of Master Tin Sun, a Chinese geomancer who frequently works with residents of Chinese Sunset Park. The symbolic colors of black and gold are intended to attract good luck.

From an office in the back of a local market on Eighth Avenue, he prescribes traditional medicines for healing. Chinese residents of Sunset Park often call upon Master Tin Sun to help them select a place of business or decorate a shop, restaurant, or home. A geomancer, he draws upon astrology, geography, and ergonomics to advise people how to bring their living and working environments into harmony with nature, based on the belief that improved efficiency and performance increase one's chances for good luck and prosperity. By combining new ways and old traditions, Brooklyn's Chinese residents are creating a home that indeed seems to be "a good place to land one's feet."

Sauerkraut and Plum Pudding: Making Brooklyn Home

Over the course of Brooklyn's history, its neighborhoods have become home to successive generations of newcomers. Sunset Park, for example, where Native Americans and Dutch colonists once lived, has long been a destination for new arrivals to Brooklyn: the Irish in the mid-nineteenth century; Poles and Scandinavians in the 1880s; Italians in the 1890s; Puerto Ricans after World War II, followed by others from the Caribbean and from Latin America; and most recently, Chinese and other Asians.

Because newcomers often look for reminders of home, Rocco Yulo and other rural-born Italian immigrants were attracted to Gravesend's open spaces in the 1920s, and Jewish Soviet emigrés in the 1970s were drawn to Brighton Beach, not just for its Jewish community or cheap housing but because for many the ocean spoke to them of home. Brighton Beach Avenue, the area's commercial strip, is now lined with dozens of Russian businesses. As Brooklyn becomes home, community ties can become impossible to break: Many Sephardic Jews who moved

to suburban Deal, New Jersey in the 1970s have returned, renewing their relationship with the local synagogue and relegating Deal to the status of summer resort.

Sometimes, newcomers have changed Brooklyn to suit their needs. In Williamsburg, brick and brownstone rowhouses that had housed a Jewish community since the early 1900s have for decades now been home to members of the Satmar sect of Hasidic Jews. Like many other Orthodox Jews, the Hasidim place a premium on strict religious observance, and Williamsburg residents have fashioned lives that combine Old World ways and ancient biblical traditions with modern technology and employment in such fields as the diamond and computer industries. Men wear garments based on eighteenth-century European styles, while women dress modestly but often fashionably. Clothing, hair and hat styles, shoes, the cut of a coat all speak a language common to community members. Subtle details, for example, can reveal the wearer's Hasidic sect, age, or marriage status.

This community provides many of its own goods and services, including newspapers, schools, ambulances, bus and car services, printers, tailors, special Kosher foods, and religious articles. The *talit katan,* a four-cornered garment with fringes tied in numerologically significant knots, worn by males in accordance with biblical commandments, is made in a local Williamsburg shop. Matzo for Passover is hand baked according to strict requirements. Each autumn, observant Jews commemorate forty years of wandering in biblical times by symbolically recreating *sukkah,* temporary shelters built under the open sky. Inventive residents design apartment buildings to accommodate staggered balconies, so that they can build their sukkah in ways that everyone has a clear bit of sky overhead.

Often, objects represent history or homeland for Brooklynites. Doña Esperanza Andón de Fuentes, who came to Cobble Hill from Piaxtla, Puebla, Mexico,

in the 1970s, knew that she could make enchiladas and tamales correctly only
with the proper utensils and ingredients. Initially, she found it difficult to find
Mexican ingredients in Brooklyn and the right kind of Mexican pots and pans
were never available. So, over the years, she and her family have stocked their
kitchen with glazed handmade *ollas, cazuelas,* and *jarritos* (earthenware pots,
casserole dishes, and mugs) from Mexico, which she mingles with modern stainless-steel containers purchased in Brooklyn. In the same spirit, when Kennet and
Elizabeth Rawson moved to Park Slope from Long Island to pursue college and
careers, he brought his family's heirloom coat of arms and she brought family
photos—tangible ways to hold onto the past. In her urban Bay Ridge home, Doris
Holvik Jensen revives the rural traditions of her Nordic grandparents by deco-
rating plates, furniture, and clothing in the tradition of Norwegian *rosemaling*,
decorative floral painting. For sale in the windows of the Nordic Deli on Third
Avenue, her delicately hand-painted items are a tie to old Norway in a community where her neighbors include people from all over the world. In a shop on
Atlantic Avenue, William del Pilar, Jr. makes cuatros (traditional Puerto Rican gui-
tars) and other instruments as instructed by his father, who came from Puerto
Rico in the 1940s.

In the process of making Brooklyn home, old-timers and newcomers often
cross cultural boundaries, sometimes in the simplest of things, like food. Wee-
kee's at Eighth Avenue and Fifty-fourth Street in Bay Ridge was once the Atlantic
Diner, which catered to a predominantly Norwegian community. Customers today can sit down at the counter and order up either a Norwegian specialty or a
bowl of Chinese wonton soup. From shops along Atlantic Avenue in Cobble Hill,
the aroma of Middle Eastern spices and fresh baked bread acts as a reminder of
home to some and a new sensory delight to others. A kosher pizza parlor in Midwood unites the traditions of one group with the food of another. And then there
is Deedee Dailey, a chef who owns a catering business in Sheepshead Bay. A sec-

Brooklynites, Real and Imagined

ond-generation American with roots in the Caribbean and the American South, she turns her family's Thanksgiving into a testimony to the diverse cultures that call Brooklyn home. Blending the culinary legacies of a Bajan grandmother and an African Cuban great-grandmother with mainstream Black Americana, she serves up saltfish, coconut loaf, sorrel beverage, pigeon peas and rice alongside roast turkey.

Brooklyn's cultural differences are not always so happily resolved. In recent years, racial tensions in the borough have produced headlines. In Bensonhurst in August 1989, a gang of whites murdered a Black teenager. And Crown Heights was in the news and the public eye in the summer of 1991 as a result of a series of tragic events. A Caribbean child was accidentally killed by a car driven by a Lubavitch man. During the shock, protest, and rioting that disrupted the residential neighborhood, a gang of Black youths attacked and fatally wounded another Lubavitch man. The events of 1991 and the publicity that followed underscored the challenges that neighborhoods can face when people of different backgrounds, such as the Caribbean, African American, and Lubavitch Hasidic Jewish communities of Crown Heights, live together. They also created an image that does not always match the experiences of its residents. Many in Crown Heights have worked hard to resolve divisive issues, and grass-roots community organizations like Project CURE, founded in 1991 after the riots in an effort to promote racial understanding, testify to residents' continued efforts.

Given the mix of diverse backgrounds, it is amazing how well Brooklynites get along. Perhaps Gabriel Furman best described the special chemistry of the borough when he wrote in 1823 of the relationship between Brooklyn's earliest

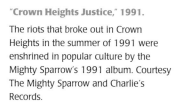

"Crown Heights Justice," 1991.

The riots that broke out in Crown Heights in the summer of 1991 were enshrined in popular culture by the Mighty Sparrow's 1991 album. Courtesy The Mighty Sparrow and Charlie's Records.

T-shirt, "Increase the Peace Project CURE," 1991.

Project CURE, a grass-roots community organization that strives to improve racial understanding, was founded in 1991 after the Crown Heights riots. Its membership includes young men from many ethnic groups.

colonial settlers, the Dutch and the English. "It is true that at first there was not so good a state of feeling existing between the Dutch and English settlers as might have been desired, but this feeling has all died away long since, and the Dutch and English, by living as neighbors and coming better to understand each other's characters . . . have become one people; and the Dutch talked English, and the English talked Dutch; and they eat sourkrout, smoked goose and kolichees, and roast beef and plum pudding together, and everything has since gone as comfortably as could be wished."

The Great East River Suspension Bridge by Currier and Ives, color lithograph, 1883.

When it opened in 1883, the Brooklyn Bridge dwarfed the skylines of Manhattan (*right*) and Brooklyn. Renowned printmakers and publishers Currier and Ives produced several different images of the new bridge for sale to a public captivated by the structure.

The Brooklyn Bridge

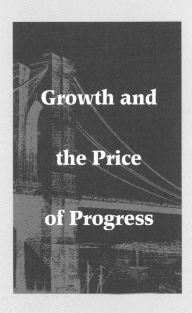

Growth and the Price of Progress

The fireworks that exploded over the East River on the warm spring night of May 24, 1883, to celebrate the opening of the massive Brooklyn Bridge reverberated far beyond the shores of Brooklyn and Manhattan. The focus of international interest, this 5,989-foot-long bridge was a testament to late nineteenth-century technology. The colossal stone and steel structure joined two of the nation's mightiest cities, solidifying a relationship born more than two centuries earlier.

Perhaps most importantly for Brooklyn, the span represented a major link in a vast urban transportation network; it would not only ease movement between Brooklyn and New York but change commuting patterns and spur real-estate development. From the steam ferry, which helped make Brooklyn Heights a fashionable suburb in the 1820s, to the speeding subway, which helped turn Sheepshead Bay into a modern suburb one hundred years later, transportation has played a pivotal role in how Brooklyn and its neighborhoods grew.

Brooklyn has also suffered losses in the process of assuming its current shape; "progress" has its downside. As the bridge's massive towers rose from the shores of the East River in the late 1870s, for instance, businesses, houses, and a church that stood in the path of its approach ramp were destroyed. Similarly, in the twentieth century, the Brooklyn-Queens Expressway ripped apart neighborhoods from Williamsburg to South Brooklyn, destroying homes and dividing communities in order to create a traffic corridor through the crowded borough. Communities like Carroll Gardens, split along Hicks Street by the expressway, still bear the scars of progress today. But great public works and public transportation innovations like the Brooklyn Bridge, trolley lines, the elevated, and subways have been at the heart of the process that gave the borough and its neighborhoods much of their contemporary shape and character.

Before the Bridge

Today, subways whisk riders under the East River between Manhattan and Brooklyn. The Brooklyn, Williamsburg, and Manhattan Bridges and their younger cousin, the Brooklyn–Battery Tunnel, accommodate thousands upon thousands of

POINTS OF INTEREST IN *THE BROOKLYN BRIDGE*

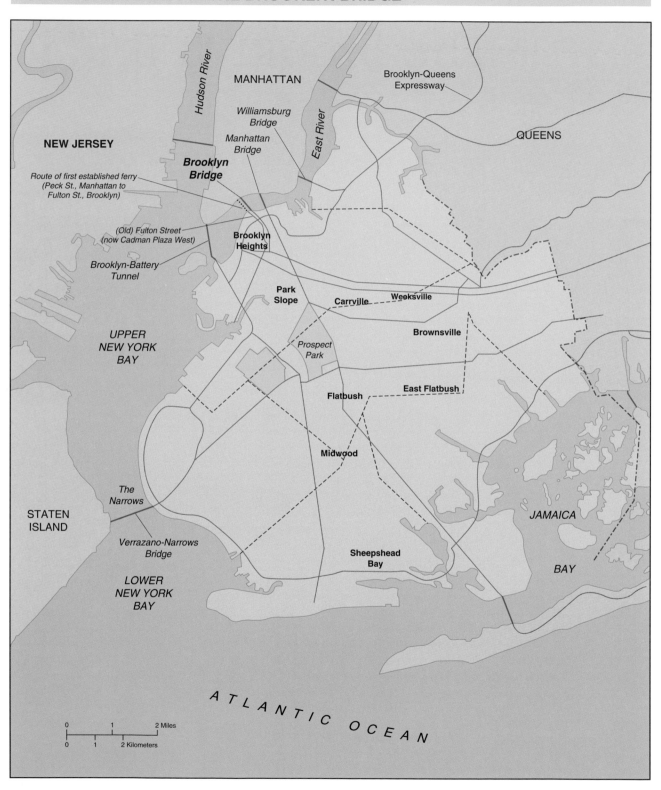

Hudson River

MANHATTAN

Brooklyn-Queens
Expressway

Williamsburg
Bridge

Manhattan
Bridge

East River

QUEENS

NEW JERSEY

**Brooklyn
Bridge**

Route of first established ferry
(Peck St., Manhattan to
Fulton St., Brooklyn)

(Old) Fulton Street
(now Cadman Plaza West)

**Brooklyn
Heights**

Brooklyn-Battery
Tunnel

UPPER
NEW YORK
BAY

**Park
Slope**

Carrville

Weeksville

Brownsville

*Prospect
Park*

Flatbush

East Flatbush

Midwood

The
Narrows

STATEN
ISLAND

JAMAICA

Verrazano-Narrows
Bridge

LOWER
NEW YORK
BAY

**Sheepshead
Bay**

BAY

ATLANTIC OCEAN

0   1   2 Miles
0   1   2 Kilometers

drivers each day. Together, the bridges over and the passageways under the river accommodate millions of commuters and travelers weekly.

Before the bridges, before the tunnel, before the subway, if you wanted to cross the East River you had two choices: pay the ferryman, or use your own boat. A permanent, public ferry service—a euphemism for a rocky ride across the choppy East River in a tiny rowboat—was opened in 1642. The ferryman was Cornelis Dircksen, who ran a ferry between Peck's Slip in Manhattan and the foot of what later became Fulton Street in Brooklyn. As Jasper Danckaerts, a visitor to Brooklyn in the late 1670s noted, "there is a ferry [a rowboat] for the purpose of crossing it [the East River], which is farmed out by the year . . . and yields a good income, as it is a considerable thoroughfare. . . . A considerable number of Indians who gain their subsistence by hunting and fishing . . . as well as others, must carry their articles to market over this ferry, or boat them over, as it is free to every one to use his own boat, if he have one, or to borrow or hire one for the purpose."

As the settlements of Brooklyn and Manhattan grew, the watery link at Brooklyn's ferry landing, located about where the Brooklyn Bridge pier stands today, became increasingly important. At that spot, Brooklyn lies closest to New York—one reason the Brooklyn Bridge was later built there. The eighteenth-century scene was captured by artist Pierrepont Bartow, whose painting shows farmers grouped on a jetty made from landfill, their carts laden with goods (perhaps the fruits and vegetables for which Brooklyn was known), waiting to make the crossing to market in Manhattan.

All routes from the outlying colonial towns of Kings County and Long Island seemed to lead to the landing, and inscriptions on milestones pointed the way and alerted travelers to how far they still had to go, precursors to the huge green

The Brooklyn Bridge

Van Pelt Milestone, New Utrecht, ca. 1917.

Travelers along the Kings Highway who gauged their journey by this 1741 milestone were colonists under the rule of King George II. Standing in front of the former Van Pelt Manor at what is now Eighteenth Avenue and Eighty-second Street in Bensonhurst, this marker directed them onward with spectral hands: "8-1/4 Mile to N York Ferry/This Road/To Denys's Ferry/2-1/2 Mile." The adjacent side offers an alternate route and reads: "10-1/2 Mile to N York Ferry/This Road/To Jamaica/15 Mile." The stone is now in the collections of The Brooklyn Historical Society. Photograph by John J. Pierrepont.

New York City Department of Transportation sign, ca. 1985.

Though it's aluminum instead of stone, this modern Department of Transportation sign functions as a contemporary milepost, pointing out the entrance to the Brooklyn Bridge as once the Van Pelt Milestone directed travelers toward the ferry to Manhattan. Loan courtesy of Bureau of Traffic Operations.

Department of Transportation signs that today direct drivers as they speed toward the Brooklyn Bridge.

As the population of Brooklyn and neighboring Manhattan grew, crossing the river for trade, business, and travel became increasingly necessary. Boat travel meant the worries and hazards of wind, water, and tides and was particularly dangerous in wintertime, when huge, jagged ice floats often made the crossing treacherous if not impossible. People began to look for ways to turn the barrier into a safe passageway. In the 1830s, for example, engineer David Bates Douglass (who went on to design Brooklyn's Green-Wood Cemetery in the 1840s) came up with an ingenious plan, a six-lane tunnel under the East River. Traffic would be divided between carts, light carriages, and pedestrians and sectioned into two directions: to New York, and to Brooklyn. Although Douglass's visionary plan never materialized, his boldness and foresight reflected the hopes of many.

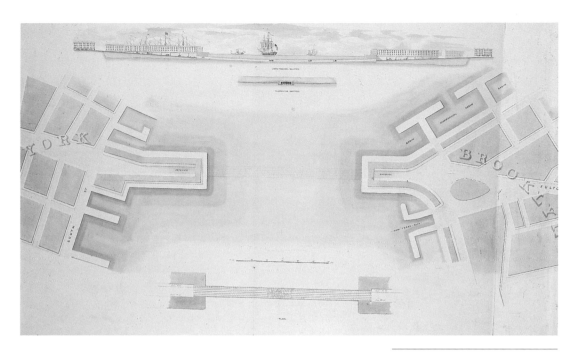

Brooklyn booster Henry Cruse Murphy shared Douglass's spirit. A founder of the company that would one day build the bridge, as well as a lawyer, one-time Brooklyn mayor, and U.S. congressman and senator, Murphy overflowed with the optimism of his era. He maintained in 1857, twenty-six years before the bridge was completed, that "it requires no spirit of prophecy to foretell the union of New York and Brooklyn at no distant day. The river which divides them will

Details from a Proposal for a Tunnel under the East River Connecting New York and Brooklyn by David Bates Douglass, ink and wash on paper, 1830s.

In this plan, horse-drawn carriages and carts would cross the river underground. Above ground is the emerging Brooklyn waterfront of the 1830s, where in addition to a commercial basin for ships, Douglass includes the New Ferry Slip, perhaps indicating that he saw his tunnel as a helpful addition to, not a replacement for, ferry travel.

Henry Cruse Murphy by unknown artist, chalk on paper, ca. 1860.

State Senator Henry Cruse Murphy, who became president of the New York Bridge Company in 1867. Founder of the *Brooklyn Eagle,* one-time Brooklyn mayor, lawyer, and businessman, corrupt New York City Democratic Party leader William "Boss" Tweed claimed Murphy paid him off to help obtain a charter so that plans for the bridge could proceed—an unlikely story.

The Brooklyn Bridge

soon cease to be a line of separation, and bestrode by a colossus of commerce, will prove a link which will bind them together."

"Our Most Durable Monument"

Although German-born bridge engineer John A. Roebling published plans for the Brooklyn Bridge before the Civil War, the project did not take shape until after the conflict ended. According to bridge lore, one factor that clinched the enterprise was a visit by William Kingsley, a contractor and influential Brooklyn Democrat, to Henry Murphy at his Bay Ridge home to persuade him to lend his support. Kingsley made the trip on a bitterly cold December night, suffering a four-mile-long drive by carriage over rutted roads; he must have felt sure his arguments would turn the tide in the bridge's favor. Whatever he said that cold night worked. Once lukewarm about the plan's validity, Murphy became an ardent supporter. With his help, plans moved ahead, and in June 1869 center-line surveys began.

The next month, John Roebling's foot was badly crushed by a docking ferry. Several of his toes had to be amputated, lockjaw set in, and on July 22, he died. Work barely slowed. Roebling's thirty-two-year-old eldest son, Washington, took over the project, and on January 3, 1870, workers broke ground for the tower foundation on the Brooklyn side of the river. When Washington Roebling was later housebound by illness, his wife, Emily, directed the project; it would be a fourteen-year endeavor.

The bridge's creation coincided with the rise of visual media for a mass market. Photographs were becoming increasingly common, lithography was still a popular household art form and commercial medium, and engraving continued to be the principal technique for cheap illustrations. For fourteen years, artists and photographers, as well as writers and journalists, kept an ongoing record of the bridge's construction. Before long no picture of the city was complete without an image of the bridge rising from the shores of the East River. The pictorial press, including *Harper's Weekly* and *Frank Leslie's Illustrated Newspaper,* also documented the activities of the workers who built the bridge. Up on the span, below the great towers, or in nearby yards, hundreds of masons, stonecutters, blacksmiths, machinists, carpenters, riggers, painters, and day laborers toiled to erect the huge edifice, working six-day, sixty-hour weeks.

While the names of people like John, Washington, and Emily Roebling have become incorporated into bridge lore, the names of these workers are not recorded in public memory. Many were immigrants, predominantly German and Irish, but also Italian, English, and at least one Chinese. Others were American-born, including African Americans. Looking at most artists' pristine renderings of the bridge, it is difficult to imagine the intensity and difficulty of its construction. Ascending the towers called for steady nerves. So did descending below the waterline in the huge caissons—bottomless wooden boxes filled with compressed air—to chip away at the stone of the riverbed. Not only was the work claustrophobic and difficult, but almost all who traveled down into the caissons at one time or another suffered from the bends, caused by coming up out of the compressed air too quickly. They called the condition caisson disease. The pain was excruciating—like being stabbed by a knife—and accompanying symptoms ranged from vomiting to paralysis. Sometimes, men died of the bends. Altogether,

INSIDE VIEWS OF THE EAST RIVER BRIDGE CAISSON, BROOKLYN, N. Y.—FROM SKETCHES BY OUR SPECIAL ARTIST.

"Inside Views of the East River Bridge Caisson, Brooklyn, N.Y.," October 15, 1870.

Frank Leslie's Illustrated Newspaper documented various aspects of bridge construction, focusing on activity in the caissons, the watertight chambers where a hundred or more men could work at a time. Around the clock, they dug away dirt and stone with shovels and picks.

Bridge cable, 1877.

A year after Charles C. Martin donated this fragment of bridge cable to The Brooklyn Historical Society, the wire used to spin it became the center of a scandal; the supplier, who procured the contract under dubious conditions, was providing faulty, cheaper wire and pocketing a considerable profit.

more than twenty workers perished building the bridge. Some of their names we do know: John McGarrity, Thomas Douglass, and John French were killed by a falling derrick; Harry Supple was knocked off the anchorage by a piece of rope and fell eighty feet; others also plummeted to their untimely deaths or died from caisson disease.

The public was fascinated by the bridge, partly because its construction was no ordinary event. Some squirreled away unlikely souvenirs, which in time became tangible, revered pieces of history. In 1877, bridge engineer Washington Roebling's second-in-command, Charles C. Martin, saved a piece of the first ca-

ble, which he presented to The Brooklyn Historical Society. For sheer size, perhaps the greatest souvenir is a carrier wheel, more than five feet across, that once drew cable across the bridge. Even an ephemeral moment was thought worthy of capture: After a salute was fired from the New York tower of the bridge to mark the landing of the first cable, an observer preserved some of the gunpowder in a small glass vial.

What contemporaries noted most frequently about the new bridge was its mechanical qualities, which fascinated the citizenry of an age characterized by enormous advances in technology and industry. As architectural critic Montgomery Schuyler wrote in "The Bridge as a Monument" in the May 26, 1883, issue of *Harper's Weekly,* "It so happens that the work which is likely to be our most durable monument, and which is likely to convey some knowledge of us to the most remote posterity, is a work of bare utility; not a shrine, not a fortress, not a palace, but a bridge." Indeed, as the longest suspension bridge ever built, with towers that dwarfed the Manhattan skyline, the Brooklyn Bridge was an extraordinary engineering feat. To the Victorians who watched from the shores as it rose, it both embodied the spirit of the age and symbolized U.S. progress.

The bridge was also an icon of Brooklyn progress, as many pointed out. As the *New-York Daily Tribune* wrote about the opening-day extravaganza on May 24, 1883 one day later, this bridge *was* "modernity"; this new span delivered Brooklyn from a "primitive" past. "On every street on the Heights and near the Bridge were masses of color for decorative purposes," wrote the paper. "In City Hall Square the decoration which attracted the most attention was a representation in front of the Park Theatre of the straggling village of Brooklyn in 1746, of the primitive ferry in 1814, of the Bridge to-day, and of the possibility in 1983 of a hundred bridges spanning the East River."

As the department store Wechsler & Abraham (later Abraham and Straus) announced in huge panels that covered the store's windows, "Babylon had her hanging garden, Egypt her pyramid, Athens her Acropolis, Rome her Athenaeum; so Brooklyn has her Bridge." Self-acclaim was not in short supply.

Brooklyn residents also celebrated enthusiastically. Samuel McLean, an importer and dry-goods merchant who lived at 47 Pierrepont Street in Brooklyn Heights, hung out a nine-foot-high canvas banner depicting the bridge. McLean had bought the enormous canvas sign—called a "transparency" because it was made to be hung with lights shining behind it—from Brooklyn banner maker E. A. Dubey, whose business was located just off Fulton Street. (The droll entrepreneur placed an advertisement in the 1884/1885 Brooklyn city directory that read "Duby or not Dubey. The Banner Painter, That is the Question!") When McLean illuminated the transparency that night, it must have been a striking sight for Heights residents, a glowing billboard gently wafting in the breeze.

While the public was welcome at much of the celebration, delicately engraved Tiffany invitations summoned only elite guests to the opening ceremonies. President Chester A. Arthur, New York governor Grover Cleveland, and the mayors of Brooklyn and New York were chief guests of honor. They marched across the bridge in a regal display, which the satirical weekly *Puck* irreverently commemorated in a take-off on the staid scenes typically published in the illustrated newspapers of the day.

Speeches turned to the predictable themes of progress and the future. Reverend Richard S. Storrs, renowned Brooklyn minister and president of The Brooklyn (then Long Island) Historical Society, whose presence alone must have be-

Gunpowder in vial, 1877.

According to the nineteenth-century *Catalogue of Antiquities,* a record of The Brooklyn Historical Society's earliest collections, this is a sample of the powder from the "only salute ever fired from the New York tower of the bridge. The occasion being the landing of the first cable."

stowed a benediction upon the new span, gave one of the principal orations, and pointedly heralded "the real builders of the bridge," the people. Representing Manhattan was the Hon. Abram S. Hewitt. He evoked contrasting images of a "primaeval scene" of three centuries before with the modern cityscape. "Could there be a more astounding exhibition of the power of man to change the face of nature than the panoramic view which presents itself to the spectator standing upon the crowning arch of the Bridge?" asked the prominent congressman and industrialist. A fourteen-year-old onlooker recalled not the speeches but the music and the fireworks: "After my Latin I got excused and . . . went to the opening of the Bridge and showed my ticket. . . . Mr. J. Levy played a cornet solo which was the best thing done and he was applauded so much that he wanted to keep it up. . . . At last the cornet stopped and Mr. Hewitt commenced to talk. . . . I went over to papa's office and . . . he told me I could go on the roof of the Equitable Building [an early Manhattan skyscraper] tonight. . . . We saw most of the fireworks. They weren't half what I thought they would be but it was fun. . . . Today was a splendid day."

The fireworks that young Reginald Fairfax Harrison described with disappointment were depicted by John Mackie Falconer, then sixty-three years old and a serious amateur artist. Once a Manhattan hardware merchant, he had retired and lived on Willoughby Street. It was particularly fitting that he paint the bridge. Writing to a friend, artist William Sidney Mount, almost thirty years earlier from his Manhattan home, Falconer had complained that he was eager to get "out of the gradually enhancing cost of living" in the city. Although Brooklyn seemed to him a logical alternative, he wrote, he had reservations about commuting on the

The Grand Opening March Over the Brooklyn Bridge. Puck follows the Example of the Illustrated Newspapers, and gives an accurate picture of the Event One Day Before It Takes Place—and Don't You Forget It! **by F. Opper, May 1883.**

Tongue-in-cheek, the humorous weekly *Puck* provided its readers with its own version of the opening march across the bridge—one day before the festivities actually took place! Former president Ulysses S. Grant is at left.

Brooklyn! *An Illustrated History*

ferries, finding "the inner fogs and detention from ice . . . somewhat of a bar." Now a Brooklynite, he was immortalizing the very structure that promised to deliver him and thousands of others from the unpredictability of wintertime ferry crossings.

To satisfy the public's keen interest in the bridge, manufacturers churned out souvenirs. Mementos often took interesting shapes—a napkin ring, a plate, a spoon, a cup: no ordinary domestic utensils these. Adorned with images of the famous span, they were lifted from the mundane world of everyday dinnerware

Illuminations at the Opening of the Brooklyn Bridge by John Mackie Falconer, oil on canvas board, 1883.

Brooklyn amateur artist John Mackie Falconer depicted the bridge from the south near the foot of Remsen Street in Brooklyn Heights. The scene is bathed in the glow of fireworks erupting over the East River until nine o'clock on the night of the bridge's opening, May 24. With the final blast of five hundred rockets, a cacophony of sound rose as bells, gongs, whoops and cheers from the crowd rang out.

Group of bridge souvenirs: Souvenir spoons, Sterling Silver Plating Co., after 1883; commemorative plate, Mayer Brothers, 1883; "Souvenir of Brooklyn" commemorative porcelain cup, ca. 1900.

The bridge evoked a range of artistic responses, from paintings, poetry, and novels to these everyday items transformed by bridge imagery into souvenirs. The porcelain cup groups the bridge with other famous Brooklyn sites: the Memorial (Soldiers' and Sailors') Arch at Grand Army Plaza and the Brooklyn Institute of Arts and Sciences (today The Brooklyn Museum).

The Brooklyn Bridge

The Great Suspension Bridge between New York and Brooklyn, New York Elevated Rail Road etc.

into the realm of the commemorative souvenir. The bridge was also appropriated by advertisers to sell everything from baking powder to liver pills. And, of course, the folkloric rube who thought he bought the bridge itself is a mainstay of American humor.

Perhaps most intriguing are the ways that people found to make the bridge their own in a less literal sense. Over the years, millions have taken advantage of the great pedestrian promenade, which Roebling envisioned as an oasis in what he called a "crowded commercial city," for a stroll, a bike ride, or a brisk walk home from a tough day on Wall Street. Others have used it as a public stage. On May 19, 1885, two years after the bridge opened, Robert E. Odlum garnered enormous press attention when he leapt from its dizzying heights. He did not survive the stunt. (One year later, Steve Brodie claimed to have jumped and survived, but there were no witnesses.) A century later, people continued to use the bridge as a stage, even transforming the span into an emotionally and politically charged space. As New York City honored the 250,000 men and women who fought in the Vietnam War by dedicating a memorial to them in Lower Manhattan in May 1985, 25,000 vets marched from Cadman Plaza in Brooklyn across the bridge to the Battery, as a wildly appreciative crowd watched and cheered. In April 1992, a convoy of ninety vans dubbed "mitzvah tanks" streamed across the bridge and through the New York Metropolitan Area to celebrate the ninetieth birthday of Grand Rebbe Menachem Schneerson, the Crown Heights figure whom the international Lubavitch community venerated as its leader. Five months later, in a display of solidarity with their former homeland, thousands of Haitians marched across the Brooklyn Bridge as their deposed president, Jean-Bertrand Aristide, addressed the United Nations General Assembly on the first anniversary of the political coup that overthrew him.

Whatever function the bridge serves today—as transportation span, advertising hook, public stage, or symbol of the borough—it all began with that eventful, memorable opening day on May 24, 1883. The bridge was up. It was a marvel. And it has continued to function as a practical conveyance and a symbol of the Borough of Brooklyn for more than a century. But what did it mean for Brooklyn?

Brooklyn and New York: Natural Rivals—and Allies

Journalists and citizens at the bridge's opening-day events created a rosy picture of peace and harmony between Brooklyn and Manhattan that belied tensions, many of them political, that had existed for years. A half-century earlier, New York City, wary of a potential rival, had opposed Brooklyn's application for a city charter, which was approved nevertheless in 1834. For years before that, the two communities had waged a running battle over control of the East River and its ferry lines. In an 1810 article in the *Long Island Star,* a writer complained about Manhattan's "injustices" toward Brooklyn. "That encroachments have been made on our water rights is true," he wrote. "That the Ferry has been wrested from us is true.—And that the inhabitants of this town have been denied the privilege of carrying their neighbors with their goods, across the east river to the city of New-York [Manhattan] by a public ordinance, is also true."

Demeaning stereotypes worsened the conflicts over transportation and self-rule. Some smug New Yorkers considered Brooklynites little more than country cousins and Brooklyn an undesirable, unsophisticated place to live. Brooklynites responded. At an 1845 meeting to wrangle yet again over East River ferry rights, Brooklyn citizens unanimously adopted a resolution: "the act of residing in the city of Brooklyn, instead of the city of New York, violates no one of the Ten Commandments." Bias on the Brooklyn side found a spokesman in Roger Mifflin, the philosophical traveling book salesman in Christopher Morley's 1917 novel, *Parnassus on Wheels:* "New York is a Babylon; Brooklyn is the true Holy City. New York is the city of envy, office work, and hustle; Brooklyn is the region of homes and happiness. It is extraordinary: poor, harassed New Yorkers presume to look down on low-lying, home-loving Brooklyn, when as a matter of fact it is the precious jewel their souls are thirsting for and they never know it. . . . There is no hope for New Yorkers, for they glory in their skyscraping sins."

Perhaps the deepest source of tension between the two cities was foreshadowed by their physical joining by the bridge. The possible political consolidation of Brooklyn and New York had been debated for years. In simplest terms, Brooklyn, a city since 1834, would lose its independence and become a part of Greater New York. Supporters claimed annexation by Manhattan would improve government, lower taxes, enhance property values, accelerate growth, and enable Brooklyn to partake of the many benefits provided by a larger municipality. A referendum in 1894 showed New York clearly in favor of consolidation. Brooklynites too preferred consolidation—but by a margin of merely 277 votes. (The vote was 64,744 for, 64,467 against.) The cover illustration of the *Greater New*

THE GREATER NEW YORK

Vol. 1. No. 1.   THE METROPOLIS OF AMERICA.   Price 5 Cents.

Father Knickerbocker:—"Welcome! Welcome! We will all dwell under one roof and be a very happy family."

"Father Knickerbocker," ca. 1894.

"Father Knickerbocker" gained currency as a symbol for Manhattan through the writings of New York author Washington Irving. On the cover of the *Greater New York,* the mythical Dutch burgher pats "Brooklyn" on the shoulder and paternally welcomes the personifications of the areas that were soon to be annexed to Greater New York. The Manhattan tower of the Brooklyn Bridge looms symbolically behind him through an open window.

York idealized the results of the referendum: Father Knickerbocker (Manhattan) places his hand upon the shoulder of young "Brooklyn," who stands politely before him. "Welcome!" he proclaims. "We will all dwell under one roof and be a very happy family."

But contention and delays marked the four-year period between the referendum and incorporation. One of consolidation's ardent supporters was department-store entrepreneur Abraham Abraham. He had grown up in New York City, the son of German Jewish immigrants from Bavaria, and had come to Brooklyn to establish Weschler and Abraham in 1865 (it became Abraham and Straus in 1893). As a businessman, he spoke for many of the city's merchants in a letter of support to Governor Levi P. Morton on May 4, 1896: "The merchants of Brooklyn representing many millions of dollars invested in realty and in various occupations, and who have the material prosperity of Brooklyn at heart, are almost a unit in favor of the union of the two cities."

Those who opposed consolidation feared a loss of community identity, sure that Brooklyn would be swallowed up by Manhattan. (Meanwhile, Brooklyn itself had been greedily annexing property, most recently absorbing Williamsburgh and Bushwick in 1855 to become the third most populous city in the United States.) Consolidation's enemies also feared that the Democratic Party machine would lose power in both Brooklyn and Manhattan. As Benjamin D. Silliman wrote the governor on December 17, 1895, "The great mass of property owners, and substantial people generally, are strongly opposed to the proposed

Union, or to any measure which will subject them to taxation for the fearful schemes of Rapid Transit, and the other enormous expenses impending over the City of New York." Opponents also appealed to an anti-immigrant sentiment, charging that Manhattan's "immigrant hordes" would overrun their community. (In actuality, the immigrant populations of the two cities were about the same.)

In December 1897, on the eve of consolidation, opponents of annexation printed a small pamphlet dominated by maudlin imagery. "In Commemoration/The Passing of the City of Brooklyn/1834/1897" borrows from Victorian tradition the dark borders that commonly appeared on death notices or on stationery and calling cards to signify that the writer or caller was in mourning. Within the black borders stands an image of Brooklyn's seat of government, City Hall (shortly to become Borough Hall). The text gives the birth and death dates for the City of Brooklyn, a fitting tribute to a little over half a century of rule.

On January 1, 1898, Brooklyn would lose its independence, but the new arrangement had its benefits. Within a few years of consolidation, both the Manhattan and Williamsburg Bridges were built, along with Brooklyn's first subway—transportation improvements Brooklyn might never have financed from its own coffers. Still, Brooklyn's pride was tinged with sadness. *Brooklyn Daily Eagle* editor St. Clair McKelway expressed what many Brooklynites felt in his hail-and-farewell oration at City Hall on New Year's Eve 1897, the last night Brooklyn was an independent city. "And, therefore, not farewell to Brooklyn, for borough it may be, Brooklyn it is," he said. "Brooklyn it remains, and Brooklynites we remain."

Brooklyn Neighborhoods and How They Grew

In 1883, Brooklyn historian and enthusiast Henry Stiles wrote of Brooklyn's promising prospects: "The town which, in 1834, had hardly one and a half square miles of closely built houses, has now about 34 miles of densely populated houses and factories, with numerous churches, school-houses, theaters, halls, and vast warehouses." And, he continued, it "is pushing forward with more energy than ever before to occupy the lands whose virgin soil is yet unbroken." The bridge provided an easy, quick, and reliable way to pass back and forth between Brooklyn and Manhattan, and not only did Brooklyn have room to grow, but that "virgin soil" was substantially cheaper than land across the river. And as one observer noted in 1883, "High rents in New York are driving merchants and working-people to Brooklyn."

Long before the bridge was built, in fact, improvements in public transport, such as the horse-drawn omnibus and horsecar, had accelerated Brooklyn's growth, for they enabled residents to commute easily to jobs in downtown Brooklyn and Manhattan while enjoying the openness of the suburbs. Together, improved transportation, cheap and available land, active real-estate developers, and the hopes and desires of prospective residents propelled Brooklyn's rapid residential development.

The seeds of Brooklyn's many neighborhoods today—by some counts over ninety—were planted with the earliest land divisions of colonial Brooklyn, when seventeenth-century European newcomers divided what is now Brooklyn into six towns (all united into Kings County in 1683). With the exception of the Town of Brooklyn—the area directly across the river from Manhattan and home to the thriving ferry district—these towns remained small rural farming communities throughout the eighteenth century. By 1800, Brooklyn had 2,378 inhabitants; the combined population of the other five towns was 3,362.

Even with the largest population of the six towns, Brooklyn was small in scale, a "walking" city where one traveled only a short distance, if at all, between home and workplace. Most people lived along the waterfront near the ferry landing, just south of where the Brooklyn Bridge now stands. Houses were interspersed with workplaces, taverns, stores, breweries, and small shops, a scene painted by British-born artist Francis Guy around 1817, undoubtedly from the window of his home at No. 11 Front Street.

Guy's townscape captures Brooklyn when it was becoming self-conscious about its growth. In 1819 the town adopted an official street map to assign some order to potential sprawl. As the pace of urbanization picked up, the need for city planning became increasingly obvious. In 1834 (the year the City of Brooklyn was incorporated), at the city's request, the state commissioned a survey of the surrounding countryside to "lay out streets, avenues, and public squares." Completed in 1839, the survey mapped the city into a rectangular grid crossed by several major diagonal avenues and dotted with small parks, just as the Commissioners' Plan of 1811 had laid out Manhattan's grid. It would serve, with little change, as the blueprint for the City of Brooklyn's growth.

In the nineteenth and twentieth centuries, Brooklyn's neighborhoods assumed their modern shapes. Some evolved from early Dutch towns; Gravesend, settled by a group of English religious dissenters in the seventeenth century, adopted its own plan. The borough developed a unique pattern of streets and radiating avenues—several gridirons in search of a city—a legacy of the grids from

Summer View of Brooklyn by Francis Guy, oil on canvas, ca. 1817–20.

A hot summer day at the intersection of Front and James Streets, roughly the site of the Brooklyn Bridge anchorage, where home and workplaces mix. At left is factory-owner Augustus Graham's brick home; Benjamin Meeker's carpentry shop and dwelling stands at the intersection. At center is butcher Abiel Titus's barn and slaughterhouse, and, behind the barn, Edward Cooper's blacksmith shop. At right is Thomas W. Birdsall's white two-story house (also the post office) and hardware store.

Brooklyn! *An Illustrated History*

the once-independent villages that now intersected at sometimes awkward angles. Within the rapidly expanding metropolis, neighborhoods took names that were sometimes influenced by natural boundaries, such as Bay Ridge; by political boundaries, such as City Line; by the local catch as in Sheepshead Bay; or by people, such as Fort Greene, named after a Revolutionary War general. People were drawn to them for a variety of reasons—overcrowding in Manhattan, or Brooklyn's lower taxes (when Brooklyn was still separate from Manhattan), cheaper, roomier housing, or jobs, or open spaces, or the presence of friends and family. And although every neighborhood has a unique history, similar factors often affected their development—not just real-estate speculation and population growth, but the shared ideals of neighborhood and community.

Above all, Brooklyn's neighborhoods owe their large-scale development to innovations in transportation. Brooklyn Heights, Bedford-Stuyvesant, Park Slope, Brownsville, Flatbush, and Sheepshead Bay are six neighborhoods whose genesis, in large part, lay in some new means of transit. From the rickety omnibus to the streamlined subway, public transportation made these communities grow, just as it would countless others throughout the borough.

Just a Ferry Ride Away:
Brooklyn Heights

"On Sunday last commenced running the new and beautiful Steam-boat *Nassau*, as a ferry-boat between New-York and Brooklyn," reported the *Long Island Star* on Wednesday, May 11, 1814, heralding the first steam-ferry service across the East River. "This noble boat surpassed the expectations of the public in the rapidity of her movement. Her trips varied from five to twelve minutes, according to tide and weather. . . . This splendid evidence of the progress of science and the arts, while it affords to all a safe and agreeable communication with the city, is a sure harbinger of the future wealth and prosperity of Long-Island."

Certain key words would appear again and again in the press and period literature with each new form of transit—progress, future, prosperity. Like the opening of the Brooklyn Bridge seventy years later, the first steam ferry drew great public acclaim, for it delivered harried riders from the small, inefficient rowboats, sailboats, and horse-powered ferries that could take up to one and a half hours for a one-way crossing, always at the mercy of wind and tide. They were also dangerous. As the *N.Y. Journal and Post Rider* noted on December 22, 1795, "On the Tuesday last, 17th Dec., 1795, one of the Brooklyn ferry boats was overset in passing the East River; one man and seven fat oxen were drowned." Now, for the first time, commuting between Brooklyn and New York promised to be reliable. Still, not everyone was convinced the steam ferries were the way to travel. In 1823, young Brooklyn lawyer Gabriel Furman noted in his diary that many people were apprehensive about the new steam-powered boats, fearing that they "may be blown up, or scalded."

Ferry-company owners, of course, foresaw hefty profits from the modern East River ferry boats. So taken were they with their new family of boats that the Union Ferry Company (the successor of the Fulton and South Ferry Companies) commissioned a series of paintings of them, probably under the guidance of company director Henry E. Pierrepont. They chose James and John Bard, twin brothers born in New York, to execute several of the works. The Bards had begun

Cartoon, company director of the Union Ferry Company, from the _Historical Sketch of the Fulton Ferry, and Its Associated Ferries_, 1879.

After the Union Ferry Company raised its fares to two cents in the 1850s, a satirist drew this cartoon showing a company director soliciting pennies from a poor laborer. The small child at left thumbs his nose at the "needy" ferry company director.

Steamboat William Cutting **by James and John Bard, oil on canvas, 1846.**

Technically a center-paddlewheel catamaran, the steamboat _William Cutting_ was the second steam ferry to run between Brooklyn and New York, added only after Brooklynites complained loudly about inadequate ferry service.

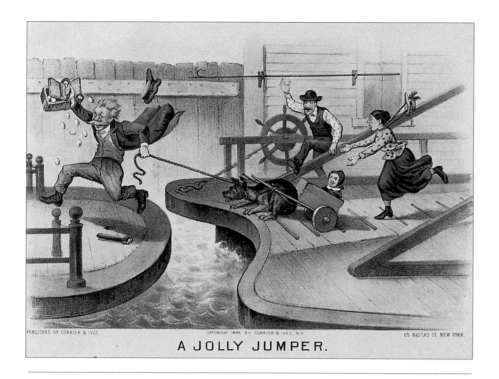

A JOLLY JUMPER.

A Jolly Jumper **by Currier and Ives, chromolithograph, 1888.**

With a caricature of a German Immigrant, this print pokes fun at the commuters who leaped after departing ferries and sometimes ended up in the East River. The boat hook in the background was used to fish out unsuccessful jumpers.

painting boats in their youth and became marine artists during the heyday of shipbuilding in New York City. Their *Steamboat William Cutting* depicts the boat named after steamboat developer Robert Fulton's partner, who took over the Fulton Steamboat Company when Fulton died in 1815. The *Cutting* hung in the directors' offices on Fulton Street for many years and was eventually donated by the company to The Brooklyn Historical Society in 1890.

While the Bards painted precise, detailed, flattering portraits of the East River vessels, others recorded everyday life on the ferries. Currier and Ives's *Jolly Jumper* pokes fun at late arrivals, frantic to catch the ferry, who often leapt from the dock to the departing deck (the nineteenth-century version of today's commuters who hurl themselves between closing subway doors). Those who didn't make it were sometimes crushed between the ferry and the dock. The *New York Times* noted another travail of ferry travel: crowds. "The Union Ferry Company lines are overcrowded," it complained in a July 28, 1867, article, packing "1,200 people on boats made to carry conveniently one-third that number. Delays are frequent. . . . The crowding on and off the boats is disgraceful and dangerous. There is no order, no system, nothing to prevent the rushing of hungry hundreds on to the boat, from which other hundreds are trying to escape. The two throngs meet, tussle, squeeze, pick pockets, tread on toes and idly swear."

The social and economic status of ferry riders was the subject of *6, 7, 8, 9 o'clock on the Fulton Ferry*. The Fulton Ferry served a largely working-class crowd,

Six O'clock.

Seven O'clock.

Eight O'clock.

Nine O'clock.

6,7,8,9 o'clock on the Fulton Ferry from *Pictures of Life and Character in New York,* ca. 1880.

Four vignettes suggest that as the morning progressed, the nature of the ferry traveler changed. The snoozing six o'clock A.M. commuter with a basket slung over one arm contrasts with the more affluent nine o'clock rider, a top-hatted businessman who sits erectly in the seat (no need to catch up on sleep, given his banker's hours).

although it also had a more affluent business ridership at certain times of the day. One observer noted that a young man's rise in the business world "was heralded when he joined the ranks of the two-cent fare payers," no longer taking the one-cent boats at earlier hours with the office boys and clerks. While people in business took advantage of the ferry's regular schedule, many others used it as well, such as farmers with their livestock and horse-drawn carts. Brightly colored ferry tickets in an array of sizes were printed and sold to commuters and to the farmers and artisans who needed to transport their goods across the river.

The new steam ferry—combined with the shrewdness and business savvy of Brooklyn businessman and ferry-company owner Hezekiah B. Pierpont—helped Brooklyn Heights emerge as one of the first modern U.S. suburbs. Pierpont (who used an anglicized spelling of his family name, Pierrepont) foresaw the Heights's potential, and in 1802 began buying property in the area. In December 1823, he advertised his Brooklyn Heights lots in the *Long Island Star:* "Situated directly opposite the southwest part of the city [Manhattan], and being the nearest country retreat, and easiest of access from the center of business that now remains unoccupied; the distance not exceeding on an average fifteen to twenty-five minutes walk, including the passage of the river; the ground elevated and perfectly healthy at all seasons; views of water and landscape both extensive and beautiful; as a place of residence combining all the advantages of the country with most of the conveniences of the city." Hoping to attract a well-to-do clientele, Pierpont also appealed to potential buyers' sense of exclusivity, noting that "families who may desire to associate in forming a select neighborhood and circle of society . . . cannot any where obtain more desirable situations."

Situated on the bluffs overlooking the East River, the Heights had long been noted for its cool breezes and spectacular views. In 1818, a guidebook to spots of special interest in the New York area commented on the vista: "Crossing over

Assorted ferry tickets and passes, early 1800s.

In all hues of the rainbow, these tickets and passes admitted commuters, farmers, and other passengers to the ferries.

The Brooklyn Bridge

Sidewheeler Peconic by Joseph B. Smith, oil on canvas, 1863.

Beyond the steamboat *Peconic* lies Brooklyn Heights with its elegant homes overlooking the water. Below stretch warehouses and the Montague Street pier and ferry house. Visible at left (below and left of the church spire) is the Montague Street Bridge. Heights commuters had easy access to lower Manhattan via the Montague–Wall Street ferry line. The painting itself may have been a subtle advertisement for Brooklyn's increased accessibility via the ferries; the boat was one of three new ones built in 1860 by the Union Ferry Company (which commissioned the painting) to carry passengers between the city and Manhattan.

the East River . . . you will extricate yourself from the narrow, dirty . . . streets . . . and turning the first road to the right leading up the hill, you will soon find yourself . . . raised above the dust and noise . . . and winding along towards the brow of the hill you will have a noble and *near* view of the city of New York." The area developed slowly—even in 1822, Gabriel Furman described Pierrepont Street and adjoining Hicks Street as "covered with grass, and enclosed on each side with post and rail fences, which gave them a very rural appearance." But over the next several decades, Brooklyn Heights became an exclusive enclave of Brooklyn's wealthy families and stylish homes, as Joseph B. Smith's 1863 painting *Sidewheeler Peconic* reflects.

Although rowhouses eventually dominated the Heights streetscape, some early homes were elegant, free-standing mansions. One of the most opulent was the home of Henry E. Pierrepont (Hezekiah's son) at 1 Pierrepont Place, built in 1857. Designed by the architectural firm Richard Upjohn and Company, its first floor held two dining areas, reception room, parlor, butler's pantry, and library. Built to replace the family's first mansion (torn down to provide access to the Wall Street Ferry), the elegant home was itself razed in 1946 to make way for a playground during the construction of the Brooklyn-Queens Expressway and the Esplanade. Not far from Henry Pierrepont lived clothing manufacturer and warehouse owner John T. Martin whose opulent home at 28 Pierrepont Street housed a private art gallery and was flanked by beautiful gardens.

Montague Street developed as the Heights's main thoroughfare. Though it appears on an 1831 map of Hezekiah Pierpont's property, the street did not take definitive form until the mid-nineteenth century. At first, it was largely residential to the east, with City Hall's financial district at its western end. Remarking on the tremendous changes, the *Eagle* noted in a February 16, 1868 article, "Twenty-five years ago corn grew on Montague Street. . . . [Now] long rows . . . of brown stone and brick buildings have risen, seemingly in the space of a single night." From the Civil War through the 1890s, the street served as Brooklyn's cultural center, but with the turn of the century it became increasingly commercial. In

Front elevation, "House for H. E. Pierrepont," 1 Pierrepont Place, 1856.

The Brooklyn Heights home of ferry owner Henry Pierrepont, elegant and expensive, with a lovely, ornamented facade, was custom designed by New York architect Richard Upjohn.

Bedroom, the John T. Martin House, 28 Pierrepont Street, ca. 1880.

Martin's bedroom suggests the opulence of upper-class Brooklyn Heights life.

Cigar store figure attributed to Charles J. Dodge, painted wood, ca. 1862.

With its feathered headdress and peace pipe, we look at this wooden sculpture as a stereotype. When it sat at 78 Montague Street in Brooklyn Heights from the late nineteenth through the early twentieth century, it was a common and acceptable advertising symbol for a cigar store.

front of a Montague Street tobacco shop, a wooden Indian, probably made by New York ship- and figurehead-carver Charles J. Dodge, greeted all who entered from 1862 to 1930. Such life-size figures were once common sights on the streets of New York and Brooklyn, where they served as three-dimensional trade signs. Montague Street, along with the surrounding neighborhood, also became home to several hotels, like the elegant 1909 Bossert with its beautiful roof garden.

While the Heights generally maintained its upscale, gentrified aura, over the years successive groups of residents altered its character, as was true of many other Brooklyn neighborhoods. While in the early decades of the twentieth century the Heights continued to be a bedroom community for many of Brooklyn's older, more well-to-do families, it underwent some drastic changes. Owners subdivided homes to accommodate tenants after the arrival of the subway in 1908 made the area more accessible, and again during the Depression, when some of the area's homes foreclosed. By the end of World War II, property values had dropped. With an influx of artists and writers in the 1940s, though, a thriving bohemian community emerged. Among its members were a group of artists and writers, many of them homosexual, lesbian, or bisexual, who shared a house at 7 Middagh Street in the 1940s. Composer Benjamin Britten, poet W. H. Auden (who ran the house), and novelist Carson McCullers were just some of the residents; prominent visitors included Salvador Dali and Aaron Copland. Artist Joseph Pennell lived in the Hotel Margaret on the corner of Columbia Heights, the street with breathtaking East River views, and Orange Street. Authors Tru-

7 Middagh Street, Brooklyn Heights, ca. 1940s.

Swiss novelist and critic Denis de Rougemont said of the house at 7 Middagh Street, in the heart of a thriving artists' community when he visited in 1941: "All that was new in America in music, painting or choreography emanated from that house." The house is no longer standing. Courtesy of the Municipal Archives, Department of Records and Information Services, City of New York.

man Capote, Norman Mailer, and Tennessee Williams all lived on Columbia Heights at one time in their literary careers. Arthur Miller wrote *Death of a Salesman* at 31 Grace Court and in 1951 sold his house to African American scholar, writer, and activist W.E.B. DuBois. In the early 1950s, many young professionals began to rediscover the Heights's charms: its proximity to Manhattan, waterfront views, tree-lined streets, and nineteenth-century architecture. Home ownership increased as newcomers, many of them Manhattanites, converted rooming houses into 1– and 2–family houses.

In 1965 thirty blocks of the Heights, with their 1820s frame dwellings and mid-nineteenth-century Italianate and Greek Revival homes, were named New York City's first designated landmark district by the Landmarks Preservation Commission. Slowly rejuvenated, by the 1970s the Heights had reemerged as a fashionable brownstone neighborhood. Today, residents and visitors enjoy walks along the Promenade (formally, the Esplanade), which rises above the Brooklyn-Queens Expressway and affords a stunning view of Lower Manhattan. Known for its nineteenth-century churches and exquisite architecture, and a thriving restaurant row along Montague Street, the Heights is a vibrant Brooklyn community and considered one of the loveliest in all of New York City.

The steam ferries that precipitated Brooklyn Heights's large-scale development enjoyed a long and illustrious reign. By 1860, when 40 percent of Brooklyn wage earners worked in Manhattan, East River ferries were carrying more than thirty-two million passengers per year. Patronage jumped to fifty million by 1870, and, when the Brooklyn Bridge opened in 1883, thirteen ferry lines were in operation. Even the new bridge did not scuttle them; until 1898 they carried 100 million passengers each year. Not until 1942 was ferry service across the East River discontinued.

Transformed by Omnibus and Horsecar: "Remarkably Healthy and Pleasant" Bedford

Uncovered by a local historian during a 1960s archaeological excavation in Bedford, a tarnished tintype from about 1870 of an elegantly dressed African American woman bears silent testimony to the fact that for well over a century Bedford has been home to an African American community.

Today's Bedford-Stuyvesant began as two distinct communities: Bedford to the west, and Stuyvesant to the east. A small sleepy farm town, Bedford developed as a suburb in the 1840s and 1850s. Part of this early development included two early African American communities, Weeksville and Carrville (now considered part of Crown Heights but then within Bedford's boundaries), both settled by free African American farmers, laborers, and artisans beginning in the 1830s. Weeksville was named for James Weeks, who bought land there in 1838; Carrville's derivation is unknown, although it is probably a distortion of "Crow Hill."

Like the Heights, Bedford would owe its growth in large part to improved public transportation. In this case, the catalysts were entrepreneur Montgomery Queen and the omnibus. Queen began buying land in the 1840s from Bedford landowners, many of whom were subdividing their farms for sale to speculators for building lots. To make his holdings more accessible and attractive to new residents, Queen established an omnibus line to the area. Essentially large stagecoaches, omnibuses were first introduced in Brooklyn in the 1830s and 1840s.

The "Weeksville Lady," tintype, ca. 1875.

A late 1960s archaeological dig near the presumed center of Bedford's early African American community, Weeksville, yielded this tintype of an elegant African American woman. Her manner of dress and the photographic technique suggest the image dates to the 1870s. Courtesy of the Society for the Preservation of Weeksville and Bedford-Stuyvesant History.

Montgomery Queen was almost certainly responsible for commissioning artist Henry Boesé to paint *The Stage Sewanhackey* just when omnibuses were coming into wider use, since he had founded the line on which the Sewanhackey ran. By picturing the stage in front of Brooklyn's City Hall, opened three years earlier, the artist makes a visual connection between the two as symbols of civic improvement. The *Brooklyn Daily Eagle* reported the omnibus's June 23, 1852, unveiling: "The [Stage Sewanhackey] is a most magnificent one capable of accommodating upwards of thirty persons, and is finished and trimmed in the richest style. . . . It was drawn yesterday by sixteen horses well matched and dressed off in plumes, flags and other showy caparison. The horses were drawn by Mr. Canfield, the head driver of Mr. Queen, who managed them with great ease and drove them along in splendid style."

While Boesé's Sewanhackey was a glamorous vehicle, most omnibuses were small and dilapidated, seating around twelve. Passengers were jostled and thrown around the unheated cars, which bounced over unpaved roads and slogged through rutted, often muddy streets. Still, with the alternatives being a horse or a private carriage, omnibuses could charge high fares and ignore schedules. The omnibus quickly became a selling point in attracting new residents to Bedford. By 1850, there were enough lines to provide a somewhat regular transit service linking Brooklyn's ferries with Bedford as well as Flatbush, Gravesend, Flatlands, New Lots, and other Kings County towns; routes to Jamaica, Flushing, and Astoria in Queens County were established by 1853.

But the fare remained too high for most Brooklynites, and public transportation was often closed to the African Americans who lived in Bedford. In August 1873, an *Eagle* reporter who went to Crow Hill (Carrville) to "collect some

The Stage Sewanhackey **by Henry Boesé, oil on canvas, 1852.**

Omnibus entrepreneur Montgomery Queen is probably the figure at left inviting members of the Brooklyn Common Council to take a ride. Its interior hung with embroidered silk drapery, the opulent omnibus was one of a line that helped attract residents to Bedford, although this particular coach was probably reserved for special excursions.

THE STAGE SEWANHACKEY

Detail, *Grand Temperance Encampment, Held at Bushwick, Long Island* by L. Strong, New York, wood engraving, 1846.

A Williamsburgh & Bushwick omnibus drops off passengers at a Brooklyn temperance camp meeting in 1846. The omnibuses were a tight fit for riders, and drivers had to sit on top, exposed to the elements.

facts" about the area coaxed a retired policeman and former omnibus driver who lived in the area to talk about the past. Using a derogatory term for African Americans, the driver recalled that twenty-five years earlier they were not allowed to ride in a public vehicle: "This was in 1854 and the stage went from there up as far as Crow Hill. Well as I was saying Montgomery Queen, who owned the stage route gave orders to the drivers not to let any darkies get in the stage and this order was made very strict. Sometimes the drivers would take pity on the poor fellows and get them a seat on the box alongside themselves but this was finally stopped by imperative orders from McQueens office and so the colored people had to walk to and from the ferrys, rain or shine, no matter if the ice paved the entire distance, they had to walk."

In 1854 the *New York Times* noted that Bedford "omnibuses are now running and soon railroad omnibuses will be in full operation . . . at the nominal fare of four cents, making it accessible and convenient to the ferries." For whites. Railroad omnibuses, or horsecars, combined the omnibus with the steel rails of the railroad for a faster, smoother ride less dependent on road conditions. They were responsible for the continuing growth of Bedford (as well as the development of such new middle-class neighborhoods as Fort Greene and Clinton Hill), making the commute to jobs in downtown Brooklyn and Manhattan quicker and easier for its residents. Meanwhile, single-family, Gothic-style frame houses became popular between 1850 and 1880, transforming the Bedford Avenue–Fulton Street area into one of the city's most fashionable neighborhoods.

Casualties of Bedford's transformation were Weeksville and Carrville. In the 1850s, as their African American populations grew, the two melded into one large, expanded community. Between 1869 and 1870, what became Eastern Park-

Hunterfly Row houses, Weeksville, ca. 1920.

These four small wood-frame homes between Rochester and Buffalo Avenues, among the oldest in central Brooklyn, were built between the 1840s and the 1870s on Hunterfly Road, a major route to New Lots and Canarsie from Bedford that marked Weeksville's eastern edge.

way cut through the area, destroying large parts of Carrville, and streets laid out between 1870 and 1875 obliterated the neighborhood. Today, the four Weeksville houses that survive conjure up images of the area's early residents, who must have passed the small wood-frame houses as they went about their everyday business—perhaps shoemaker Charles C. Louis, who lived on Hunterfly Road, or Isaac Dozier, a laborer; perhaps cigar maker J. Giles, or a widow, Catherine Griffen.

Just as Brooklyn Heights developer Hezekiah Pierpont had appealed to prospective buyers with notions of shared ideals of community, Bedford promoters assured potential residents that this growing "first class district" was filled with "enterprising and God-fearing" people just like them. Advertisements in the *New York Times* in 1854 noted that the area offered "first class improvements . . . elegant and costly dwellings . . . convenient and easy of access of New York . . . [in] a remarkably healthy and pleasant part of the city of Brooklyn."

This sense of rural seclusion attracted William Payne, a decorator who in England had worked on the Crystal Palace. He immigrated to the United States in 1858, and later, in Bedford, he and his son opened a carpet-repair business. His house, on the former Rem Lefferts estate, once served as a parsonage for the Bedford Dutch Reformed Church in a spot known for its pears and raspberries. While in 1865 the family was able to buy an existing house with some character and charm (that they later turned to face Halsey Street, away from the increasing noise of Bedford Avenue), most Bedford homes were built in rows for sale on speculation, although some early homes were custom built for the well-to-do. By 1880, Bedford had over 14,000 residents. As more people moved in, elegant brick and brownstone rowhouses replaced earlier freestanding homes, establishing much of the area's present-day architectural character.

With the opening of the Brooklyn Bridge in 1883 and the completion of elevated railways in the same decade, Bedford's population soared and its residential areas expanded. Until the end of World War I, the neighborhood maintained its reputation as an area for the more prosperous, with fine homes, elegant parks and clubs, and a network of hospitals and schools (like Girls High School on Nostrand Avenue and Boys High School on Marcy). Then brownstones lost fashion, and newer suburban neighborhoods with trees and yards attracted Bedford's middle- and upper-class residents, who were replaced by people of more limited means. Speculators carved up single-family brownstones and rented them to working-class newcomers, many of them Jews, Italians, and Irish. Beginning in the 1920s, a significant number of West Indians, spurred by eased immigration laws, settled in Bedford-Stuyvesant. African American singer Lena Horne, who grew up in Bedford-Stuyvesant on Chauncey Street, recalled the diversity of the neighborhood when she described suppertime walks to the Jewish deli from her grandparents' house: "Granddaddy would take me by the hand and we would walk down Chauncey Street to the delicatessen on Reid Avenue, where we would buy potato salad, cold cuts, baked beans, some kosher dills, anything we didn't have to cook. Then we would walk home, my grandfather nodding in his grave, dignified way to the neighbors, spread our feast on the kitchen table and go!"

The opening of the IND subway line in 1936 attracted a large, African American population to the area, mostly former Harlem residents who saw Bedford-Stuyvesant (the hyphenated designation had taken hold in the 1930s) as an alternative to their Manhattan neighborhood, increasingly crowded and run down. Over the next thirty years, the area's African American population tripled. At the same time, the white residents moved in huge numbers to suburbs in Long Island, New Jersey, and other outlying areas.

Bedford-Stuyvesant before long was labeled undesirable. Although there were social problems, the reputation was not fully deserved. Many whites regarded any area where African Americans lived as a "bad" neighborhood. For the incoming Black residents, the neighborhood promised the very benefits that so many Brooklynites of all eras looked for: decent housing and the chance to own a home. Bedford-Stuyvesant was one of the few places African Americans could buy homes in the 1950s and 1960s, given their de facto exclusion by most white neighborhoods.

Bedroom, William Payne House, 22 Halsey Street, Bedford, ca. 1880.

Compared to John T. Martin's opulent Brooklyn Heights home, the Bedford house of English immigrants William Payne and his wife Elizabeth seems cozy but modest.

Both the people who stayed in Bedford-Stuyvesant and those who arrived in the post–World War II era faced steadily declining services and many residences that had been deteriorating since the Depression, when few owners could spare money for fixing up homes. But church and community organizations banded together, creating such institutions as the Paragon Credit Union, which offered residents a way to borrow money more easily. Revitalization programs created in the 1960s, such as the work of the Bedford-Stuyvesant Restoration Corporation, have helped to revitalize the area. The Black church also continues to serve as a powerful voice for community reform and activism. Today, Bedford-Stuyvesant is largely a neighborhood of middle- and working-class families; most own their own homes, many of which are architectural gems.

When author Paule Marshall in 1972 wrote in *Brown Girl, Brownstone* about the block where she grew up in Bedford-Stuyvesant, she recalled a certain "brown monotony" in the homes. But she also reveled in their small variations and the vibrancy of the neighborhood: "Looking close, you saw that under the thick ivy each house had something distinctively its own. Some touch that was Gothic, Romanesque, baroque or Greek triumphed amid the Victorian clutter. Here, Ionic columns framed the windows while next door gargoyles scowled up at the sun. There, the cornices were hung with carved foliage while Gorgon heads decorated others. Many houses had bay windows or Gothic stonework; a few boasted turrets raised high above the other roofs . . . in those high rooms, life soared and ebbed."

Kings County Court House, Brooklyn, Long Island, George F. Nesbitt & Co., New York, lithographers and printers, color lithograph, 1861.

The horsecar in this lithograph of the Kings County Court House designed by Brooklyn City Hall architect Gamaliel King represents the latest in transportation. The rails made horsecars ride much smoother than omnibuses—and faster, too, to the dismay of this latecomer.

By Horsecar to Litchfield's Land:
Aristocratic Park Slope

An 1861 lithograph of the Kings County Courthouse in downtown Brooklyn shows a hapless soul chasing a horsecar as it rounds the bend. He had to run fast: after the ambling pace of the omnibus, the vehicle probably seemed like it was racing along. The horsecar (a popular name for the horse-drawn railroad) was a huge improvement over the omnibus, not only faster but less dependent on road conditions since it ran on rails, so that it kept to reliable schedules. In 1854, the Brooklyn City Rail Road Company bought out the omnibus lines and began to replace them with horsecar routes.

Park Slope, today known for its rows of elegant Victorian brownstones, owes much of its initial development in the post–Civil War era to the horsecar. The entrepreneurial force behind Park Slope's eventual growth was railroad magnate, lawyer, and industrialist Edwin C. Litchfield, who lived in a mansion high above the area. In the 1850s, Litchfield began buying up large tracts of farmland, which

Plan of Prospect Park by M. Dripps, New York, lithograph, ca. 1865.

In this plan for Prospect Park, never carried out, Park Slope is at the top left. Several Litchfield lots are marked, especially near the Gowanus Canal in the lower Slope. A few sites in the area between Twelfth and Sixteenth Streets were developed by this time.

House at Union and Plaza Streets, Park Slope, ca. 1890.

With its tiled roof, columned porch, and large yard, this elaborate single-family dwelling typified the lavish homes erected in the mid 1880s in Park Slope along Plaza Street and Prospect Park West. The multistory rowhouse at left rear foreshadows the huge apartment buildings that rose in the area after World War I.

he planned to develop for residential use above Fourth Avenue and for industrial use below that line, close to the Gowanus Canal. After the Civil War, he began selling his properties to developers, and by the 1880s, newspaper advertisements were describing Park Slope as an aristocratic district of brownstone homes. Transit lines along Fifth Avenue, Seventh Avenue, Ninth Street, and Prospect Park West provided frequent service to downtown Brooklyn and Manhattan for the neighborhood's predominantly professional population. Early homes, especially those along the northern crest of Park Slope and Prospect Park, were extremely elegant.

Advertisements described homes with billiard rooms, libraries, and sewing rooms, parquet floors, full baths, and burglar alarms. Real-estate dealers promised value at far lower prices than across the river. "Houses on Eighth Avenue, four story brownstone residences, we sell for $28,000 and $30,000," noted one, Leonard Moody, in the November 2, 1888 *Tribune.* "The same class of dwelling in New York on the West Side, from Seventieth Street up along that fashionable section, command from $50,000 to $55,000 each, while some sell for $60,000. Well, now, you see our properties are about the best investment, being about fifty per cent less than New York." The nearby 526-acre Prospect Park, which opened in 1874, offered beautifully landscaped areas of lawn, groves of trees, a pristine lake, and scenic rustic benches and shelters. The prestigious Montauk Club, built on Eighth Avenue in 1891 just a few blocks from the park, hosted social activities for the more well-to-do.

More modest rowhouses were later built on the lower Slope, nearer to the Gowanus Canal, to accommodate the growing population of Italian and Irish working people, many of whom earned their livelihood along the waterfront and in the numerous industries in the area. People with limited resources and without funds to commute needed work and home within walking distance of each other.

As mass-transit lines pushed suburban development further into Brooklyn in the nineteenth and early twentieth centuries, many Park Slope residents moved on. Two-family homes and once privately owned brownstones were divided into boarding houses to accommodate new residents. Some of the elegant mansions of the northern Slope were razed in the 1920s by builders who erected apartments on the huge lots. After World War II, many upper-middle-class residents moved to more suburban areas outside of Brooklyn, where modern suburban homes offered attractive alternatives to the neighborhood's now unfashionable brownstones. Park Slope's population became older and less affluent, rooming houses multiplied, real-estate disinvestment became more common, and some buildings were even abandoned. In the 1960s and 1970s, however, "brownstone pioneers" began to buy homes and fix them up, first in the northern Slope and then in the southern.

Today, Park Slope is once again an upscale middle-class neighborhood, with lush tree-lined streets and some of the nation's finest examples of Queen Anne and Romanesque and Rennaissance Revival style rowhouses and mansions. Seventh Avenue, its main commercial thoroughfare, boasts restaurants, supermarkets, shops, and banks; along nearby streets are public and private schools, churches, and synagogues. The revitalization that has swept the area between Seventh Avenue and the park from Flatbush Avenue to Fifteenth Street is expanding.

The neighborhood is also home to one of the largest lesbian communities in the country, as well as the Lesbian Herstory Archives, the most extensive collection of lesbian research materials in the United States. The organization moved from Manhattan and opened in Park Slope in 1993 to become part of this growing community. Park Slope's combination of cityscape, space, affordable housing, and more scenic charms has also attracted many artists, writers, and literary types, many emigrés from Manhattan's Upper West Side, as well as families and commuters to Manhattan drawn by its easy accessibility. With the beauty of Prospect Park nearby, and sources of inspiration like the main branch of the Brooklyn Public Library, The Brooklyn Museum, the Brooklyn Botanic Garden, and the elegant arch at Grand Army Plaza all within walking distance, Park Slope continues to draw a varied population—even without horsecars.

"They Are Buying and Selling Real Estate Like Mad": The El to Brownsville

It is easy to imagine Charles Brown, Brownsville's namesake, visiting the area's rolling farmland in the late 1850s and envisioning rows of houses rising on the landscape. By 1865, he had built over a hundred homes, most of them modest in scale. In its October 7, 1867 issue, the *Brooklyn Daily Times* assessed this remarkable development: "Brownsville . . . numbering about one hundred houses, has had its principal growth in the last eighteen months. It is almost exclusively settled by mechanics, who have come out of the city to secure homesteads of their own. The rapid growth of Brownsville is largely due to the liberal policy pursued by Charles S. Brown, the original proprietor. He built cottages for purchasers, and lent money to others who preferred to build their own houses, giving easy terms of payment. Purchasers have not only found pleasant homes, but profitable investments." Although the housing development failed and Brown fled the country, he had set the stage for Brownsville as a neighborhood for working people (the "mechanics" mentioned by the *Daily Times* were most likely skilled artisans or even early factory workers). Extensive development came at the end of the nineteenth century, with the sale of land to New York real-estate developer Aaron Kaplan.

Kaplan envisioned the area as a working-class community. He arrived in Brownsville in the 1880s and persuaded several Lower East Side garment manufacturers to relocate there. As they came, attracted by cheaper land and the proximity to Manhattan, small single-family homes sprang up around the factories and the proposed elevated-train route along Atlantic Avenue. (The term "elevated railroad" was coined in 1868 to describe a railroad that operates chiefly on an elevated structure.) More manufacturers and workers followed, many of them Eastern European Jewish immigrants from Manhattan's crowded Lower East Side.

The Kings County Elevated Company's line opened in 1891, connecting Brownsville to downtown Brooklyn and accelerating development. More newcomers came with the completion of the Williamsburg Bridge in 1903 and the Manhattan Bridge in 1909, links that made travel from Manhattan to Brownsville fairly easy. Another reason for the influx lay in bridge construction itself. The entrance ramps to the bridges destroyed numerous tenements in their paths, dislocating thousands of Jews from their Manhattan homes, and forcing them to look for new housing. It was the elevated, though, that was at the heart of Brownsville's transformation.

Powered by steam, and raised high above city streets away from the congestion of horsecars and other traffic, the elevated railroad, or "el," made travel quicker and easier than surface transit. *Harper's Weekly* captured its debut on May 13, 1885: Well-dressed prospective riders hovered over the tracks as the train pulled into the station. The *Brooklyn Daily Times* noted that while there had been "a thousand difficulties and drawbacks" in the process, the opening of the elevated was "an event of supreme importance to the city." By the 1890s, elevated lines extended east from the downtown area, through Bedford, to the newly developing neighborhood of East New York, south along Fifth Avenue to the border with New Utrecht, and along Broadway from downtown Williamsburg through Bushwick to East New York. In 1898 elevated routes were extended directly over the Brooklyn Bridge to the terminal at Park Row, Manhattan, providing an uninterrupted trip to New York for many Brooklyn commuters.

A boon to travelers, the els that ushered in the age of rapid transit proved a nuisance to those who lived near them, typically the less well-to-do, and they could be dangerous. Trains were noisy and dirty; the towering elevated structures cast permanent shadows, and as the *Brooklyn Daily Eagle* noted on July 22, 1891, "In bad weather the streets under the elevated are the last to dry up after storms, and they are generally very dirty, and dampness and foul odors arise from them. . . . I have no doubt we shall soon hear of a new disease caused by the foulness of the streets under the roads." One of the most devastating accidents in the history of the New York City transit system involved a BRT (Brooklyn Rapid Transit) Brighton Beach elevated train, which sped down the approach into the Malbone Street tunnel at Flatbush Avenue on November 1, 1918; when it could not negotiate the curve and derailed, its "old wooden cars . . . crumbled like fruit cases when they struck the concrete wall of the Malbone Street Tunnel," according to the next day's *New York Post.* Ninety-seven people died, and more than a hundred were injured. The cause was human error. The operator had been hastily trained, foolishly recruited by management at the last minute to take the place of the regular driver who was out due to a motormen's strike. To ease bad memories, Malbone Street was renamed Empire Boulevard.

Opening of the Brooklyn Elevated by W. P. Snyder, hand colored, 1885.

In this illustration from the May 23, 1885, *Harper's Weekly,* excitement fills the air as prospective passengers for the new elevated train line the platform on May 13, waving and doffing their hats.

As the elevated kept drawing more newcomers to Brownsville, the area grew densely populated, with crowded business streets—like Pitkin Avenue, the main thoroughfare—and packed pushcart markets. In December 1903, the *Forward* reported that "only yesterday everybody laughed when you mentioned Brownsville. But today business is booming. They are buying and selling real estate like mad. Lots are sold by the hundreds; houses are sold and resold every minute." The paper failed to mention that most of the dwellings built for the initial influx in the late 1800s were often hastily constructed. Rows of wood-frame houses, backyards with frame privies, and small frame tenements lined the muddy streets. As the area became more accessible, two-family homes and small tenements with storefronts at street level replaced earlier houses. By 1910, Brownsville was a community of large multifamily buildings where life had come to resemble the Lower East Side, including the crowding so many had tried to escape. By 1916 more immigrant Jews lived in parts of Manhattan, the Bronx, and Brownsville than on the Lower East Side. Brownsville's last building boom followed World War I.

The Brooklyn Bridge

Belmont Avenue, Brownsville, 1910.

This jostling street scene is reminiscent of the Lower East Side, the former home of many Brownsville residents, with signs in English and Hebrew. Perhaps it was Thursday or Friday, when crowds of people shopped for the Sabbath, choosing from baskets of bread and barrels of salted herring sold by street vendors. Photograph by Irving Underhill, courtesy of the Brooklyn Public Library–Brooklyn Collection.

Typically, Jews who moved on and up the residential ladder left Brownsville for East Flatbush and from there went on to Flatbush or Eastern Parkway. As one contemporary observer noted, "If God is good, a Brownsvillian moves to Eastern Parkway." In the 1930s, Italians settled in the northern part of Brownsville, often in the Ocean Hill section. But after World War II, many residents left for Canarsie and suburban communities on Long Island and in New Jersey. African Americans, many from the South, moved in during the late postwar period. They came seeking better jobs in the garment and related industries but found dwindling factory jobs and exclusion. Old housing stock, mostly poorly built working-class homes, could not withstand the strain of rapid disinvestment and soon deteriorated.

Large-scale publicly sponsored high-rise housing constructed in Brownsville in the 1950s and 1960s in an effort to relieve its housing problems was less than successful. Some city officials even discussed the idea of consolidating residents into other Brooklyn neighborhoods, leaving Brownsville fallow. Fortunately, there was some relief, such as the government-sponsored Marcus Garvey Village, a low-rise development built in 1976 whose more human scale was a better solution to housing problems. One of the real successes was the result of the combined effort of a consortium of churches working with the local community, the city, and the federal government. East Brooklyn Churches' Nehemiah housing, single-family dwellings that began to rise in the 1980s, provide home ownership to thousands. Residents and merchants have also organized to improve the community. Pitkin Avenue remains an active retail district, with shoe, clothing, and furniture stores, restaurants, and other small enterprises. There, long-time Jewish business owners have been joined by Israeli newcomers who now dominate the garment industry, along with Korean, East Indian, and African American merchants. The bustling activity recalls the crowded Brownsville street markets of old.

Trolley Lines to a "Garden of Eden": Flatbush

Destined to become one of Brooklyn's most cherished features, trolleys began to glide along rails on Brooklyn streets on April 19, 1890, when directors and several stockholders gathered for an inaugural ride. The *Brooklyn Daily Eagle* dubbed it a "thorough success." The trolley reigned until it was phased out beginning in the 1930s with the introduction of buses and made its last run in 1956. In the process, it changed the face of transportation in the borough and earned a reputation as one of the model street-railroad systems of the United States. Faster and larger than the horsecars and propelled by mechanical power, the trolley offered quick and easy travel to outlying areas of Brooklyn.

While in 1887 a line from Queens had dipped into East New York, the trolley line that opened in April 1890 was the first electric line wholly in Kings County. By 1892, the move to electric cars was underway in earnest; by 1895 horsecars had virtually vanished; and by the turn of the century, it was possible to travel to New York over the Brooklyn Bridge from almost anywhere in Brooklyn for a five-cent trolley fare. The fare was much more affordable at the turn of the century than fifty years earlier, in part because real income for working-class Americans doubled between 1880 and 1920. They were no longer confined largely to Brooklyn's congested downtown area or to the neighborhoods in which they worked. By 1919, a Brooklyn resident could choose among forty trolley lines.

While a few trolleys were quite elaborate, such as the special cars that could be chartered for excursion parties, most were not, although a certain novelty lay

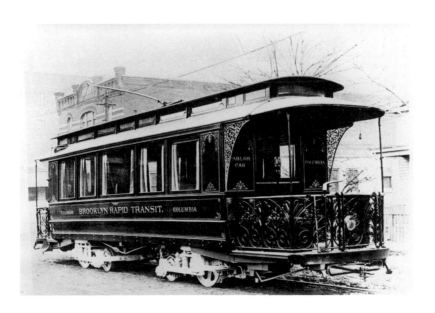

Parlor Car Columbia, ca. 1895.

Like the Stage Sewanhackey, the Columbia was intended for special trips. Its decorative foliate ironwork, curtained windows, and a special buffet replete with fancy table linens were not features of ordinary trolleys.

#6148 Flatbush Avenue Line–Livingston Street looking east to Nevins Street, 1946.

Heading east on Livingston Street from downtown, number 6148, on the Flatbush Avenue line, was a later model than the Columbia; Brooklyn's growing population demanded ever-larger cars.

in the "trolley" itself, the device that carried electric current from an overhead wire to every car and gave the vehicles their name. But novelty and speed came at a price. Although the trolley could travel significantly faster than its predecessor, the horsecar, the results could be deadly. A broadside entitled "Crop of Murders," issued in 1894, uses rows of tiny coffins to symbolize deaths in trolley accidents. Newspapers frequently carried stories of disasters on Brooklyn streets. "The weekly victim of the trolley lines to Coney Island for yesterday was Patrick McGrath, a 50 year old laborer," reported the *Brooklyn Daily Eagle* on May 9, 1910. "He was run over and killed instantly early yesterday . . . by a car of the Smith Street line of the Coney Island and Brooklyn Railroad. The body was dragged a hundred feet."

Even when trolleys moved more slowly on streets congested with cars, wagons, and trucks, pedestrians often cut and dodged in front of them. This behavior and the many miles of track in Brooklyn earned locals the label "trolley dodgers" from their Manhattan neighbors, a nickname eventually assumed by Brooklyn's professional baseball team, the Dodgers.

Flatbush, one of Brooklyn's six original colonial towns and the governmental center of Dutch Long Island until the early nineteenth century, owes much of its development to the trolley. Although horsecars and the steam railway had served the area since the 1850s, it was still comparatively undeveloped in the 1890s. Besides the advent of trolley service, growth was spurred by the annexation of Flatbush by the City of Brooklyn in 1894, whose new tax rates forced

Broadside, 1894.

Trolleys could be dangerous business. Each year people were knocked down and run over by the vehicles, which shared the already crowded streets with pedestrians, wagons, and later, automobiles.

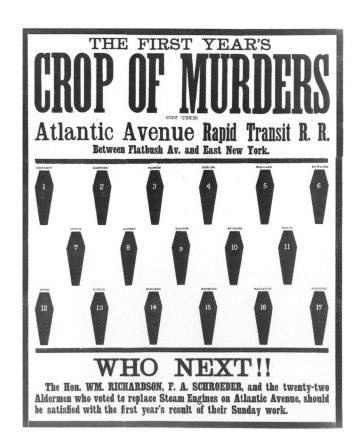

Brooklyn! *An Illustrated History*

T hen he turned and saw the papers. With half a sigh he picked up the *World.*

"Strike, Spreading in Brooklyn," he read. "Rioting Breaks Out in all Parts of the City."

He adjusted his paper very comfortably and continued. It was the one thing he read with absorbing interest.

Through the words of George Hurstwood, the character who sinks to personal ruin in Theodore Dreiser's 1900 novel *Sister Carrie,* Brooklyn's trolley car strike of 1895 entered popular literature.

Called by a local branch of the Knights of Labor, the strike paralyzed service for weeks in January and February 1895 as workers fought for better wages and hours. The special committee appointed to investigate its causes called it the culmination of negotiations that had been going on for eight years; its participants included "five thousand motormen, conductors, car cleaners, switch-turners, truckmen and other employees on four of the largest systems of street-surface railroads, embracing nearly 50 different lines of cars." *Harper's Weekly,* apparently promanagement, ran a cover illustration that pictured the Seventh Regiment, called out by the mayor to secure order, as guardians of a trolley. Filled with newspapermen, it is driven by a strike breaker along Gates Avenue.

Questioned about the outcome, motorman Joseph W. Parisen recalled at age ninety, in a letter printed in the *New York Daily News* on December 27, 1957:

> And did we win? Well, I'll say we did not. The company imported strike-breakers from all over, some from Syracuse, some from Buffalo, and all points east or west. . . . The strike was pretty well broken up after Mayor Charles A. Schieren ordered out the militia. They took possession of the car barns and almost of everything. . . . After it was settled, the strikers had an offer to come

down to the main office on Montague St. and take their chances on getting back.

I went with a few other fellows and got a little slip telling me to report on a certain date and perhaps I might get appointed. Well, thank God, I never went back.

The caption that ran with this *Harper's Weekly* cover for February 2, 1895, read: "The Strike in Brooklyn—Firing at the Mob . . . A Detail of the Seventh Regiment escorting Car filled with Newspaper Men on Gates Avenue, Evening of January 1st."

Advertisement, Brooklyn Heights R.R. Co., 1898.

The old-fashioned stage "with its clatter and rattle" looked decrepit beside the modern wonders of the trolley in 1898 "with its elegance comfort and ease"—in this persuasive advertisement in the *Brooklyn Gazette.*

farmers to sell to developers, and by a demand for more housing. In 1892, local grocer and developer Henry A. Meyer's Germania Land and Improvement Company laid a grid across sixty-five acres of the former Vanderveer potato farm and erected rows of cottages. Just six years later, the *Brooklyn Gazette* advertised the advantages of the quick and easy trolley ride to Flatbush.

In 1899, developer Dean Alvord created Prospect Park South, a planned mini-community that became the prototype for Flatbush's suburban growth. The area was marketed as a rural park within the city, and promotional literature boasted of landscaped malls and stately detached homes. Restrictions forbade "the erection of factory and objectionable business structures or low class tenement houses," noted the real estate section of the *New-York Daily Tribune* in April 1906. Potential buyers had to produce references "to protect the families of lot purchasers against undesirable social and moral influences," essentially codewords for the less well-to-do. According to *The Realm of Light and Air,* a 1905 periodical about Flatbush, "It is quite certain that had Columbus preceded Adam, Eve would have founded the Garden of Eden not in the Far East, but in Flatbush."

By 1910 almost no open land remained in the northern part of Flatbush. Before and after photographs of Flatbush Avenue looking south to Church Avenue, taken in 1877 and in 1920, chronicle the striking effects of development. Within a little more than thirty years, Flatbush had evolved from a small, almost rural hamlet to a crowded, bustling town. When the Brighton Beach subway line cut through the neighborhood in 1920, linking Flatbush with Manhattan and the oceanfront at Coney Island, development accelerated even more. From 1920 to

Assorted postcards, Flatbush, ca. 1910.

Popular enough to warrant their own postcards, these suburban subdivisions established within Flatbush were marketed as rural parks dotted with substantial turn-of-the-century single-family homes.

1930, the Jewish population—many the children of earlier immigrants—increased 250 percent, mixing with the largely Irish residents who had been in the area since the mid–nineteenth century and white Protestants.

With little room to expand out, Flatbush built up in the 1920s, often replacing mansions with the fine ornate apartment buildings that now line Ocean Avenue from Prospect Park to Kings Highway. But many of Flatbush's single-family homes with yards remain, a stabilizing factor as new residents move in, often to raise families. Along streets like Marlboro and Cortelyou Roads, huge Victorian-era wood-frame homes that went out of favor after World War II have charmed new owners, eager to renovate these striking reminders of turn-of-the-century life.

Today, Flatbush is itself a collection of neighborhoods—Ditmas Park, Prospect–Lefferts Gardens, Prospect Park South, and more. Midwood, with the

Flatbush Avenue, looking south to Church Avenue and beyond, ca. 1877.

most extensive tract of detached houses in New York City, became home to many Italian and Jewish Americans in the 1930s and 1940s; over the last few decades, the Jewish community has expanded and includes Orthodox, Hasidic, and Reform Jews. Sephardic Jews from Bensonhurst created a new community, for which the Sephardic Community Center at 1901 Ocean Parkway is now a cultural focus. Brooklyn College, incorporated in 1930 to provide higher education for the children of immigrants, is in Midwood. Asians and Latinos have also recently settled there and in Ditmas Park, and Cambodian refugees settled in northern Flatbush in the 1980s. The largest group of relative newcomers, though, are Carribbean Americans, and along East Flatbush streets like Church Avenue,

Flatbush Avenue, looking south near Church Avenue, 1920.

In thirty-three years, the small town of Flatbush, surrounded by farmland, became a commercially developed, urban area.

Brooklyn!   *An Illustrated History*

bakeries, businesses, and vegetable stores bright with island produce give new life to old buildings. As its eclectic mix of housing styles—art deco apartment buildings, elegant Victorian mansions, attached brick bungalows, homes with yards and porches—makes Flatbush one of Brooklyn's architectural gems, its fascinating blending of cultures and traditions makes it one of the borough's most diverse and vibrant neighborhoods.

End of the Line for the Subway: Sheepshead Bay

By the first decade of the twentieth century, Brooklyn had one of the most comprehensive and affordable rapid-transit systems in the country. But it was the subway that significantly changed the borough's commuting patterns. Four years after Manhattan's IRT (Interborough Rapid Transit) debuted, the subway extended through a tunnel under the East River to open in Brooklyn on January 9, 1908. The celebration matched the fervor of the Brooklyn Bridge inauguration almost twenty-five years earlier. An eight-car train was "greeted by a crowd of upwards of 5,000 at Borough Hall, flashlights from the *Brooklyn Eagle* tower and blazes of light from surrounding buildings," reported the *Eagle Almanac*'s 1909 "Gazetteer of Long Island." While "the formal celebration by Brooklyn of the opening was postponed until 12 o'clock of the day, upon the arrival of the official train," it was worth the wait. "The features of this celebration were the immense throng that had gathered around Borough Hall; the elaborate decorations throughout the downtown districts of public buildings, business houses,

Unsung Heroes

The unsung heroes of the early subway system were people like Big John DeMarco who, according to the note scribbled on the back of the photograph, stands at left. He and his co-workers take a break in front of a shield in a tunnel beneath Brooklyn's Temple Bar Building at Joralemon Street, built in 1901 and at the time the borough's tallest skyscraper. When the line was finished, Manhattan and Brooklyn were connected—underground. DeMarco was one of hundreds of workers, many of them Italian and Irish, who built one of the most extensive rapid-transit systems in the country, often with only hammers, picks, and shovels.

Subway shield below Temple Bar Building, 1907.

churches; the lining of the streets with gay colored bunting, flags and streamers; the ringing of bells, shrieking of steam whistles and bombs—all of which led up to the reception of the official party of the train."

Four months later, on May 1, 1908, a "Citizens' Celebration" took place. *Opening of the Brooklyn Subway,* a special brochure printed for the day, touted the benefits of rapid transit: "The new subway will have the immediate effect of stimulating growth and development and of enforcing in the public mind the superior advantage of Brooklyn for residence."

Four years later, at the groundbreaking for the Fourth Avenue line on October 26, 1912—just one of many track extensions—some quick-thinking entrepreneur hawked felt pennants depicting the improvement. (By 1915, the Fourth Avenue line connected Park Slope, Sunset Park, and Bay Ridge with Manhattan over the Manhattan Bridge.) Between 1893 and 1936, more than five thousand subway and elevated cars were built for use on Brooklyn's nearly endless miles of track. The vast system allowed people to travel almost anywhere in Brooklyn and New York City in less than an hour. Subways, and later automobiles, opened up even the most distant regions of Kings County to suburban development.

Pennant, Extending of Brooklyn Subway, October 26, 1912.

Since the Fourth Avenue subway did not arrive in Bay Ridge until 1915, this pennant probably heralds the groundbreaking. It depicts Forty-third Street, now part of Sunset Park; at the time the pennant was made, everything south of Thirty-ninth Street was called Bay Ridge.

Sheepshead Bay, located along Brooklyn's southern shore, owes much of its early large-scale development to the subway. The once sleepy fishing and farming village emerged as a popular vacation spot in the late nineteenth century because of its fine beaches and easy summertime access via the Coney Island Railroad. Small, wood-frame houses faced the marshy, grass-lined waterfront and the pristine bay beyond. Primarily a farming and fishing community until the 1920s, Sheepshead Bay blossomed with the extension of subway and elevated lines, the advent of the automobile, and government policies that encouraged new construction and home ownership.

The housing boom ignited in 1923 with the auctioning off of the Sheepshead Bay Racetrack, a horse-racing track that had later been converted to a car speedway. Instead of stressing aesthetics and quality, real-estate promotional materials hawked new developments as "big" or "dynamic," calling Sheepshead Bay the "New Flatbush," perhaps a reference to Flatbush's recent phenomenal growth. By 1925, a thousand homes had been built (in 1922 and 1923 Brooklyn led the nation in housing construction). To keep profits high, developers built on large

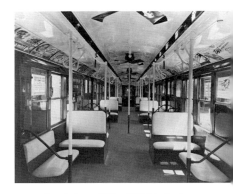

Interior of subway car #1208, July 2, 1940.

Next to the earliest subway interiors, with their wooden floors and rattan seats, this 1940 car appears modern and squeaky clean. Subway ridership dropped off during the Depression but soared in the 1940s.

Auction poster, August 30, 1924.

Conjuring up seaside images and cashing in on the recent popularity of housing developments in Flatbush, this 1924 real-estate poster announces the sale of the Harkness estate, formerly a horse-racing track and car speedway.

Brooklyn's Last Farmer, 1949.

Surrounded by apartment buildings, Frank Albanese of Sheepshead Bay poses for an *Eagle* photographer in 1949, who depicts him as the last farmer in Brooklyn. For generations, most Brooklynites had been farmers, a way of life that had almost disappeared by this time. Photograph from the *Brooklyn Eagle,* December 4, 1949, Courtesy of the Brooklyn Public Library—Brooklyn Collection.

tracts using standardized designs and materials. Sellers emphasized houses equipped with driveways and garages and interiors designed for "modern" living. Before long, the area's rural character had changed. In December 1949, the *Brooklyn Daily Eagle* carried a photograph of Frank Albanese of Sheepshead Bay, "Brooklyn's last farmer."

Sheepshead Bay saw further massive development with the advent of the automobile. By the 1920s, increased availability and affordability put a car within the reach of many (in 1905, there were 8,000 registered cars in the United States; in 1925, 17,481,001). At the same time, public policies supported an emerging car-oriented society and a decentralized city. After World War II, low-cost GI loans enabled more people to buy their own homes. The automobile (as well as new highways like the Belt Parkway, built in 1940 and later extended) encouraged Brooklynites first to settle in areas outside mass-transit routes, and later to move out of Brooklyn altogether, to nearby New Jersey, Long Island, and Staten Island. Besides Sheepshead Bay, distinct automobile neighborhoods such as Canarsie, Gerritsen Beach, and Flatlands had begun to take shape as early as the 1920s. They shared many of Sheepshead Bay's suburban features: driveways, garages, and single-family detached homes. The last areas in Brooklyn to develop, they offered Brooklynites newer suburban environments as they left older crowded neighborhoods.

An apartment building boom in the 1950s made Sheepshead Bay one of the few Brooklyn neighborhoods to gain in population. By then, its houses and apartment buildings were becoming home to a large Jewish population, including many from Williamsburg, Crown Heights, and Bushwick, who erected numerous synagogues in the 1950s. Today, winterized summer cottages built in the early twentieth century and semi-attached houses with yards and driveways stand alongside newer condominiums. Longtime Italian, Irish, and Jewish residents have been joined most recently by Chinese and by Russians from nearby Brighton Beach looking for affordable housing.

Today, Sheepshead Bay residents enjoy the area's still-beautiful waterfront. When Emmons Avenue, the main thoroughfare, was widened and paved in the 1930s, the city built concrete piers for fishing and ferry boats, and early risers can catch day-fishing boats from the Sheepshead Bay piers. These piers have since been revitalized, and Lundy's, the area's famous fish house, has reopened under new management. Along Sheepshead Bay Road, the area's commercial strip, are numerous shops and boutiques, and strollers along Ocean Parkway can appreciate the huge houses that were home to the silent-film stars of the 1920s who worked at the nearby Vitagraph Studios.

"Great Changes Have Taken Place around Rose Cottage"

The Brooklyn Bridge, the ferry, the horsecar, the elevated, the trolley, the subway—each in its own time was a tremendous advance, adding new impetus to Brooklyn's growth. But Brooklyn's evolution into a major urban center—the product of transportation growth, new housing, industry, social, political, economic development, and population growth—was a complex process with many

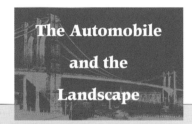

The Automobile and the Landscape

I n 1910, the *Brooklyn Daily Eagle* called automobiling "the last call of the wild." By the 1920s, cars were fast becoming a standard feature of middle-class American life.

While Brooklynites into the 1950s continued to rely on trolleys to get around, the automobile had an enormous impact on the borough. Cars and highways—encouraged by federal policies in the 1940s—made it easier to move not only within Brooklyn, but through and out of it to new suburbs in Long Island, Staten Island, and New Jersey.

The automobile also brought changes more subtle than highways to the borough's landscape. Gas stations, public parking lots, garages—and, of course, car showrooms—sprang up all over Brooklyn.

Janet Parker, Miss Brooklyn 1963, in front of the showroom of Central Lincoln Mercury, 2001 Coney Island Avenue.

Brooklyn in 1851 by Francis H.
Heinrich, oil on canvas, 1851.

Heinrich's romanticized portrayal of the
view from Lookout Hill (later part of
Prospect Park), facing north toward
Gowanus Bay and New York Harbor, includes all the facets of a landscape
changing from country to city: wilderness in the foreground, farm animals
grazing in the middle ground, and in the
distance, the church spires, rowhouses,
and belching factory smokestacks of the
urban streetscape.

ramifications. Some mourned the passing of an older Brooklyn and asked a question that remains pertinent today: Have the gains outweighed the losses?

Brooklyn businessman Alden Spooner was one of those who voiced the
question. In 1830, he complained in the *Long Island Star* about the development
of Brooklyn Village. Its building up, he felt, "has been accompanied with too little reference to its future interests. The whole object seems to have been to cover
every lot of 18 × 22 with a house . . . [and] to tumble the hills into the valleys,"
a reference to leveling ground to make way for new streets.

Almost twenty years later, Swedish writer and women's-rights champion
Fredrika Bremer echoed Spooner. "Brooklyn is as quiet as New York is bewilder-
ing and noisy" she wrote in a letter to her sister in 1849. "Rose Cottage lies just
on the outskirts of the town, . . . and the country, with wooded heights and green
fields, may be seen therefrom on three sides." Two years later, Bremer noted with
alarm that "great changes have taken place around Rose Cottage . . . a hundred
houses, certainly, have sprung up around it in all directions, and a regular street
runs now in front. . . . When I first came to Rose Cottage, it stood in the country;
now it lies in the very middle of the city."

Viennese artist Francis Heinrich depicted this rapidly changing Brooklyn on
canvas. In 1851, he set up his easel on Lookout Hill, an elevated area in what is
now Prospect Park, and painted a sweeping panorama encompassing Gowanus
Bay, New York Harbor, the skylines of Brooklyn, Manhattan, and the towns of
New Jersey. In the distance, smoke billows from factories, and buildings seem to
creep further and further into the rural Brooklyn in the foreground. The real focus of the painting is the place where city and country meet. Heinrich shows that
boundaries between rural and urban, while still apparent, were growing less dis-

Ruins of the Simon Aertsen de Hart House by John Mackie Falconer, oil on board, July 19, 1886.

Falconer was fascinated with the disappearing remnants of early Dutch and English life in Brooklyn. He painted the de Hart House, built around 1660, first intact, on Third Avenue near Gowanus Bay, then in ruins the day it was demolished in July 1886.

tinct. His "gleaming" city was in fact a threat to the countryside and would gradually overwhelm it.

As Brooklyn grew, many other artists and photographers chronicled its changing landscape. The tranquil scene captured by Francis Guy in his 1817 *Summer View of Brooklyn* was shattered during the construction of the Brooklyn Bridge, when workmen tore down the old homes and shops in the 1870s to make way for a storage yard for Brooklyn Bridge wire. Brooklyn's John Mackie Falconer, an antiquarian at heart, documented the remains of Brooklyn's Dutch and English heritage. Over the course of a few days in 1886, he recorded the demolition of the seventeenth-century Simon Aertsen de Hart House near Gowanus Bay, showing the home in ruins when it was knocked down to make way for the Thirty-ninth Street ferry house. With a modern apartment house rising behind the ruined home, the painting grieves for the time when Dutch homesteads were scattered all over Brooklyn, and gives a nod to the way of the future.

Since the eighteenth century, residents have protested public projects, from road, highway, and bridge construction to grand new complexes such as MetroTech, built in the 1980s. One of Brooklyn's earliest protesters was Dutch butcher Jacob Patchen, known in his day for his unfashionable leather breeches and for a long series of legal maneuvers he engineered to halt "progress." For instance, he blocked village road construction in 1826 by refusing to give up his house lot. Ultimately, he was evicted—but not without a final act of defiance. As the *Long Island Star* wrote in a May 11, 1826 article, even as Patchen's house was being torn down, even as "the bricks were rattling over his head," he stayed

Jacob Patchen, lithograph by A. Brown & Co., New York, 1865.

Everyone in Brooklyn seemed to know Jacob Patchen; most considered the butcher, shown here in *Henry McCloskey's Manual of 1865* as he appeared around 1826, somewhat eccentric. His was an early voice against development.

Construction of the Brooklyn-Queens Expressway, ca. 1940s.

This huge public-works project, of a scope unlike anything Brooklyn had ever seen, required the leveling of numerous buildings.

"calmly seated in his chair," until "two stout administrators of justice took him up bodily, and carefully placed the chair with its contents on a cart!"

One of the most controversial projects of the twentieth century was the construction of the Brooklyn-Queens Expressway in the 1940s, which destroyed parts of such communities as South Brooklyn and Williamsburg. Even the home of the man who oversaw the creation of the Brooklyn Bridge fell prey to the new highway. "The fifty-foot bluff of staid Brooklyn Heights is undergoing alterations as bulldozers and steam shovels scrape away century-old structures to make way for the modern features of the triple-tiered Brooklyn-Queens connecting highway," reported the *New York Herald Tribune* on May 9, 1947. "The houses slated for demolition include . . . 110 Columbia Heights, the house from which Washington A. Roebling, telescope in hand, directed the building of the Bridge after he was injured." Brooklyn Heights was more fortunate than most. Concerned citizens in this well-to-do, politically connected neighborhood forced a change in the planned route, so that the BQE ran under the Heights instead of through it. Others with less political clout were not so fortunate.

History seemed to come full circle in the 1960s with the construction of the Verrazano Narrows Bridge, which spanned the Narrows from Brooklyn to Staten Island and eventually eliminated the ferries on that route. As Brooklyn Bridge construction had destroyed buildings in its path, eighty years later, whole swatches of Bay Ridge fell to make way for the Verrazano Narrows Bridge. While many celebrated the sheer technological triumph of the bridge—it was, like the Brooklyn Bridge, the longest suspension bridge of its time—others opposed this link between Brooklyn and Staten Island at Brooklyn's southern end. Construction destroyed hundreds of houses in Bay Ridge and, as one old-time resident put it, "knocked out the heart of the Norwegian community." Residents now looked out their windows and saw stark bridge approaches instead of their neighbors' homes and uninterrupted views of New York Bay and the Narrows. As the *Daily*

News reported on May 13, 1955, "Bay Ridge residents have launched a petition and letter writing campaign as part of an attempt to prevent construction of the $200,000,000 [Verrazano] Narrows Bridge linking Brooklyn and Staten Island. The drive is being conducted by residents along 68th and 69th Streets, and by storekeepers along Eighth Avenue."

But change was inevitable. Just as the great Brooklyn Bridge had spelled an end to an older way of life and ushered in a new one, so did twentieth century "improvements" bring their own havoc and rebirth. Out of it all came Brooklyn, a metropolis where the dynamic exchange among transportation, housing, and people created the neighborhoods that are today home to 2.3 million Brooklynites.

Navy Yard workers, 1945.

Workers stream from the docks of a ship under construction as the noon whistle blows at the Navy Yard. Every day, yard workers ascended the ways to assemble the ships' outer structures, the hammering of riveters and the clang of foundries ringing in their ears. Photograph courtesy of the National Archives.

The Brooklyn Navy Yard

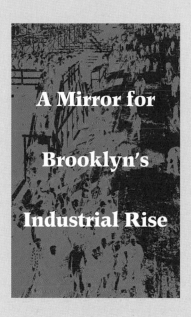

August 27, 1942. The grandly festooned battleship *Iowa* slipped from the Brooklyn Navy Yard's building ways into the chilly waters of Wallabout Bay. The workers who had built it and the dignitaries gathered for the launch sent it off with a great cheer, and tugboats steered the *Iowa* toward the East River, the gateway to the Atlantic, and to its uncertain fate in battle.

The launching had special significance for the Brooklyn Navy Yard. Responding to President Roosevelt's order to operate defense plants around the clock, Navy Yard workers met their pledge to speed up production and completed the *Iowa* a full seven months ahead of schedule. The first of many battleships built in Brooklyn after the United States entered World War II, it represented the combined efforts of thousands of workers and a new efficiency. The *Brooklyn Daily Eagle* credited the accomplishment to recent advances at the yard, especially mass production. "The 'secret' of the yard's faster production was mainly due to new sub-assembly shops," it wrote. "These brought mass production to the yard, hitherto groaning under growing obsolescence, for the first time in its history. In place of the crawling method whereby a monster warship was put together piece by piece, whole ship sections, made in the shops, were carried by crane to the ways where they were riveted and welded together."

As the Brooklyn Navy Yard reorganized for wartime production, it expanded not only its facilities but its work force—to some seventy thousand men and women—and its operating schedule to three shifts, twenty-four hours a day, seven days a week. Mobilized for defense work, the yard represented the zenith of Brooklyn's industrial might.

Brooklyn had long been a manufacturing and commercial powerhouse with national and international reach; the yard itself had been established in 1801. From a few scattered ropewalks and shipyards along the eighteenth-century waterfront, Brooklyn had grown by the mid–nineteenth century into an industrial city whose shores were lined with factories and warehouses from Williamsburg in the north to Red Hook in the south. As city chronicler Henry Stiles pointed out in his 1867–70 *History of the City of Brooklyn*, "The oft-repeated saying that Brooklyn is only a large bedroom for the business men of New York, may pass for a joke, but as a fact it is not tenable, when we consider the immense amount of manufacturing which is here carried on." By 1880 a vast waterfront, ready

POINTS OF INTEREST IN *THE BROOKLYN NAVY YARD*

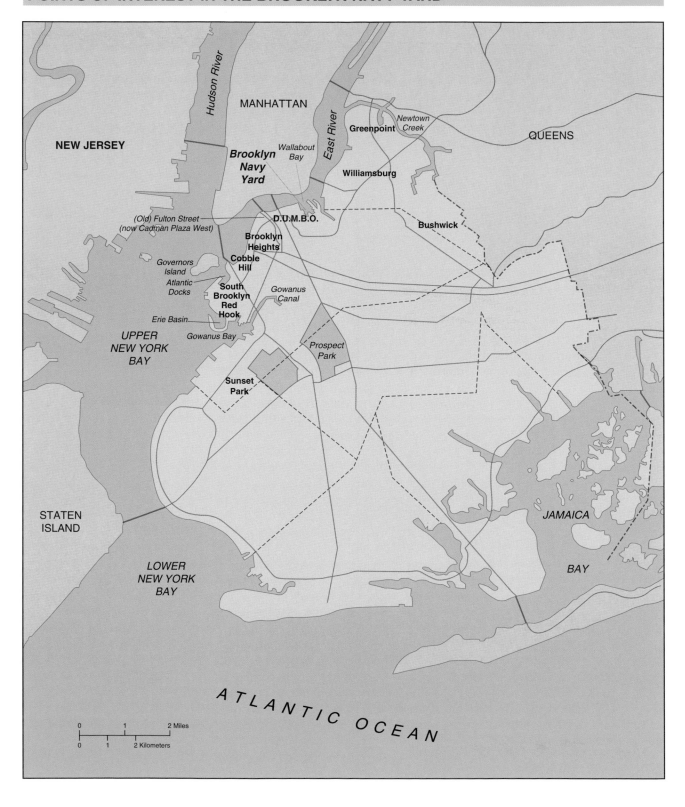

NEW JERSEY

Hudson River

MANHATTAN

East River

Brooklyn
Navy
Yard

Wallabout
Bay

Greenpoint

Newtown
Creek

QUEENS

Williamsburg

(Old) Fulton Street
(now Cadman Plaza West)

D.U.M.B.O.

Bushwick

Brooklyn
Heights

Cobble
Hill

Governors
Island

Atlantic
Docks

South
Brooklyn
Red
Hook

Gowanus
Canal

Erie Basin

Gowanus Bay

UPPER
NEW YORK
BAY

Prospect
Park

Sunset
Park

STATEN
ISLAND

JAMAICA

BAY

LOWER
NEW YORK
BAY

ATLANTIC OCEAN

0   1   2 Miles

0   1   2 Kilometers

The *Iowa* after leaving the ways, 1942.

The mighty battleship *Iowa* slipped into New York harbor on August 27, 1942, accompanied by tugs.

workforce which multiplied with a steady influx of immigrants and newcomers, and complex transportation networks had helped make Brooklyn the fourth-largest industrial city in the country—although it sometimes suffered from an image problem. Much of its commerce was erroneously credited to Manhattan, and fancy corporate addresses in New York obscured the fact that plants were actually in Brooklyn. As writer Julian Ralph observed in the April 1893 issue of *Harper's New Monthly Magazine*, "Brooklyn really has great manufacturing interests, and many of the goods that the people of the country buy as of New York are really made in Brooklyn." Nevertheless, by the twentieth century, Brooklyn was an industrial giant that turned out everything from warships to bubble gum.

Brooklyn's complex industrial story was shaped both by forces that affected the entire country and by more local ones. While Brooklyn's story was one of expansion into the mid-twentieth century, progress did not always trace a straight upward line. Apart from major shifts in the U.S. economy (like the Panic of 1857 or the Crash of 1929), its fortunes also were linked to such major events as the opening of the Erie Canal in 1825 and such national policies as the ban on African Americans in defense-plant work prior to World War II. Local labor conflicts resulted from management pitting workers against each other or competition between successive waves of immigrants. And local catastrophes were not uncommon: Work and the promise of prosperity were abruptly ended by the explosion of the Ames and Moulton Hat Factory on February 3, 1860, that demolished the two-week-old plant, killed six people, and injured a dozen others. It was jut one tragic incident out of numerous others that marked Brooklyn's history.

And what once seemed a given—that Brooklyn would continue forever as an industrial powerhouse—proved an illusion, for in 1966 the yard closed, the victim of a changing urban industrial economy and redefined defense priorities. At the same time, numerous manufacturers were closing their doors or leaving

Brooklyn. Manufacturing continues to be a Brooklyn mainstay (and the yard, newly converted, is host to numerous small-scale manufacturers), but service industries have replaced it in importance; a utility like Brooklyn Union Gas or a hospital like Kings County Medical Center is today a more typical workplace than a mammoth industrial complex like the Brooklyn Navy Yard of the 1940s.

The diverse material records of this long story range from rare nineteenth-century oil paintings of Brooklynites at work to 1940s snapshots that capture the camaraderie of yard workers striving to get the job done. People have not always recognized the value of recording or preserving the records of their work lives. Few images depict the downside: pollution, factory accidents, the grind of low-paid work, discrimination. So much has gone unrecorded. But the surviving images, products, and memories offer a tantalizing glimpse into Brooklynites' work and community—in the yard, on the waterfront, and in the thousands of large and small industries operating in Brooklyn from the eighteenth century to the twentieth.

The Early Yard

***The Brooklyn Navy Yard* by [Miss] A. M. Walker, oil on canvas, 1839.**

Beyond the watermen's small craft a frigate enters the protective enclave of the Brooklyn Navy Yard. *Left,* the large covered ships with their masts removed are probably old vessels used for storage. On the shore behind them, in two huge wooden structures, as an observer noted in 1840, "ships-of-war of the largest class are protected from the weather while they are building."

The East River looms large in mid-nineteenth-century images of Brooklyn, for as a route for commuters and a pathway to the ocean and international ports beyond, it was central to the lives of the communities on both its shores. In 1839, marine artist A. M. Walker captured in oils and canvas the river from the New York side. The central figures are two oarsmen for hire, known as watermen, transporting passengers to Manhattan. But the real focus of the painting is the

imposing Brooklyn Navy Yard, a conglomeration of masted ships, machine shops, and storage sheds, which owed its genesis to the river.

Walker depicts the yard almost four decades after the U.S. Navy had bought the land in 1801 from local shipyard owner John Jackson. Apparently working through a mediator, Francis Childs, Jackson charged $40,000 for what amounted to roughly forty acres on Wallabout (Dutch for "bend in the river") Bay; the navy paid Childs $5. After a slow start, the navy began to convert the property into a facility where it could build, repair, and supply its ships. In choosing the Brooklyn site, the government wanted to "bestow a proportion of its patronage" on the area, especially in terms of expanding employment opportunities. The East River shorefront offered a large site along a sheltered stretch of the river, convenient to New York and close to a ready work force of skilled shipbuilders in both Manhattan and Brooklyn. The official name, New York Navy Yard, indicated a Manhattan-centered view as well as the growth potential of the Port of New York. But the yard itself translated into thousands of jobs for Brooklynites.

While early yard workers had their hands full fitting privateers and men-of-war with cannon for forays against Barbary and Caribbean pirates and for raids on British merchant shipping during the War of 1812, no ships were built until after the war ended, with the likes of the frigate *Fulton* in 1815 and the *Ohio* in 1820, the first U.S. ship of the line, that is, a battle-worthy warship. By 1852, the yard at Brooklyn was called the "second in importance in the country" by Captain Mackinnon in his two volume *Atlantic and Transatlantic Sketches Afloat and Ashore.* Shipbuilding was in full swing. It was a complex operation that required the talents of skilled artisans, including shipwrights, riggers, sailmakers, ropemakers, caulkers, and blockmakers. Life at the Navy Yard was periodically featured in popular illustrated papers, such as *Harper's Weekly,* which in 1859 ran a biting satirical piece, "Ye story of Ye Navy Yard Wh[ich] Is at Brooklyn," that lampooned charges of political favoritism brought by a federal investigating committee. In 1861—the year that marked the start of the Civil War—*Harper's* took a

**"Orders are received at ye Navy Yard to fit out nine ships for sea,"
1859.**

Throughout much of the yard's history, coveted jobs were often political plums. In this detail from a cartoon inspired by a federal inquiry, *Harper's Weekly* lampoons the practice, describing the dozing hired "friends" as working "with a will." From "Ye Story of Ye Navy Yard Wh Is at Brooklyn, Laboriously and Faithfully Compiled from Ye Records of Ye Investigating Committee, 1859," *Harper's Weekly,* March 12, 1859.

more serious look at shipbuilding operations. In the illustrations, workers are shown shaping timber and working on the wooden frame of a gunboat on stocks. They use saws, axes, and adzes to perform backbreaking work: The navy preferred to use live oak for the parts of a ship's frame that bore the greatest strain, and this southern wood, prized for its toughness, was difficult to shape.

Between the beginning of the war and its end in 1865, workers built and launched fourteen large vessels and fitted out as cruisers over four hundred commercial vessels before taking up a less active postwar pace. When *Harper's* again documented yard workers in 1870, the weekly told of massive changes in con-

Top left, a decade before the shift from wood to iron vessels, workers shape the ship's timbers. *Top center,* cordage, used largely for rigging, arrives from one of the many ropewalks along Brooklyn's shore. *Top right,* using oakum—hemp or jute fibers impregnated with tar—caulkers fill the seams of the planking to make the hull watertight. From *Harper's Weekly,* August 24, 1861.

Brooklyn! *An Illustrated History*

struction (not without some trepidation at the new technology): "The change from the use of wood to that of iron in naval structures has effected prominent changes in the requisites of this as of every navy-yard in the country," *Harper's* reported. "The machines which handle that metal are, of necessity, formidable. Hideous monsters, mechanical ogres, stand ready with savage jaws to bite out mouthfuls of solid metal. The metal shrieks as chisels pare it away while sliding under the planing tools."

The workers hired to build and refit ships of the fleet under naval supervision were largely civilians, a circumstance that would hold true throughout the yard's history. Jobs at the yard were greatly prized, in part for their comparatively short hours. By 1872 yard workers, many of them local Irish immigrants, put in eight-hour days at a time when workers elsewhere were still working twelve-hour days. (In 1872, workers elsewhere had intensified a campaign for an eight-hour day, the law in New York State since 1867, mounting strikes throughout New York City. The movement collapsed in the face of widespread opposition from the largest manufacturing employers, and most workers went back to twelve-hour days.)

Like those in other craft industries, for much of the early nineteenth-century yard workers had some control over the pace of their work. Their environment was fairly unstructured, with breaks for food, alcohol (an accepted aspect of early nineteenth-century work), and socializing. While perhaps somewhat romanticized, a typical day at a New York yard such as Brooklyn's in the 1830s was recalled by a ship's carpenter in *Fincher's Trades' Review,* an 1860s labor publication, and reprinted in 1887 in George E. McNeill's *Labor Movement: The Problem of To-day:*

> In our yard, at half-past eight a.m., Aunt Arlie McVane, a clever kind-
> hearted but awfully uncouth, rough sample of the "Ould Sod," would make
> her welcome appearance in the yard with her two great baskets, stowed
> and checked off with crullers, doughnuts, ginger-bread, turnovers, pieces,

and a variety of sweet cookies and cakes; and from the time Aunt Arlie's baskets came in sight until every man and boy, bosses and all, in the yard, had been supplied, always at one cent a piece for any article on the cargo, the pie, cake and cookie trade was a brisk one. Aunt Arlie would usually make the rounds of the yard and supply all hands in about an hour, bringing the forenoon up to half-past nine, and giving us from ten to fifteen minutes "breathing spell" during lunch; no one ever hurried during "cake-time."

After this was over we would fall to again, until interrupted by Johnnie Gogean, the English candyman, who came in always at half-past ten. . . . Johnnie usually sailed out with a bare board until 11 o'clock at which time there was a general sailing out of the yard and into convenient grog-shops after whiskey. . . .

In the afternoon, about half-past three, we had a cake-lunch, supplied by Uncle Jack Gridder, an old, crippled, superannuated ship carpenter. No one else was ever allowed to come in competition with our caterers. Let a foreign candyboard or cake basket make their appearance inside the gates of the yard, and they would get shipped out of that directly.

At about five o'clock p.m., always, Johnnie used to put in his second appearance; and then, having expended money in another stick or two of candy, and minutes in its consumption, we were ready to drive away again until sundown; then home to supper.

Such agreeable sounding days were actually on the wane by the 1870s, as work at the yard, as elsewhere in industry, became increasingly regulated and ruled by the clock.

The work force at the Navy Yard ebbed and flowed, peaking in times of war. During the Civil War, over six thousand mechanics (skilled handicraftsmen) and laborers toiled there. The numbers rose again with the Spanish-American War and again during World War I, when more than eighteen thousand skilled workers strained to meet the challenge posed by the early submarine. In June 1915, one year after the start of the war, the yard launched the *Arizona*, and the *Brooklyn Daily Eagle* described the event.

Uncle Sam's greatest naval creation—the superdreadnought *Arizona,* mightiest war craft ever wrought by the hand of man—was successfully launched at 1:11 o'clock this afternoon at the Navy Yard, while 50,000 persons roared a mighty cheer.

A whistle blew a signal, Miss Esther Ross, one of Arizona's fairest daughters, sent a wicker bottle crashing against the huge steel hull, and with a white feather of champagne—mixed with water—on her steel plates, the biggest warship of them all slipped smoothly down the greased ways into the Wallabout Basin.

The "Can Do" Yard: World War II

The busiest era in the yard's history began when the United States entered World War II. On December 7, 1941—"a day that will live in infamy"—Japanese warplanes destroyed the yard-built *Arizona* and other ships at the American Naval base at Pearl Harbor, with 3,700 casualties. Just two days later, President Franklin Roosevelt called on all defense plants to switch to a twenty-four-hour, seven-day-a-week schedule of operations.

On December 24, at a lunchtime rally, 2,000 yard workers pledged to speed up work, especially on the warship *Iowa*. The result: They finished the ship seven months ahead of schedule. To meet new demands, the yard expanded from its original forty-odd acres into a complex covering almost three hundred acres that housed several dry docks, two building ways, enormous storehouses, shops, furnaces, and forges. Altogether, some three hundred buildings were connected to the water's edge by thirty miles of standard and narrow-gauge railroad track, "the largest single industry in the bustling commercial borough of Brooklyn," as *Life Magazine* pointed out in its February 23, 1942, issue. Not only that, but the civilian workforce at the yard was the highest of all U.S. Naval shipyards during World War II, surpassing Philadelphia, Boston, and Charleston, among others. Between 1941 and 1945, the final year of the war, yard workers repaired more than 5,000 ships, converted more than 250 for wartime usage, built four aircraft carriers, and produced three of the greatest battleships afloat: the *North Carolina,* the *Iowa,* and the *Missouri.* Their efforts earned the yard the title, the "Can Do" yard.

Wartime ship launchings were bittersweet; the ultimate purpose of these magnificent vessels was to go to war. In Shop 11-12-16's "Launching Bulletin," Master Shipfitter H. F. Connor described the launch of the *Missouri* on January 30, 1944:

> In former years, the launching of a ship was the signal for thousands of persons to wind their way into the Navy Yard to watch the traditional bottle of champagne smashed across the bow as the ship began slowly to slide down the Ways. . . . How different, then, was the launching of the U.S.S. *Missouri.* The hilarity generally prevalent, the usual jovial attitude of those present, these were missing. It was, no doubt, the most quiet launching of the past decade, yet it was comforting to know that those in attendance realized the purpose of this ship. As this mass of protectiveness began slowly to slide towards the water, a spontaneous cheer went up and as she smoothly cut her way out into the stream, the crowd, to a man, was again silent. They may have been awed, they may have been pensive, they may have been reassured, whatever the reason, they were silent as the ship disappeared from sight when the tugs got a line on her.
>
> As one looked upon the magnificent ship, it was difficult to realize that soon her mission would be to take her place on a fighting front. If these were not war times, she could be looked upon as a thing of beauty. For the time being, we shall be content to consider it as a potent weapon and a comforting asset.

Many yard workers saved the special pins fabricated especially for such launchings to identify the wearers' place to view the event and to serve as tiny souvenirs.

Launches meant welcome breaks in routine, for most days at the yard offered only hard work at a driving pace. "We worked seven days a week and when you came home you wanted to rest," remembers former machinist Henry Tatowicz. "We had only . . . one day off for twenty-one days of work . . . we all had to do our part." Solomon Brodsky, who packed supplies for naval vessels and supply depots during the war, remembers how the hectic schedule affected his life: "For quite a while we worked at seven days [per week]; there was no such thing as time off, except emergencies," he recalls. "In fact, I'm Jewish, and we had the Jewish holidays coming up . . . Yom Kippur and Rosh Hashanah, and the rabbis at the time told us we should work, we were at war. It was the only time in my life

Buttons worn at launchings of U.S.S. *Arizona*, U.S.S. *Kearsarge*, U.S.S. *Missouri*.

These small pins worn at ship launchings were easy-to-save pieces of U.S. history. The *Arizona* pin that belonged to James F. Kelly, a World War I–era yard worker, later became a tragic reminder. Launched at the yard on June 19, 1915, the ship was sunk at Pearl Harbor on December 7, 1941; more than a thousand men were lost.

The Brooklyn Navy Yard

Equipment, tools, and coveralls of workers at the Navy Yard and at Todd Shipyards.

As a Navy Yard machinist, Henry Tatowicz over the years filled this elaborate oak toolbox lined with green felt with many of his own handmade tools. Alfred Yanone, who worked at the yard from 1940 through the mid 1960s, used the lunch box. The coveralls and visor belonged to Edward Volpe, who worked at nearby Todd Shipyards, which converted to wartime production during World War II.

Friends at the Brooklyn Navy Yard, ca 1942.

Catherine Hennings Sarnowski, *lower left,* and her friends Anne Harper, Lucille Kolkin, and Ida Pollack suit up for work in clothes traditionally worn by men. In 1944, the *Navy Yard Shipworker,* the yard's house newsletter, reported that the yard sold regulation overalls, low-heeled shoes, and "trim clothing" that helped the women stay "good looking." (The graffiti about New York's Patrick Cardinal Hayes on the wall behind the group may be a reaction to his well-known opposition to "smut.")

I ever worked on a Yom Kippur or Rosh Hashanah." He also remembers what drove him and others to keep going. "There were days I felt like a zombie," he said. "You work; there was a war. I had my kid brother in the war. So you feel like you're working for him." The intensity of those days prompted many workers to save reminders of their time at the wartime yards—such as tools they had made and items of clothing.

Catherine Hennings Sarnowski, a welder, remembers not only the driving pace but the need for versatility and quality control: "We were really on some

very tough jobs. I myself was working on the hot rod, and that was working on the turrets and . . . also on the diving bells. Our work had to be excellent, because if it wasn't, the chipper was right there to chip it out and you had to do it over." Sarnowski treasures the bracelets made of CRS (corrosive resilient steel), the stainless-steel rods used by welders, made for her by some of the men she worked with in the welding shop.

Through all phases of production, the yard maintained a high standard of safety. Strict regulations dictated that workers wear hard hats, visors, goggles, and steel-tipped shoes. The Navy Yard house newsletter, the *Shipworker,* published the cartoon "Dopey Dan" to encourage on-the-job safety through a little comic relief. But accidents happened. While the loss of lives at the front was well publicized, most people were unaware of the life-threatening hazards of work in the wartime industrial complex that included the Navy Yard. Former yard worker Leo Skolnick started as an apprentice in the sheet-metal shop in 1936 and eventually moved into design coordination, where he stayed until 1948. He worked on many ships—the *Brooklyn,* the *North Carolina,* the *Iowa,* the *Missouri*—often under deadly conditions. "It was a hard place," he recalls. "I was primarily concerned in new construction, and the closest thing to describe it was like Dante's *Inferno,* between the noise and the conditions and the fumes and the welding and everything. I don't think we built a big ship without losing people." He re-

Dopey Dan cartoon, "Hair Tear Affair," by Phil L. Jagust.

This regularly featured *Shipworker* cartoon chronicled the workday experiences of Dopey Dan and his Navy Yard cohorts and made points about safety through the mishaps of Dan and such regular characters as his girlfriend, Ann, who spoke in "Brooklynese." From *The Navy Yard Shipworker,* October 17, 1944.

members in vivid detail one horrifying incident: "They were building a ship up on the building ways and they were pulling in the propeller shafts . . . using what they call chain blocks with cables. And they were pulling them, and one, they strained it, and the cable snapped and . . . just whipped and took one kid's head right off." Nationally, between 1940 and war's end, nearly 90,000 workers were killed in accidents on the homefront and millions were injured.

Some dangers were less apparent, emerging only years after the war. Asbestosis, or cancer of the lung caused by exposure to asbestos particles, eventually devastated the lives of many workers who had applied the asbestos to ships and of welders who worked with the material daily. Today, those suffering from asbestosis, while proud of their work at the yard, blame the government and the suppliers. With shipyard workers as their initial membership base, the White Lung Association, a nonprofit public health and public interest organization was formed in the early 1980s largely to find caring, competent, compensation lawyers for asbestos victims filing claims. Today, it serves the interests of asbestos victims, asbestos abatement workers, and people currently exposed to asbestos.

Given government concerns over security and the potential for espionage, yard workers were also subject to searches. Clerk-typist Frances Haber recalls that "the Sands Street entrance was manned by uniformed Marines who inspected our IDs and the contents of our pocketbooks." One worker remembers that "you weren't supposed to talk about the job. There were signs saying 'Be careful—if you are talking, someone may be listening.'" Photo identification cards, shop colors, and numbers indicated the buildings in which employees worked or the ships they worked on and enabled security workers to distinguish between insiders and outsiders.

Navy Yard security check point, February 1945.

Two U.S. Marines in winter gear rigorously search persons not connected with the yard before they are allowed to enter. Photograph courtesy of the National Archives, photo no. 80–G301735.

Brooklyn! *An Illustrated History*

In spite of job hazards and tensions over security, yard workers seemed to share with other Brooklynites a willingness to make sacrifices for the common good. These were hard times. Gasoline was rationed, often making it difficult to get to work. Many items were not available—goods such as sugar and coffee were also rationed. And Brooklynites, like millions across the country, feared for loved ones at the front. But workers at the yard recall a camaraderie that grew out of sharing such challenges. Not only was the battleship *Iowa* completed ahead of schedule, but Brooklyn Navy Yard workers became the first in the nation to win the Navy's "E" for excellence in production, an award they continued to earn annually until war's end. Catherine Sarnowski said that winning gave them a "feeling of pride . . . that we were really doing something for our boys." The sense of patriotism spread beyond the confines of the yard. "Every morning when I was leaving [the yard after my shift]," Henry Tatowicz said, "they had a bugle blow taps and a flag raising ceremony, and all around the yard, no matter what area, as far as a person could see, all the trains, buses, cars stopped while the taps were going, and people walking the streets stopped to face the area where the flag was."

Memories of the Depression were still fresh: few jobs, layoffs, business failures, and Hoovervilles filled with the jobless in places like Brooklyn's Erie Basin. Many yard workers were pleased just to have a steady, paying job, regardless of working conditions. Frances Haber, who worked in the pipe shop, recalls hot and humid summers without fans or air conditioning, and freezing winters when icy winds blasting across the bay chilled the shop, which was perched on an exposed

"E" for Excellence pin, 1940s.

Many yard workers valued their mementos of the navy's awards for excellence in wartime production, tiny pins that bear a small gold "E" and the word "PRODUCTION."

dock. For Haber, it was okay: "Most of us had never had better anyway as this was right after the Great Depression."

Especially for women, the war opened up new horizons. On a much larger scale than during World War I, job opportunities emerged as men left for the front. Although not new to industry, most women in manufacturing had been limited to work in the needle trades and light assembly work. Now, at the yard alone, six thousand women took jobs that would otherwise have been filled by men. Women like oxyacetylene burner Hazel Licouri, welder Alberta Daye, and typist Frances Haber represent a national female labor force that jumped 57 percent as women replaced men gone to war. In industries like shipbuilding, traditionally dominated by men, increases were even more remarkable. The dozen women in ship construction at the start of the war became more than 160,000 nationally by December 1942. Discrimination persisted in the form of pay scales,

Working Women: The Needle Trades

Lucila Padrón came from Ponce, Puerto Rico, in the 1930s and found a job in Brooklyn's garment trade. With her favorite scissors, she cut patterns and sewed laces and appliqués to wedding dresses at a Williamsburg factory. For her and many others—particularly recent immigrant women—the garment industry offered work.

At the turn of the century, the garment industry employed largely Eastern European Jewish immigrants, many of whom had been skilled workers in their native countries. While African American women worked as dressmakers in their homes, they were largely excluded from factories and unions. A telling incident occurred during the 1909–10 Shirtwaist Strike, when garment-industry

Lucila Padrón's appliqués, laces, and threads.

manufacturers tried to keep on their few African American women workers and enlist others as scabs. In a unified gesture with their white sisters, the African American garment workers met at a Black church in Brooklyn and passed a resolution, later printed in the *New York Call.* Not only did they refuse to be strikebreakers, but they urged that "in the event of the successful termination of the strike, organized labor exercise a proper consideration of the claims and demands of the men and women of color who desire to enter the various trades in the way of employment and the protection of the various labor unions."

By the 1930s, the industry was hiring more African Americans from the South and people from the Caribbean. With the economic boom of the 1950s, job recruiters even traveled to Puerto Rico in search of garment workers, and by 1969, 33 percent of workers in the New York apparel industry were Puerto Rican. Today, many immigrant Chinese work in sewing factories in Sunset Park, New York City's third Chinatown.

While apparel manufacturing has been a major Brooklyn employer since the nineteenth century, much of the work has taken place in small factories or even in homes. When manufacturers discovered they could reduce overhead by having work done outside their factories, they often distributed piecework to contractors who gave it to workers to complete in their tenement rooms.

even though the National War Labor Board had endorsed the principle of equal pay in 1942. The policy was rarely implemented, and job titles were often changed for women. Men who had been "mechanic learners" at the Navy Yard were replaced by women called "helper trainees" at lower pay.

When huge numbers of servicemen returned after the war, women were deluged by federal propaganda that encouraged them to return to the home and to give their jobs back to men. Haber recalls her last days at the yard: "On V.E. [Victory in Europe] Day I came to work and crowds of civilians and sailors were outside Sands Street gate and people were kissing, shouting and dancing in the street. . . . Then the day came I got a pink slip notifying me of a reduction in force, namely me. I don't know why I was surprised, but I was devastated and it was the end of an era." While Haber was one of many women to lose their jobs, women had made some gains. Even though labor-force participation rates for women dropped between 1945 and 1950, they remained higher than prewar rates.

The same labor shortages that opened up new opportunities for women brought some relief for African Americans, long excluded from manufacturing jobs. But theirs was a struggle perhaps more deeply rooted in prejudice and injustice, and opportunity came only after an incident that in many ways signaled the beginning of the civil-rights movement. In 1941, powerful labor leader A. Philip Randolph, president of the Brotherhood of Sleeping Car Porters, organized the March on Washington Movement. In his keynote address to the movement, he said, "Our nearer goals include the abolition of discrimination, segregation, and jim-crow in the Government, the Army, Navy, Air Corps, U.S. Marines . . . and defense industries; the elimination of discrimination in hotels, restaurants, on public transportation conveyances, in educational, recreational, cultural, and amusement and entertainment places such a theaters, beaches, and so forth. We want the full works of citizenship with no reservations. We will accept nothing less."

Randolph threatened President Roosevelt with a massive march on the nation's capital if he did not desegregate the armed forces and defense industry.

Hazel Licouri, oxyacetylene burner, February 1945.

Hazel Licouri traveled from her home at 2915 Avenue M to work as an oxyacetylene burner at the yard. Unlike most comparable photos of men at work, she is smiling for this posed public relations shot, typical of features in print media of the time. Photograph courtesy of the National Archives.

Alberta Daye, welder, 1944.

Photographs of workers that appeared in the yard organ, the *Shipworker*, were typically upbeat, such as this one of welder Alberta Daye in the June 9, 1944 issue. African American women had limited opportunities in industry before the war, but defense work provided some employment mobility for both them and their white female co-workers.

Roosevelt signed the Fair Employment Practices Act in June 1941, prohibiting racial discrimination in the defense industry. The National Association for the Advancement of Colored People (NAACP), many African American United Automobile Workers (UAW) union leaders, and others then stepped in to push for the act's implementation. While the armed forces did not integrate until President Harry S. Truman signed an executive order barring segregation in 1948, the defense industry opened its doors to Black people in the early forties for the first time in U.S. history. Brooklynite Reverend Daniel A. King, who had come to New York from New Orleans in 1929, was one of those who benefitted. Hired as a welder from 1943 to 1944, he worked on the *Missouri,* among other ships. The force at the yard was so focused on getting the job done, he said, that there was no friction between African American and white workers. To his mind, the bottom line was a person's qualifications, not his color, since all of their lives were at stake. Still, during the late 1930s and 1940s, civil-rights action fired many African Americans in the North. Most Black people were adherents of the Double V campaign: victory over enemies overseas, and victory over discrimination and segregation at home, two "V"s seen as a route to basic social change.

The war was the catalyst for the yard's becoming Brooklyn's biggest industrial facility during those years, but the domestic call to arms reverberated throughout the borough. Almost half of all U.S. wartime personnel headed overseas sailed from Brooklyn, and the borough had some of the largest training centers. It sent 326,000 army and navy fighting men to war and was home to a huge number of volunteer women. Brooklyn industries helped make everything from combat helmets to the atomic bomb, hiring thousands of additional workers to meet the demand. As the *Brooklyn Daily Eagle* noted in a December 9, 1945, supplement to the paper, "Brooklyn, a city that made pencils and linotypes, razors and fancy cakes, baking ovens and men's ready-to-wear suits, found itself asked, all of a sudden, in 1941, to make guns and ships and shells and all the other accouterments of war."

Many firms changed course to meet the challenges of the war. Todd Shipyards, which even by World War I was one of the leading ship-repair organizations in the world, now built and repaired cargo vessels for the fleet on nearly three hundred acres of Brooklyn waterfront. Huge plants like Mergenthaler Linotype became defense plants. The Murray Manufacturing Corporation in Bedford-Stuyvesant, which once produced radiators, welding machines, and electrical distribution products, now fabricated trench mortar shells for U.S. infantrymen. The firm adapted its manufacturing process (using conventional power presses made by Brooklyn's E. W. Bliss) to take the heaviest work out of the shell-making operation in order to accommodate women workers as its male workers left for the front. Out of 1,800 employees during the war, almost 90 percent were women, who took part in almost all aspects of production.

One of Brooklyn's most important civilian contributions to the war effort came out of Pfizer Inc, a fine-chemicals manufacturer founded in Williamsburg in 1849 by German immigrants. Through an unprecedented collaboration with other chemical and pharmaceutical companies brought together by the U.S. government, Pfizer produced penicillin on a large scale for the first time ever and by 1944 was producing significant amounts of the medicine. Much of Pfizer's work took place at what was once the Rubel Ice plant at the corner of Marcy Avenue and Lorimer Street in Williamsburg. The firm converted the plant into a penicillin-production facility in just four months. A notice to workers posted at the

Souvenir trench mortar shells, made by Murray Manufacturing Corporation of Bedford-Stuyvesant, 1940s.

These scale-model trench mortar shells are replicas of the 25 million made for the U.S. Army infantry during World War II. They were created by tool-and-die makers at Murray, who machined and plated the miniature shells on their own time as a display of their skill.

Chuck-loading operation at Murray Manufacturing Corporation, 1940s.

Lottie Szkoda of Greenpoint worked on the 8-Spindle New Britain Gridley at Murray, cleaning off the welding flash on the sides of the shell and packing the shells in wooden boxes.

site during construction cited the project's immediacy: "The completion of this project is a vital necessity to provide the life-saving drug 'penicillin' to the fighting men of our armed forces who are wounded in action. . . . Please help to complete this job at the earliest possible date. By doing so you will take part in the saving of lives which otherwise could not be saved."

By the end of February 1944, the plant was in full-scale production, the largest penicillin producer in the United States. Pfizer's penicillin went ashore with the Allied troops on D-Day, June 6, 1944.

Some of the grateful penicillin recipients were Brooklynites. Peter DeConza, who fought with C Company, 473rd Regimental Rifle Team, Fifth Army, was hit with shrapnel in Italy; penicillin warded off infection following surgery to remove it at a hospital in Liverno. Elliott Rogel, who served in the navy and was part of the occupying forces in Japan in August 1945, felt that he would have died of pneumonia without the antibiotic: "I really do earnestly believe the penicillin had indeed saved my life."

Pfizer's discovery also touched the lives of Brooklynites on the homefront. While in the United States we now often take penicillin for granted, before it and other antibiotics became available infected burns and wounds could be life threatening. As a newborn at Brooklyn Jewish Hospital in 1947, Fred Miller was accidentally scalded with steam by a trainee nurse. When he underwent surgery later to correct the scarring, the penicillin he took successfully warded off infection. Besides such infections, diseases such as scarlet fever were also often fatal. Brooklynite Angelo P. Casano, who as a child in the 1940s lived on Court Street, recalls his bout with scarlet fever: "Our family doctor (who made house calls) was Dr. Peter Gallo. . . . Dr. Gallo together with my dad visited many pharmacies and hospitals in order to locate the 'wonder drug.' It took them all day and mom wor-

Penicillin made by Pfizer Inc, 1940s.

Frank Michel, in charge of quality control at Brooklyn's Pfizer Inc, during the 1940s, saved this sample of penicillin, probably from one of the first batches produced at the new Marcy Avenue plant in Williamsburg. The yellow color—due to early impurities—earned it the name "Yellow Magic" in the 1940s.

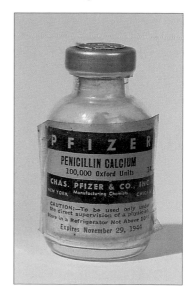

ried where they were (we had no phone at the time). They returned late at night with the Penicillin. . . . My life was saved. For years afterward my family praised God, Dr. Gallo and Penicillin for saving my life."

On the Waterfront: Docks, Factories, and Foundries

Over the course of almost 150 years, the Navy Yard grew from a tiny enclave of ships and storage facilities to a sprawling plant employing tens of thousands of workers. Its rise from a small parcel of waterfront land to an industrial behemoth during World War II, however, is just one chapter in Brooklyn's industrial history. Alongside the yard, and up and down the shore from Williamsburg to Red Hook, industrial and commercial enterprises were fostered by the same advantageous conditions that had helped spawn the yard: excellent port facilities, inexpensive land, and proximity to Manhattan. The waterfront provided jobs, attracted workers, and was, through the mid–twentieth century, key to the borough's economic vitality.

Brooklyn's first, small industries began to develop toward the end of the eighteenth century. They clustered near the foot of Old Ferry Road, or Fulton Street, where the ferry linking Manhattan with Brooklyn docked (about where the foot of Water Street is now, in the shadow of the Brooklyn Bridge). Moreau de St. Méry described one of these industries, an early ropewalk—a long covered walk or building where rope is made: "At the northern end of Brooklyn and so close to the edge of the river that part of it is on pilings, is a rope-walk belonging to Sand Brothers, who own a large part of the real estate in Brooklyn," he wrote. "This rope-walk, established in 1791, is 1175 French feet long, 24 feet wide at the south or entrance end, and 18 feet wide at the other end. It employs forty people, who as a rule are paid three fourths of a dollar a day."

Hezekiah B. Pierpont by J. C. Buttre, engraver, after painting by H. Inman, engraving, ca. 1865.

New York City line engraver H. C. Buttre produced this portrait after a painting by Henry Inman of Brooklyn Heights resident Hezekiah Beers Pierpont (1768–1838), a distillery owner and prominent Brooklyn land developer and speculator. Pierpont used the anglicized spelling of his name; his heirs used the original spelling, Pierrepont.

Distillerie de M. Pierpont sur l'isle Longue

Pierpont's Distillery on Long Island

In Insula Longa Pierpont officina.

Das Distillirt Hauss von herr Pierpont auf dem Lange Insuln.

Pierpont's Distillery on Long Island by J. Milbert, lithograph, 1825.

Hezekiah Pierpont's waterfront gin distillery, across the river from Manhattan, was a well-known geographic landmark for Brooklynites. The windmill was not a remnant of Brooklyn's Dutch culture; it was built by Pierpont. From *Amérique Septentrionale–Etat de New-York,* from the series *Itinéraire Pittoresque du Fleuve Hudson* (Paris, 1825).

By 1810, the valuable waterfront property between Red Hook and Wallabout Bay was dominated by Brooklyn's economic elite, most of them not descendants of the Dutch families who had settled Brooklyn, but a new breed of entrepreneurs. Many were New Englanders, among them Hezekiah Pierpont. The cosmopolitan grandson of a founder of Yale University, Pierpont was an astute but not always lucky businessman. While he amassed a fortune as an importer in France, he lost it all when pirates captured one of his cargo ships in 1797. In 1800, he returned to America and married Anna Marie Constable, the daughter of New York State's largest landowner, merchant William Constable, and acquired huge tracts of land in upstate New York as a wedding present. In 1804, he moved to Brooklyn and bought a large segment of land in Brooklyn Heights (including portions of a former farm) and a shorefront gin distillery located at the foot of Joralemon Street (today, the East Side Lexington Avenue subway runs beneath the site on its route to Lower Manhattan). Around 1820, French artist J. Milbert depicted the site of the distillery, including with it a stretch of the waterfront. It was a prime location for the distillery, with easy access to water and transportation to Manhattan and beyond. At the terminus of a network of rutted roads that ran from the scattered settlements to the west, it was also convenient for Long Island farmers who brought Pierpont grains.

Now in the collections of The Brooklyn Historical Society, the distillery's ledger of accounts clearly reflects the ethnic and occupational divisions of early nineteenth-century Brooklyn. Pierpont, the distillery owner, was typical of the non-Dutch, largely Yankee-bred merchants and manufacturers who lived along the shoreline and in the ferry district. The Long Island farmers listed in his ledger were part of the more rural farming population largely made up of descendants of Brooklyn's early Dutch settlers—people with names like Vandyke, Stoothoof, and Duryea—who lived outside the town.

Alongside factories such as Pierpont's, piers and warehouses were built along the waterfront to receive goods from incoming ships. The goods were then shipped out again or transported inland. As early as 1810, Brooklyn served as a point of exchange for an enormous variety of goods, as a July 5 advertisement in that year's *Long Island Star* for William Furman and Benjamin Birdsall's warehouse indicates: "Stores and Wharf. At Brooklyn, directly South of the Old Ferry [Fulton Ferry] . . . these stores are eligibly situated, in good repair . . . and ready for the reception of all kinds of goods, such as Cotton, Hides, &c. Also a yard for the reception of all kinds of Naval stores, such as Pitch, Tar, Rosin, Spars and other ship timber. Also, all kinds of provisions, such as Beef, Pork, Fish, &c." Such facilities were joined by the shops of artisans; the 1812 Brooklyn directory notes the presence of rope makers, carpenters, coopers (barrel makers), blacksmiths, and watchmakers, along with others who served the growing waterfront community: cartmen (one-man movers and shippers for hire), laborers, grocers, butchers, tailors, tavernkeepers, and boarding house owners.

Shortly before the War of 1812, Yale president Timothy Dwight marveled from the vantage point of Brooklyn Heights at the activity on the East River. "The immense number of vessels, assembled at the numerous wharves, anchored in the streams, or moving in a thousand directions over their surface, and over the great bay, in which they terminate present to the eye one of the liveliest images of vigorous activity, which can be found in the world." The war spurred com-

Robert Story's trade card, ca. 1830s.

On his business card, Robert R. Story displayed the products of his trade: saddles, tack, even a leather trunk. Craftspeople like Story had long clustered near the ferry landing to serve the early Brooklyn community.

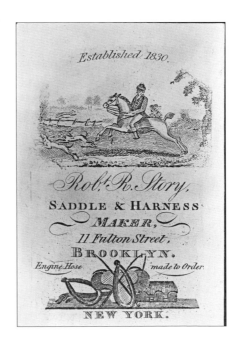

Winter Scene in Brooklyn by Francis Guy, oil on canvas, ca. 1816.

In a rare early portrayal of African American workers, Francis Guy includes several laborers in his depiction of the snowy intersection at James and Front Streets, crowded with white men and women going about their daily activities. Of the Black workers, one saws, one carries a pail, one leans on a shovel, and another is a chimney sweep. Courtesy of The Brooklyn Museum 97.13 (gift of the Brooklyn Institute of Arts and Sciences).

mercial development, and by the mid-1820s port-related businesses flourished, such as the ropewalks that furnished ships with rigging. By the 1830s waterfront factories produced tinware, iron railing, steam engines, chairs, oilcloth, Britannia metal, dresses, brass, and other goods, many employing over one hundred workers. Interspersed among them were the shops of craftspeople.

In a trend that continued with little change into the twentieth century, though, jobs in factories or as apprentices to artisans were largely denied to Black people, at the time almost 10 percent of the population of Kings County. Francis Guy's depiction of African American workers in his *Winter Scene in Brooklyn,* from around 1816, is an extremely rare visual record of Black labor. In a clear reflection of social roles, Guy identified the whites in the scene in an accompanying key, but not the African Americans. When Henry Stiles reprinted the view in his 1884 history of Kings County, he noted that the chimney sweep was Samuel Foster, and the man carrying the pail "Abiel Titus' negro servant, Jeff."

In 1831, H. C. Thompson, one of the first Black landowners in the African American communities of Weeksville and Carrville, asked some pointed rhetorical questions in a letter to the *Long Island Star:* "In our village and its vicinity, how many of us have been educated in colleges, and advanced into different branches of business; or taken into mercantile houses, manufacturing establishments, &c.? are we not even prohibited from some of the common labor, and drudgery of the streets, such as cartmen, porters, &c.?"

Brooklyn, N.Y. 1854 by B. F. Smith, Jr., artist, H. Fern & Co., publishers, engraving, 1853.

Watermen carrying passengers competed for space on the crowded East River with sailboats loaded with barrels, a packed steam ferry, and a huge array of ships. Beyond the Brooklyn shore lined with warehouses and factories rise the church spires of residential Brooklyn.

The 1831–32 Brooklyn city directory provides some answers. First, it placed small asterisks next to the names of African Americans—a reflection of the pervasive discrimination against these early Brooklynites. A review of the occupations listed along with residents' names shows such jobs as dyer and scourer, steam scourer and boot cleaner, milkman, blacking manufacturer, rope maker, hairdresser, carpenter, and whitewasher held by Black men along with one entry for a female, Sarah Johnson of 13 James Street, a "washwoman" and one for an educator, George Hogarth, a "teacher, African school 147 Jay." The rest—the vast majority—are listed simply as "laborer," shorthand for low-paying, unskilled physical work. Low-level jobs do not translate into insignificant lives, of course. Brothers Peter Croger, listed as a laborer, and Benjamin Croger, listed as a whitewasher, for instance, were founders and trustees of the first African American church in Brooklyn, the High Street (later Bridge Street) A.W.M.E. Church. Each was also involved in other religious and educational pursuits, helping to operate or establish schools, a magazine, and the Brooklyn Temperance Society for Free People of Color.

The period from the 1830s to the 1870s marked heavy commercial and manufacturing growth in Brooklyn. The waterfront was further transformed, and prints of Brooklyn during the time focused on the frenetic activity of the East River, as did *View of Brooklyn, Long Island from the U.S. Hotel, New York* (see Introduction) in 1846, or *Brooklyn, N.Y. 1854.* The river is a mighty, trafficked thoroughfare, packed with ferries steaming between Brooklyn and Manhattan and fully rigged ships headed out to sea, bound for distant shores. An unusual feature of John Bornet's panorama of the city, published in 1855, is that the foundry chimneys have no smoke billowing from their stacks. Their usual fiery glory inspired Brooklyn poet Walt Whitman to describe them in "Crossing Brooklyn Ferry" in 1856: "Burn high your fires, foundry chimneys! cast black shadows at nightfall! cast red and yellow light over the tops of the houses!"

Such prints visually underscore just how close Brooklyn and Manhattan were both physically and economically. The success of Brooklyn's active, crowded waterfront was directly related to New York's establishment as the nation's leading port following the War of 1812. Linked to vast markets by the Hudson River and, after 1825, the Erie Canal, Manhattan blossomed commercially, and so did Brooklyn. At midcentury, in fact, Brooklyn in some ways had the advantage. New York's port facilities were older, frequently dilapidated, and severely strained by the demands of a burgeoning shipping trade. Cramped conditions put space at a premium and drove up storage prices; Manhattan warehouse owners began to specialize in storing high-priced goods that required less space. Brooklyn, with its spacious waterfront and newer facilities, was able to handle the bulky goods that Manhattan could not—such as grain, sugar, and coffee—and at more reasonable fees. With much of Brooklyn's shoreline still open and undeveloped, huge stores, or warehouses, were built right on the water to easily move goods in and out. By contrast, the narrow streets of Lower Manhattan made maneuvering goods difficult, and merchants had to pay extra to have goods carted from the waterfront across busy streets to their inland warehouses, running the risk of theft along the way.

After Williamsburg became part of the Consolidated City of Brooklyn in 1855, more ships tied up at Brooklyn's docks than at Manhattan's. In 1884, Brooklyn historian Henry Stiles boasted of the new, modern facilities that attracted vessels from virtually everywhere: "The building of the great warehouses along the river and water front has been almost wholly the work of the last thirty years," he wrote. "In solidity and strength, as well as in capacity, they surpass the far-famed London Docks. One of them (Dow's stores), at the foot of Pacific street, is said to have no equal in extent, capacity, and all the appliances for the rapid

***City of Brooklyn, L.I. Taken from Rush Street* by John Bornet, artist, A. Weingartner, printer, color lithograph, 1855.**

John Bornet presents a detailed view of Brooklyn, with its factory- and warehouse-lined shores, from Rush Street just north of the Navy Yard looking south. Beyond the yard, featured prominently in the foreground, stretches Brooklyn; to the right, Manhattan.

transference of grain to and from the vessels which lie at its docks, in the world. The bricks and mortar put into these 250 great warehouses, are sufficient to build an ordinary city." Pierrepont Stores, on the waterfront below Brooklyn Heights, was typical of the warehouses, or stores, that Stiles describes, gloomy, cavernous holding bins for goods from all over the world.

Various stores specialized in the goods they warehoused: for instance, Pierrepont Stores in sugar and molasses; Woodruff & Robinson's at the foot of Congress Street in sugar, guano, and fish; De Forest's between the Fulton and South Ferries in hides and wool. The U.S. Warehousing Company had an immense grain warehouse, or elevator, while the great Empire Stores, located along the waterfront near what is now the Brooklyn Bridge anchorage, held general storage.

Sometimes at odds with waterfront development were the interests of the area's residents, particularly in fashionable Brooklyn Heights, which looked directly down on the vast stretches of warehouses. As Brooklyn residents argued for years over the idea of turning the edge of the Heights into a publicly accessible promenade, the opportunity was slipping away. Reformer and feminist abolitionist Lydia Maria Child wrote in September 1841 in *Letters from New York* about the desecration of the waterfront by warehouse developers. "Brooklyn Heights . . . command a magnificent view of the city of New-York, the neighbouring islands, and harbour; and being at least a hundred feet above the river, and open to the sea, they are never unvisited by a refreshing and invigorating breeze. A few years ago, these salubrious heights might have been purchased by the city at a very low price, and converted into a promenade of beauty unrivalled throughout the world; but speculators have now laid hands upon them, and they are digging them away to make room for stores, with convenient landings from the river."

Farther south, one of Brooklyn's greatest mid-nineteenth-century developments was taking shape directly across from Governor's Island, along the South

Brooklyn waterfront: the great Atlantic Docks. The huge storefront facility was once a swamp so shallow that only small boats could navigate it. The dredging required to build the docks, the biggest enterprise in 1840s Brooklyn, destroyed the homes of squatters who lived on some of the elevated hummocks of the swamp. In May 1844, the stockholders of the Atlantic Dock Co. held a ceremony attended by Brooklyn and Manhattan authorities plus a large contingent of merchants, and laid the cornerstone of the first block of warehouses. Begun by Daniel Richards, the project was taken over by James S. T. Stranahan (later a major force in the creation of Brooklyn's Prospect Park and the Brooklyn Bridge). Stranahan, Voorhis and Company, an Irish firm, hired many Irish workers to transform the swampy area into the impressive new facility.

Friction among workers escalated into bloodletting in 1846. Management not only brought in German laborers at lower wages than the Irish but housed them in the shantytown on the site, commonly erected for workers on such long-

View of Atlantic Dock and Vicinity, Port of New York **by E. Whitefield, lithographer, and F. Michelin, printer, colored lithograph, ca. 1850.**

Stranahan, Voorhis and Company's workers transformed swampy ground into the Atlantic Docks, a modern complex that appears to straddle the urban landscape and the rural countryside in this lithograph. The passageway into the basin was two-hundred feet wide, with a depth of more than twenty feet at low tide to accommodate even very large ocean steamers; there was room for 150 vessels; and it was all convenient to Manhattan via the ferry that ran to the foot of Hamilton Avenue (left of the basin in the print). English-born artist Edwin Whitefield's depiction confers a magnificence on the facility typical of Victorian celebrations of invention and achievement.

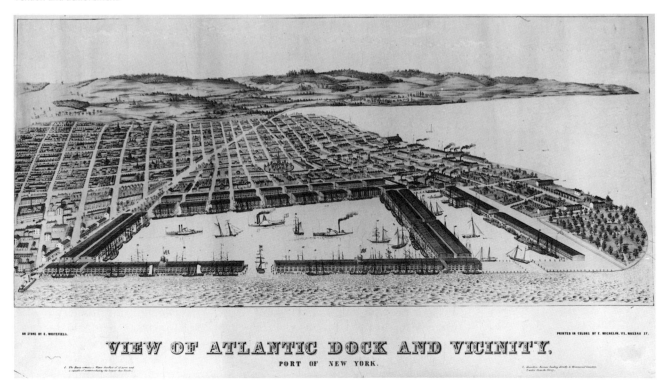

ON STORE BY E. WHITEFIELD.   PRINTED IN COLORS BY F. MICHELIN. 111. NASSAU ST.

VIEW OF ATLANTIC DOCK AND VICINITY,
PORT OF NEW YORK.

term projects. This was not an unusual strategy in nineteenth-century Brooklyn–to keep costs down by pitting already poorly paid members of different ethnic groups against one another. Violence erupted the night of April 19, when a German employee was shot. The *Eagle* speculated that he was "instrumental in the engagement of the German laborers, and this was probably the cause of the attempt upon his life." On the 21st, in a speech at an Irish laborers' protest meeting on Bergen Hill, Reverend N. O'Donnell of St. Paul's Catholic Church of Brooklyn addressed one of the roots of the problem while beseeching the workers not to use violence. He pointed out that wages were indeed pitiful and the hours fierce: "Every man knows that five shillings a day is not enough to maintain a man and his wife and four or five children, and that working 13 hours a day, for any lengthened period of time, will break down the strongest constitution," he said. Nevertheless, he cautioned, "You have no right to take the law into your own hands . . . it is the privilege of the contractors to get the work done in the cheapest manner, and to the best advantage for themselves. It is also the privilege of the Germans . . . to seek for work there as well as you, and they are at liberty to work for half a dollar a day; nay, for 25 cents, if they choose, and from sunrise to sunset, if they think proper to do so." Eventually, management assuaged the workers by hiring Germans and Irish in a fifty-fifty ratio, which translated into about 250 members of each group.

Once completed, the Atlantic Docks–inspired in part by the great London and Liverpool Docks in England–were magnificent, with over forty acres of basin protected on all sides against winds, huge grain elevators, and hundreds of warehouses with safe on and off loading at water's edge. As an 1846 promotional piece also pointed out, "insurance can be effected at lower rates here, than on the New York side," and access to Manhattan was easy: "The direct communication to, and from these Warehouses, is by the New Ferry from the foot of Hamilton Avenue . . . and requires but 12 to 15 minutes to go from the Atlantic Docks to the Custom House, the Banks, & Exchange on Wall Street."

The Atlantic Docks gave Brooklyn a clear advantage over Manhattan in commercial shipping. Other waterfront improvements soon followed. The Erie Basin was built in Red Hook, the Gowanus Canal was widened, and Newtown Creek on the Brooklyn-Queens border was developed. At the same time, manufacturing continued to expand, and each of the districts along the waterfront developed a particular flavor. By the 1870s, Greenpoint was largely dominated by shipyards. The Williamsburg shore, between the Navy Yard and Bushwick Creek, was lined with distilleries and sugar refineries, with lumber, brick, and coal yards, and with shipyards and gas works. South Brooklyn had extensive planing mills, distilleries, breweries, plaster mills, foundries, and machine shops, as well as wood, coal, stone and lumber yards. Out of these districts at midcentury and later came some of the finest ironwork, glass, porcelain–even beer–made in the United States.

The glowing foundries that Walt Whitman described in his poem "Crossing Brooklyn Ferry" in 1856 had their origins in 1840s Brooklyn, when producers rushed to meet the demand for cast iron. New methods of mass production made cast-iron products available to more people at reasonable prices, and by 1845, Brooklyn had seven foundries (by 1880, it would have well over one hundred) near the East River, a location ideal for receiving the coal and pig iron essential as raw materials. The difficult and often dangerous work in the foundries called on the skills of a variety of craftsmen (supported by the toil of young boys), who created finished cast-iron pieces for homes, public buildings, parks, and cemeteries.

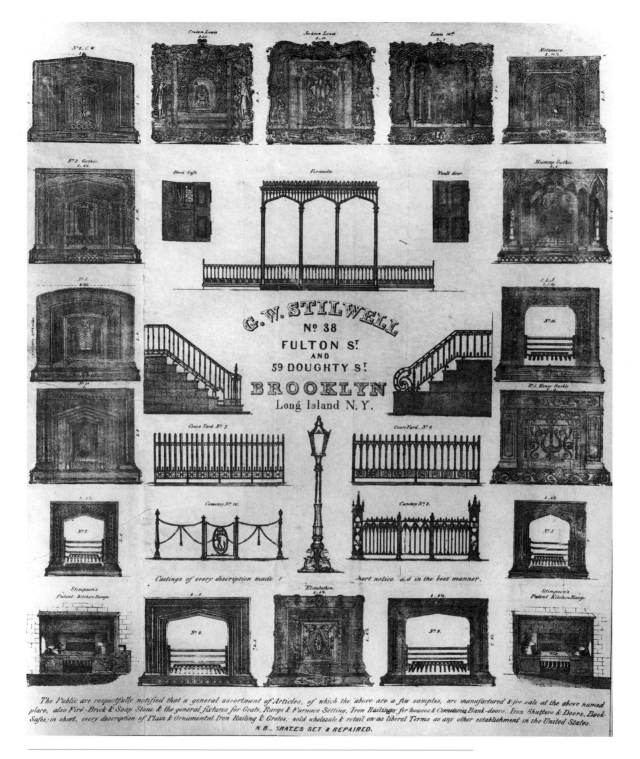

Broadside, 1840.

Promising "castings of every description made," Brooklyn's G. W. Stilwell advertised a variety of iron items to consumers, including stoves with elaborate names like "Croton Louis" and "Mummy Gothic," which may have enticed buyers more accustomed to their cast iron in the form of ordinary pots and kettles.

Launch of the Monitor at the Continental Iron Works by Endicott & Co., lithograph, 1860s.

After a celebratory launching from Greenpoint's Continental Iron Works, on its first night out, heavy seas rolled over the *Monitor's* low-lying deck, washed out the caulking in the turret, and gushed into the berth deck. Collection of The New-York Historical Society.

The demand and uses for cast iron went far beyond iron stoves and railings. Workers at the Continental Iron Works, established in Greenpoint in 1859, produced the *Monitor,* the first ironclad warship of the U.S. Navy. They assembled the ship in just three months in 1861 after its keel was laid at Greenpoint, using iron plates shipped from the Albany Rolling and Slitting Mill in Troy, New York. Its iron hull and a revolving turret mounted on a low-lying iron deck made its design revolutionary. Launched by a crew of volunteers recruited from the Navy Yard's receiving ships (where officers and men waited until they were able to join their ships), the *Monitor* slipped into the East River on January 30, 1862. Endicott and Co., the prolific New York lithographers and publishers who recorded numerous city scenes, commemorated the event, giving the ship monumental proportions to signify its importance. Although the *Monitor's* confrontation with the

Fragments of the Monitor, 1862.

In 1894, more than thirty years after the *Monitor* was launched in Brooklyn, M.V.B. Swart donated these fragments to The Brooklyn Historical Society. They are some of the only known remains of the ship, destroyed by a storm off Cape Hatteras at the end of 1862.

South's *Virginia* (formerly the *Merrimac*) on March 9 ended in a draw, its arrival at Hampton Roads probably saved the Union fleet. At the end of 1862, on its way to Charleston, South Carolina to take part in an attack, the ship went down in a storm off Cape Hatteras, North Carolina.

By midcentury, Brooklyn had also gained a reputation as one of the country's leading glass producers (by 1880, it would be the country's third-largest manufacturer of glass). Today's Corning Incorporated began as the Brooklyn Flint Glass Company in 1823, with a warehouse on South William Street in Manhattan and the works until 1868 on the Brooklyn waterfront south of Brooklyn Heights, at Columbia Street and what is now Atlantic Avenue. There, workers produced glass of all kinds, from plain, cut, and pressed glassware to lamps, chandeliers, and lantern lenses. Over on Concord Street, Christian Dorflinger established a glass works that turned out such items as flint glassware, druggists' wares, and cologne bottles. The factory's products were so highly respected that when Mary Todd Lincoln refurbished the White House, she ordered Dorflinger glassware especially designed for her husband, President Lincoln.

The often delicate glass produced by such works as Dorflinger and Brooklyn Flint Glass contrasted with the harsh working conditions endured by the companies' artisans and workers, boys and girls (girls worked finishing the glass). They breathed air full of floating glass particles fine as powdered sugar in suffocatingly hot conditions, and even for the most careful workers burns were a constant danger, as suggested in June 1863 by the *Brooklyn Daily Times,* which described a scene at Williamsburg's Empire State Flint Glass Works. "Two great

Brass oil lamp, ca. 1852.

U.S. Patent Number 9,184 was for the manufacture of a "dioptric lens," the first glass-related patent registered by Brooklyn Flint Glass Company founder John Gilliland. Used in this brass oil lamp, the lens is described in his patent as "in use for sea lights and for other lights requiring great intensity."

Glass-Blowing, Brooklyn, N.Y., 1877.

The frenetic pace and uncomfortable temperatures at glass houses were effects of young boys carting finishing bottles, craftsmen blowing molten glass into hinged molds, and fires raging in furnaces. A steady, even heat allowed fumes and smoke to be carried away by the draft so that smoke did not damage the finished glass. From Edward H. Knight, *American Mechanical Dictionary,* (New York: Hurd and Houghton), vol. 2, 1877.

The Brooklyn Navy Yard

Porcelain pitcher, Charles Cartlidge and Company, Greenpoint, ca. 1850.

New technology allowed porcelain makers to adorn such goods as pitchers, teapots, and coffee pots with organic patterns and embossed designs. The all-white cornstalk pattern of this molded pitcher with an applied handle, embellished with gilding, is a distinctively Cartlidge design. Courtesy of Mr. and Mrs. Jay Lewis.

furnaces with a dozen glaring eyes each warn the curious that their vicinity is not agreeable. Half a hundred boys are running to and from with long iron pipes, the same being laden with the molten glass at one end. One would suppose that dreadful burning accidents must frequently occur from what seems to be confusion; but a little observation will disclose the fact that there is method and order in every movement."

By 1860 Greenpoint had become something of a pottery center; its firms produced some of the finest porcelain in America. Before 1850, almost all high-quality porcelain available in the United States came from overseas, first from China, and by the end of the eighteenth century largely from England. But by the mid–nineteenth century, Brooklyn firms were producing porcelain comparable to European wares, bolstered by the immigration of expert English potters. One of the earliest makers, an English immigrant, founded Charles Cartlidge and Company in Greenpoint in the 1840s. Although his porcelain was largely mass produced in a factory (typical of early porcelain manufacture), Cartlidge trusted old European craft skills and manual labor above machine technology.

The post–Civil War Union Porcelain Works, also in Greenpoint, was founded by U.S.-born Thomas C. Smith. Over the entrance to the factory, the word *China* appeared above the works' name, a reference to the years before European and American production when all porcelain was imported from that country. (The word soon came into use as an umbrella term for porcelain, regardless of its origin.) Unlike Cartlidge and more typical of a new generation of porcelain makers, Smith relied heavily on mechanization. His company became the first U.S. firm to succeed over the long term as a manufacturer of high-quality porcelain. While it largely turned out mass-produced commercial wares, the works also gained a reputation for its art pottery, such as the elaborate Century Vase designed by German-born sculptor Karl Müller and manufactured in 1876 for the U.S. Centennial.

By the 1870s Brooklyn had become a major force in American beer brewing, as numerous establishments, largely run by Germans, flourished in the borough's Eastern District (Williamsburg, Greenpoint, and Bushwick). Otto Huber, the New York and Brooklyn Brewing Company, and Samuel Liebmann (founder of Rheingold Breweries) were all on Brewer's Row, a twelve-block stretch from Bushwick Place to Lorimer Street covering Scholes and Meserole Streets. By the 1880s, thirty-five breweries had been established in Brooklyn. This veritable explosion was triggered by German immigrants who arrived bearing the technology for lager-beer brewing. Lager was a distinctly German drink that called for different kinds of yeast and a different process than beverages in the English tradition—ale, porter, and stout—to which most Americans were accustomed. As Walt Whitman wrote in 1862, tastes changed. "There are fifteen to twenty breweries in the eastern district, in the Neighborhood of Bushwick; these are the sources of the mighty outpourings of ale and lager beer, refreshing the thirsty lovers of those liquids in hot or cold weather."

Many breweries featured beer gardens next to their plants, huge outdoor beer halls where brewers could sell their product. They were also community gathering places: German immigrants could meet to drink beer, socialize, and feel at home in a new environment. They drew other locals and New Yorkers as well. On March 16, 1861, the *Brooklyn Daily Times* ran a piece titled "Opening Day of the Lager-Bier Gardens." While its tone is somewhat patronizing, it provides a wonderful description of these extensive establishments, as it describes the scene at Schneider's:

The Union Porcelain Works and Wares, 1884.

This print of the extensive Union Porcelain Works features the Century Vase, *top right,* designed by the firm's German-born sculptor, Karl Müller, and displayed at the Centennial Exhibition in Philadelphia in 1876. This magnificent piece incorporated four American icons, including George Washington, bison (a symbol of the American West), the Boston Tea Party, and workers building the Brooklyn Bridge. In Henry Stiles, *History of . . . the County of Kings,* 1884.

One of the most popular if not the most fashionable places of resort this summer, in the vicinity of New York, will be Schneider's extensive gardens and halle in the 16th ward [Williamsburg]. Every one who has ever traveled through this ward, knows the genuine enjoyment experienced by its inhabitants in these gardens in which it abounds. During the winter they are closed up, and where the thousands of Germans who frequent them stow themselves in evenings, or how they amuse themselves, has often puzzled us to know. These gardens and halles are always attached to breweries. They are opened in the spring, generally after being renovated, enlarged, or made more attractive by some new decoration. The opening of a new three cent railroad through the heart of the ward, has caused a great commotion among the proprietors of these places, and with the setting in of mild weather, a greater influx of visitors from New York than ever occurred before, is expected. . . .

Schneider's brewery is known far and near as the largest, the one making the best lager, and having the jolliest, best natured, proprietor of any in this city. His gardens and his halle are also the largest, finest, and most aristocratic of any in the State. During the warm weather thousands daily visit them, lounge around, play billiards, listen to the sweetest of music and—drink lager of course.

The Brooklyn Brush Manufacturing Company, founded by Freeman Murrow, was one of Brooklyn's many smaller industries. For African Americans, largely excluded from white-owned industry, entrepreneurship had become a necessity, although discrimination often prevented firms from expanding. Incor-

Advertisement, 1855.

Company cofounder Freeman Murrow describes the advantages of the brush he invented in an advertisement in the "Rules of Association of the Brooklyn Brush Mfg. Co. N.-Y." Founded and run by African Americans, the company was awarded numerous medals for the invention, including one at the Crystal Palace exhibition of 1854.

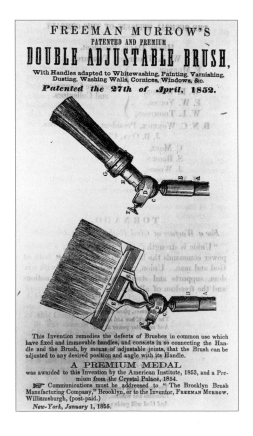

porated in 1854 by trustees Anthony Gale, C. W. Trainer, William L. Thompson, Henry Davis, William E. Wilson, Francis W. Young, and Freeman Murrow, the company's "Rules of Association," bound into a small pamphlet, set forth its statement of purpose. Referring to the freedom and equality promised in the U.S. Constitution, the pamphlet states that the firm was established "to provide other means of support for our wives and daughters than perpetual servitude as scrubbers and washing servants to others, and to alleviate ourselves from our former and present low condition—as we are disenfranchised by this Government,—that we may enjoy our rights as free Citizens of the United States, and that by means of productive labor . . . whereby we may cultivate, strengthen and employ our inventive genius, as authors and producers, equally with other men."

Addressing both male and female workers, the rules go on to note that "with Brush-making of all kinds, there is also a number of other branches of the highest art connected with this Company, adapted to male and female labor, such as designing, die sinking, engraving, brass finishing, casting, plain and ornamental painting, gilding, workers of wood and cement, etc. etc." The pamphlet locates the firm in "Brooklyn and Williamsburg," undoubtedly written when the two were separate cities—they merged in 1855. At the back of the pamphlet, the trustees include what may have been the company's driving philosophy, a poem titled "Tornado: For a Warfare of Civil Rights and not Bloodshed," which extols labor as a means to equality.

The expansion of Brooklyn manufacturing—the teeming waterfront, the huge number of products, from beer to brushes—often had disastrous by-products. One of them was industrial pollution, concentrated at two particularly nasty sites: Newtown Creek on the Brooklyn/Queens border, and the Gowanus Canal in Red Hook. Factories and refineries lining Newtown Creek threw off sludge that covered its banks with silt; their emissions filled the air with a foul stench. In 1881, *Harper's Weekly* pictured the numbing scene of oil refineries along the waterway spewing forth thick smoke. Farther south, in Red Hook, lay the Gowanus

Canal. Once a tidal creek teeming with wildlife, by the late 1800s it was a filthy waterway polluted with the refuse of the paint manufacturers and paper mills along its shores. In *Plunkitt of Tammany Hall*, a series of talks on politics delivered by the garrulous Tammany Hall (a powerful New York Democratic political organization) sachem George Washington Plunkitt in 1905, the senator offers up his tongue-in-cheek description of a Brooklynite's relationship to his environment: "Brooklyn don't seem to be like any other place on earth. Once let a man grow up amidst Brooklyn's cobblestones, with the odor of Newtown Creek and Gowanus Canal ever in his nostrils, and there's no place in the world for him except Brooklyn."

Fourth–Largest Industrial City in the United States

Odoriferous it might be, but Brooklyn had evolved, by 1880, into one of the leading producers of manufactured goods in the country, surpassed only by New York, Philadelphia, and Chicago. By that decade, industrial growth in Brooklyn seemed almost contagious. Brooklyn's largest industry—sugar refining—was outputting enormous amounts of both molasses and sugar, producing over half of all the sugar consumed in the United States. The slaughter houses too had a huge annual output. Book publishing had taken off, partly because New York houses were moving their manufacturing operations to Brooklyn. Lain and Company, for example, who printed Brooklyn's city directory, kept its composition and electrotyping functions in New York but did its press work in Brooklyn. Hat and cap manufacturing was expanding; thirty-two establishments employed 1,392 workers, 487 of them women and children. Improved national transportation networks meant that the city was increasingly connected with the rest of the nation, making possible a wide exchange of goods. Brooklyn was a powerhouse that provided products not only to customers on Bedford Avenue in Brooklyn, or Broadway in Manhattan, but to consumers across the country and around the world.

Perhaps one of industrial Brooklyn's greatest assets at the time was its diversity. Unlike many other cities, whose economies were based largely on one product—like New Bedford, Massachusetts, and textiles, or Lynn, Massachusetts, and shoes—Brooklyn produced a little of everything, a circumstance that would help it stay on its feet industrially through the Great Depression. Contributing to the diversity was the huge Ansonia Clock Company, which expanded its Connecticut operations to Park Slope in the late 1870s and by the turn of the century claimed to be the largest clock factory in the world. There were whole industries, like shoemaking; Brooklyn was a leading shoe and boot manufacturer through the late nineteenth and early twentieth centuries. In tenements throughout the city, cigar makers rolled tobacco leaves, and their output made Brooklyn a major cigar producer. Drake Bakeries was just one of the city's many baking and confectionary firms; founded in 1896 near the Navy Yard, it introduced to America mass-produced slabs of cake sold through local groceries. The Eberhard Faber factory in Greenpoint, many of whose workers were women, turned out hundreds of thousands of pencils a year.

The variety of Brooklyn's industrial enterprises continued from the nineteenth into the twentieth century. But many Brooklyn businesses, like their counterparts across America, consolidated into larger enterprises to better meet

the demands of a growing national and international economy. Vast stretches of privately owned waterfront warehouses and piers were united under the Brooklyn Wharf and Warehouse Company in 1890 (the trust was reorganized one year later as the New York Dock Company), creating a huge, linked system of storage areas. Sugar companies formed a sugar trust in 1887. The petroleum refineries also formed consortiums, one of which had a particularly wide-ranging impact on Brooklyn through the work of its owner, Charles Pratt.

Overview of New York Dock Company, ca. 1930s.

Buildings of the New York Dock Company line the Brooklyn shore below residential Brooklyn Heights, with the Brooklyn Bridge looming in the background. As the painted, billboard-like advertisement on the side of the building at center reads, the New York Dock Company featured vast stretches of "BUILDINGS FOR MANUFACTURING AND DISTRIBUTING, STORAGE AND PIERS" and was connected with "TEN [railroad] LINES." Note how the rail lines go directly to the water's edge—at *rear center*, a train turns to its left as it leaves a pier.

Workers at the Brooklyn refinery of the Pratt works, 1893.

This posed group probably includes skilled workers, coopers, and tinsmiths, as well as laborers, who were paid substantially less for their work. The children (except the toddler, *right*) may also have worked at the refinery. This is probably the day shift, paid slightly less than those who worked night shifts. Courtesy of the Mobil Oil Corporation.

Originally from New England, Pratt had risen from machinist to clerk to successful owner, in 1867, of Charles Pratt and Company. In 1874, Pratt went into partnership with John D. Rockefeller, head of Standard Oil, and began to buy competing refineries in Brooklyn under the Pratt name. (Pratt's relationship to Ohio's Standard Oil as its New York branch was not made public, however, until 1892.) Of the more than fifty petroleum refineries that had lined the Williamsburg, Greenpoint, and Newtown Creek waterfronts in 1875, many smaller firms were driven out of business by the competition or bought by Pratt and other large firms; Pratt's refinery, the Astral Oil Works, was located along the Williamsburg waterfront.

At the same time he and Rockefeller were buying up refineries, Pratt decided to streamline operations. When the coopers' union—whose members were the craftsmen who made the barrels that held the oil—opposed his efforts to cut back on certain manual operations, he busted the union. Pratt's strategies for breaking this powerful organization were soon adopted by other refineries.

Pratt's influence extended beyond the industrial scene to housing and education. For workers at his Astral Oil Works, he created the Astral Apartments, model, low-income housing named for his trademark Astral Oil, a high-quality kerosene used in lamps and noted for its safety—similar petroleum derivatives used for lamp fuels were typically highly flammable and dangerous. Built in 1886 on Franklin Street between Java and India Streets in Williamsburg, the apartments were patterned after similar housing designed by Alfred Tredway White and built just south of Brooklyn Heights.

In 1887, Pratt founded Pratt Institute in what is today Clinton Hill, probably modeled on businessman and philanthropist Peter Cooper's 1859 Cooper Union in Manhattan. (Cooper also had Brooklyn connections—in the 1840s he moved his glue factory to the Bushwick-Ridgewood area, where land cost less than in Manhattan.) To address the need for trained industrial workers, Pratt conceived of the institute as a school to accommodate Brooklynites of all backgrounds and

diverse skills. Innovative from the start, it offered classes to all races, both men and women (a sound move, considering that one-fifth of Brooklyn's labor force was female). Pratt also founded the Pratt Institute Free Library, as well as a savings and loan company where workers could obtain mortgages at reasonable rates.

In this era of consolidation, Bush Terminal, located in today's Sunset Park, emerged as a modern conglomerate of unified waterfront activities. The site along the Brooklyn waterfront was just south of the area painted in oils by A. G. Fabian in 1897; Fabian depicts the South Brooklyn warehouses and factories just across the bay from an area whose rural nature the artist probably exaggerated.

***South Brooklyn, Gowanus Bay* by A. G. Fabian, oil on canvas, 1897.**

As development moved south along the waterfront, the South Brooklyn area around Gowanus Bay became the site of breweries, foundries, and coal and lumber yards. Fabian focuses on the rural foreground, a simple and serene contrast to the factories and warehouses, pierced by smokestacks and ships' masts, in the distance.

Development began in the 1890s, when Irving T. Bush put together a motley enterprise consisting of a warehouse, a pier, a tugboat, and an old railroad engine on land that had once housed his father's oil business. The terminal ultimately occupied about two hundred acres, a huge complex of warehouses, piers, manufacturers, and railroad sidings sprawled along an enormous section of the Brooklyn waterfront. Bush's innovative thinking brought together under one umbrella at Bush Terminal all the functions related to receiving and distributing goods, making it the port's largest commercial and industrial facility. It employed thousands of workers—many of them Norwegian and Polish immigrants who lived in the area, as well as Italians hired to unload ships and move cargo. During World War I, the U.S. Government even used it to store and move equipment and supplies, hiring women to work as locomotive drivers and crane operators to take the place of men gone to war.

Bush's advertising relied on key words such as *modern, efficient,* and *convenient,* promising that Bush Terminal offered relief from the crowded conditions and high cost of business in Manhattan (by then a familiar Brooklyn vs. Manhattan refrain); at Bush Terminal, goods were loaded directly from huge manu-

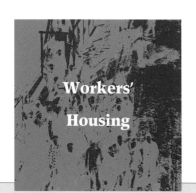

Workers' Housing

While industrialist Charles Pratt and other wealthy Brooklynites lived in elegant Clinton Hill, home to some of Brooklyn's most famous industrialists and merchants, as well as similar affluent neighborhoods, most of Brooklyn's working people had little choice but to live in tenements in the oldest parts of the city, near the docks, shops, and factories where they worked. Working-class neighborhoods established in nineteenth-century Brooklyn included large parts of Williamsburg, Bushwick, Greenpoint, and South Brooklyn. Few workers owned their own homes; many lived in boarding-houses.

Disgusted with tenement overcrowding and the resulting filth and disease, businessman and philanthropist Alfred Tredway White financed the first low-rent housing in New York: the Tower (1878–1879) and Home (1876–1877) buildings in Cobble Hill, and Riverside (1890) in Brooklyn Heights. All stand today, although part of Riverside was demolished for the Brooklyn-Queens Expressway construction in the 1940s. White's buildings, modeled on English precedents, incorporated towers, balconies, a central courtyard for light, windows in every room, kitchens, toilets, and separate entrances for privacy (amenities few working-class people of the time ever had).

While workers in many ways welcomed such housing, in instances where work bosses were also landlords, the arrangement was potentially a difficult one. Workers' problems at home might well jeopardize their jobs; being a labor "agitator" could endanger both job *and* home.

Tenements in Greenpoint, ca. 1920s.

facturing lofts onto waiting boxcars, which were carried by barge across the harbor to New Jersey and its railroad connections to all parts of the United States. By the 1930s, almost 20 percent of all the port's imports and exports passed through Bush Terminal, and some thirty-thousand workers were employed there by assorted companies.

Like the port itself, complexes such as Bush Terminal were essentially arenas of exchange, not just for goods but for the people from all over the world who passed through them: crews aboard ships; sailors on leave; and the Brooklyn workers, like the longshoremen and dock workers, many of them recent immigrants. Cheek by jowl with the docks, factories, and warehouses, districts grew up that catered to those who worked on or passed along the waterfront and offered them equipment and clothing, places to drink and eat, tattoo parlors, and brothels. In a March 17, 1907 article, the *Brooklyn Daily Eagle* described "the waterfront and the streets that neighbor it [as] a separate world from the usual city world that stretches almost down to it, a world that smells of salt and tar and old rope, and where every person one meets has the weather worn air of the sailor. . . . The dirty, narrow streets that skirt along in the rear of the docks and the side

The Riverside Buildings at Columbia Place, Furman Street, and Joralemon Street, Brooklyn. "Living-Room, Riverside Buildings."

From Alfred T. White, *Sun-Lighted Tenements. Thirty-five Years' Experience as an Owner* (National Housing Publications 12, New York City, March 1912).

Loading cars, Bush Terminal, ca. 1910s.

One of the great advantages of Bush Terminal was that railroad cars could be loaded directly at the loft buildings for eventual distribution throughout the United States.

Corner of Sands and Navy Streets, ca. 1900.

Perhaps early in the morning following a late night at Elliott's Curio Tavern, four loungers groggily survey the scene. A woman looks on from the tavern balcony, *right.* Just a few blocks from the Navy Yard, this intersection lay at the heart of the area's red-light district. Courtesy of the Brooklyn Public Library—Brooklyn Collection.

streets that lead to them are the backyards of the shipping world that reaches along the bay front. They have filled themselves up with grimy little ale and beer shops the doors of which are constantly on the swing for longshoremen, the workers on the docks and the crews of the ships. . . . [As to] the longshoremen in their . . . blue caps . . . [one] sees in their faces the hints of . . . every nationality." Near the Navy Yard along Sands Street, the hotels and saloons of Brooklyn's most famous stretch became known as a cruising ground for both heterosexuals and homosexuals.

Brooklyn! *An Illustrated History*

Sands Street swarmed with sailors during wartime. Michael Faiella of Reliable and Franks Naval Uniforms—one of the many military supply stores that once lined Sands Street, it is now located on Flushing Avenue, opposite the yard—recalls that "when the fleet was in, from the gate to the Navy YMCA at the top of Sands Street, all you could see was a sea of white hats. Some of [the supply stores] stayed open all night. Business was booming." In her 1955 novel *The Mortgaged Heart,* Carson McCullers captures the special flavor of the street:

> Here in Brooklyn there is always the feeling of the sea. On the streets near the water-front, the air has a fresh, coarse smell, and there are many seagulls. One of the most gaudy streets I know stretches between Brooklyn Bridge and the Navy Yard. At three o'clock in the morning, when the rest of the city is silent and dark, you can come suddenly on a little area as vivacious as a country fair. It is Sand Street, the place where sailors spend their evenings when they come here to port. At any hour of the night some excitement is going on in Sand Street. The sunburned sailors swagger up and down the sidewalks with their girls. The bars are crowded, and there are dancing, music, and straight liquor at cheap prices.

With the closing of the yard in the 1960s, the construction of the Brooklyn-Queens Expressway and Farragut Housing, and the general decline of the waterfront in recent years, the swagger that was Sands Street is only a memory. Only the occasional waterfront bar or clothing supply store—like Reliable and Franks—survives to recall an earlier era.

Modern Brooklyn: Closings and the Container Revolution

By 1900, only .5 percent of the borough's workers were involved in agriculture, a far cry from the colonial era, when farming had dominated Kings County. Brooklyn moved into the twentieth century firmly established as a major industrial center and a thriving international port. By 1920, tens of thousands of factory workers, longshoremen, warehousemen, and truckers worked in waterfront-related jobs, and the port of Brooklyn handled more than 25 percent of the foreign commerce of the United States. In a November 1946 article, the *Brooklyn Daily Eagle* gave this concrete example of Brooklyn's contribution to the world's economy: "The foreign newspaper the Brooklyn traveler picks up on his first morning abroad will be printed from type set by a typesetting machine shipped from Brooklyn. The cigarette he smokes as he scans the headlines was rolled by machinery manufactured in Brooklyn. And if he opens a can of coffee to top off his morning meal, he will find that the can came from Brooklyn and possibly the coffee as well."

In 1954, employment in manufacturing peaked at roughly 235,000 jobs, and stayed close to that level into the 1960s. Port employment also peaked, with almost 15,000 jobs for waterfront workers and thousands more in related fields, such as trucking and warehousing. By then, as a 1962 aerial view shows, the waterfront was a dense concentration of docks, warehouses, and industrial buildings. Four years later the Brooklyn Navy Yard closed. Once a symbol of Brooklyn's industrial and economic strength, its shutdown reflected the borough's decline. In February 1966, the *Brooklyn Times* echoed the sentiments of many

Workers at Sone and Fleming Refinery, ca. 1950s.

Near the peak years of Brooklyn's reign as a center of manufacturing and commerce, workers move cases of Mobil Oil at Sone and Fleming Refinery, a descendant of Pratt/Standard Oil.

Aerial view of the Brooklyn waterfront, 1962.

Looking north from a point just south of the Atlantic Basin, this view captures the culmination of years of manufacturing and commercial development—huge piers, massive roads, and three enormous bridges. But there was no room to grow.

Broadside, ca. 1964.

Inexpensive flyers like this "gloom and doom" broadside were easily reproduced and distributed when the yard was threatened with closing. "Can Do" refers to the yard's World War II nickname as the "Can Do Yard," when the huge complex was at its peak.

GLOOM at the famous BROOKLYN NAVY YARD!

- Will the 162 year old "Can Do" yard be closed in the name of "economy"?
- What lies ahead for 11,000 civilian workers?
- What can workers do to change the picture?
- Can new uses be found for this famous naval installation?

Brooklynites, who had watched as, one after another, borough mainstays had crumbled or left: "The closing of the Yard ranks with the traitorous departure of the Brooklyn Dodgers [in 1957], and the shuttering of the *Brooklyn Eagle*."

So long a stable force in Brooklyn's economy, the yard did not close without a fight. Workers organized, groups churned out and distributed leaflets, posters, fliers, and buttons, and, at gatherings large and small, irate workers and citizens sounded off. The Brooklyn Metal Trades Council (a member of the AFL-CIO), which represented more than eleven thousand yard workers, organized rallies and a newspaper and media campaign to keep the yard open: In June 1964, a bus caravan traveled to Washington, D.C., to protest, and in October 1964, organizers orchestrated a huge rally at Madison Square Garden. New York senator Robert F. Kennedy became a vocal advocate for saving the yard, and workers mounted demonstrations outside the yard's gates. But the effort was in vain. The devastating news was finally spelled out in a *Daily News* headline in oversized type: "NAVY YARD LOST." On February 1, 1966, the *World Telegram* noted that "the shipyard has earned 6 Navy 'Es'—given during World War II for 'excellence for work'. . . . On June 30 her last 'E' will mark END for the Brooklyn Navy Yard."

The closing was part of a trend in the borough and beyond; industrial cities along the entire northeastern seaboard lost manufacturing and shipping jobs in the 1960s. Mergenthaler Linotype, whose enormous factory on Ryerson Street produced a good share of the typesetting machinery used by newspapers all over the world, moved to Long Island from Brooklyn in 1959. Some factories relocated outside of New York. Drake Bakeries, Inc., moved its baking operations to New Jersey in 1977, and others left for the South's lower labor costs, taxes, and utility rates, drawn too by government incentives. Some, like the brewing industry, were dealt blows that ultimately spelled their death. Prohibition in the 1920s, a major strike in 1949, competition from national giants and their ad campaigns, sky-

Tickets and rally protesting yard closure, 1964.

Adopting some of the strategies of the civil-rights movement, irate Navy Yard workers organized rallies, marches, and a bus caravan to Washington, D.C. to protest the closing of the complex, more than a century and a half old. At a Cumberland Street rally, workers crowd behind a police barrier.

rocketing costs, a lack of room for expansion, and inadequate rail transportation all contributed to the industry's decline. While Brooklyn's beer was still well known—like Piels, "the Beer Drinker's Beer"—the last of Brooklyn's breweries, Rheingold and Schaefer, closed in 1976. By then, two thirds of manufacturing jobs from only a decade earlier were gone.

There were problems along the waterfront, too, where organized crime was allegedly siphoning off profits. As the *New York Times* reported on January 22, 1970, the "Waterfront Commission of New York Harbor was created in 1953 to combat half a century of crime and corruption on the waterfront, or kickbacks, usury and labor racketeering, of bloodied heads and murder. Now, 17 years later, the commission concedes publicly that there are 'still certain Mafia influences on the waterfront' and its members privately believe that every facet of the Brooklyn waterfront is run by organized crime."

But more importantly to the fate of the waterfront, shipping began to relocate to New Jersey's larger, more modern facilities. The container revolution of the 1970s meant that goods once packed in sacks, crates, or boxcars were now

Organized Labor

Brooklyn's earliest labor organizations were artisans' groups, like the Rope Makers' Benevolent Society, organized in 1821 to aid "widows, orphans, and distressed workers." These gave way to more extensive trades movements by the mid–nineteenth century and to national organizations by the late nineteenth century. Many Brooklyn workers, for example, joined the Knights of Labor in the 1880s and 1890s, before the rise of the American Federation of Labor (AFL). Such groups addressed the changing conditions of the nineteenth-century workplace—low pay, long hours, job security, and safety.

Despite a history full of conflict, the AFL pulled together various trade organizations in Brooklyn from the 1890s through the 1930s. Independent efforts at the same time were mounted by the Metal Workers Industrial Union, which organized larger machine shops, and by one of the most powerful unions in Brooklyn's history, the International Longshoremen's Association. Throughout much of the twentieth century, the ILA was a strong waterfront presence. Its most lasting monument may be the Guaranteed Annual Income, which guarantees full wages for all workers displaced by the container revolution of the 1960s and 1970s. With the loss of thousands of union jobs as Brooklyn industry and shipping have declined in recent years, labor organizing is shifting to workers in the rising service sector, such as hospital employees and teachers.

ILA workers at Brooklyn headquarters, 1955.
Courtesy of the Brooklyn Public Library—Brooklyn Collection.

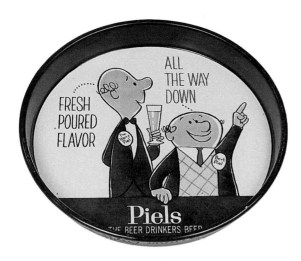

Piels's Beer tray, ca. 1957.

"Piels, the Beer Drinkers Beer" was a slogan well-known to a generation of beer lovers, as were the comedy team Bob and Ray, who portrayed brothers Bert and Harry Piel in advertisements and on beer trays and coasters. When production at the Brooklyn plant ceased in September 1973, Schaefer bought the Piels name and label.

pre-packed in metal containers that required more space but, with increased automation, less than one-sixth the workers to handle, resulting in the loss of thousands of jobs. As vice-president of the International Longshoremen's Association and president of its largest local, Brooklyn, Anthony M. Scotto looked at the big picture in 1977: "How to preserve jobs in the teeth of the container revolution is the question that haunts the waterfronts not only of the United States, but the world." Even though Brooklyn constructed containerports along the East River—such as the Red Hook Container Terminal and the South Brooklyn Marine Terminal, with investment from the City of New York and the Port Authority of New York and New Jersey—the borough, congested and crowded, could never compete with New Jersey's vast open spaces and easy highway and rail access.

Today in Brooklyn, as in much of the United States, manufacturing and employment opportunities for blue-collar factory workers are giving way to jobs in service industries—health, social services, and education. Brooklyn's top employers are now places like hospitals, utilities, and retail trade firms. Some companies that have opted to keep plants in the borough continue to thrive, like pharmaceutical giant Pfizer Inc on Bartlett Street, or Domino Sugar, formerly Havemeyer and Elder and today one of America's major sugar producers. Industry still flourishes in Brooklyn, but on a much smaller scale, and industrial rebirth, while slow, is ongoing. Elsewhere, developers have converted old sites to suit new needs. In a former matzoh factory on North Eleventh Street, the Brooklyn Brewery gears up to join the handful of small specialty manufacturers that now call Williamsburg home—and revives Brooklyn's brewing tradition. Greenpoint's Eberhard Faber Pencil Company, once the largest manufacturer of pencils in the United States, left Brooklyn in 1955; today, the building where five hundred people once worked houses a thriving group of smaller manufacturers and brings new life to the neighborhood. Numerous small companies are spearheading a modest but thriving manufacturing revival at places like the remodeled Brooklyn Army Terminal. Under the guidance of the Brooklyn Navy Yard Development Corporation, old multi-storied loft buildings at the former yard have been subdivided into smaller units to house a wide variety of small businesses—and reinvigorate the complex that so many had called obsolete. The borough still offers lower rents than Manhattan, which continues to be an attraction. As always, manufacturing jobs offer

Nurses at Long Island College Hospital, 1989.

Today, many Brooklynites work in service industries rather than in factories or shipyards. Brooklyn's many modern hospitals and health-care facilities have become some of the borough's largest employers. Photograph courtesy of Long Island College Hospital.

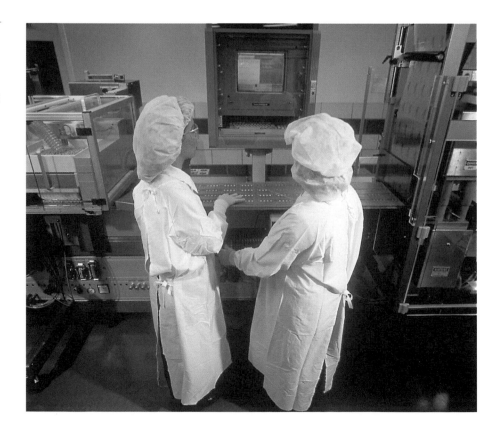

Workers at Pfizer's Bartlett Street plant, 1994.

Marisol Vazquez, operator, *left,* and Miriam Almeyda, line handler, monitor physician samples of Procardia XL being packaged at Pfizer's plant in Williamsburg. Photograph courtesy of Pfizer Inc.

recent immigrants and unskilled people an opportunity to start with little or no skills and move up.

Brooklyn still looks like an industrial city; along with the skeletons of waterfront piers stand industrial buildings, rows of workers' housing, and the transportation system that served them. Only today, the industrial loft in DUMBO (Down Under the Manhattan Bridge Overpass) may house an artist's studio, and the immense brick building in Williamsburg where a single manufacturer once did business now accommodates the work spaces of many craftspeople. Brooklynites have never lacked ingenuity or adaptability. As today they transform and redefine Brooklyn's economic underpinnings, the interesting question is not whether the city can change, but what that change will look like.

Postcard, "Entrance to Luna Park, by Night," ca. 1905.

Visitors passed through Luna's gates into a city of play.

Coney Island

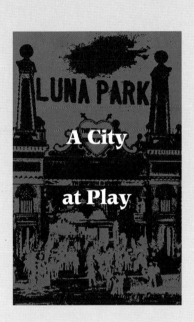

LUNA PARK

A City at Play

"Coney Island is only another name for topsyturvydom," wrote U.S. art critic James Gibbons Huneker in 1915. By the turn of the century, this spit of land at the southern tip of Brooklyn was already the most famous amusement center in the world, and it has never been equaled. The place where the world was turned upside down, an odd combination of glamour and honky-tonk, drew gamblers and entrepreneurs, artisans and wax-museum proprietors, old money and new immigrants. Although the amusement area has shrunk, and high-rises and single-family homes now stand where horses' hooves once pounded the racetrack and thousands of thrill seekers enjoyed dazzling amusements, the words "Coney Island" still conjure up images of death-defying rides, beaches packed with sun worshipers, raucous vendors, and miles of boardwalk. Coney has served as inspiration for numerous other amusement parks—including Canarsie's short-lived "Golden City," built on Jamaica Bay in 1907—and as a standard against which all others are judged.

Coney developed as an amusement area about the same time that Brooklyn itself was emerging as a major urban center. Bounded on three sides by water, the site seemed a world away from the smoky factories of industrial Williamsburg or the commercial hustle and bustle of downtown Brooklyn, but Coney was connected to the city and urban life in important ways. Its enormous audiences came from Brooklyn and neighboring Manhattan, whose populations surged with incoming immigrants. Transportation innovations like trolleys and subways, which played such a major role in Brooklyn's residential and industrial development, also brought growing crowds of pleasure-bound visitors to the amusement area. In the name of fun, people clambered aboard rides at Coney that mimicked the jostling and speed of the elevated trains and trolleys they commuted on, and put their money down for other attractions—dime museums, arcades, vaudeville—that had begun as urban amusements.

Over the course of the nineteenth century, as Coney became a huge city of play within the city, it competed with numerous other pastimes and places where Brooklynites spent their leisure hours—Coney did not appeal to everyone. As Brooklyn burgeoned into a major American city at the turn of the century, it offered commercial entertainment like vaudeville shows at newly built theaters in dozens of neighborhoods and open green spaces for fresh-air walks. Prospect

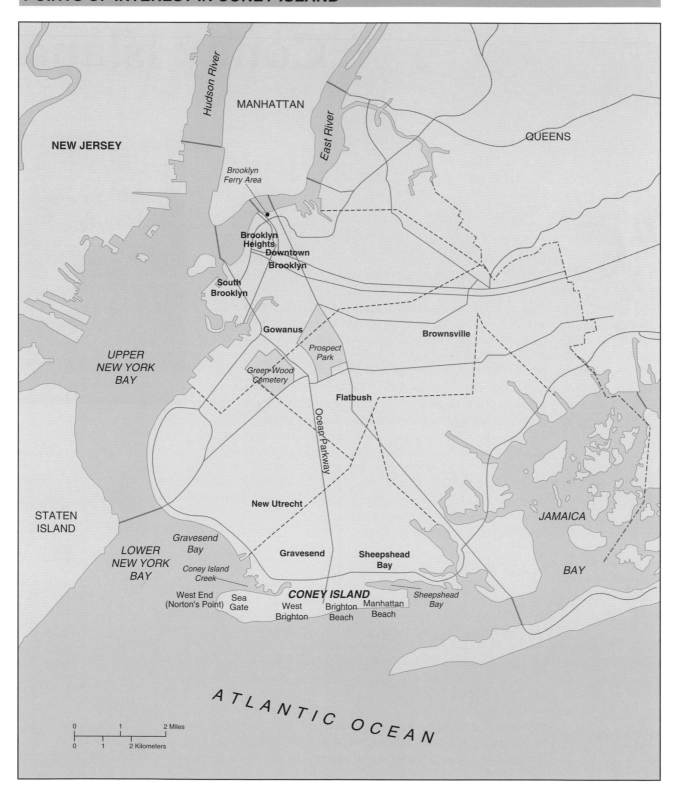

NEW JERSEY

MANHATTAN

QUEENS

Hudson River

East River

Brooklyn
Ferry Area

**Brooklyn
Heights**

**Downtown
Brooklyn**

**South
Brooklyn**

Gowanus

*Prospect
Park*

Brownsville

*Green-Wood
Cemetery*

*UPPER
NEW YORK
BAY*

Flatbush

Ocean Parkway

New Utrecht

JAMAICA

STATEN
ISLAND

*Gravesend
Bay*

*LOWER
NEW YORK
BAY*

Gravesend

**Sheepshead
Bay**

BAY

*Coney Island
Creek*

West End
(Norton's Point)

Sea
Gate

CONEY ISLAND

West
Brighton

Brighton
Beach

Manhattan
Beach

*Sheepshead
Bay*

A T L A N T I C   O C E A N

0	1	2 Miles
0	1	2 Kilometers

Park, the greatest of these urban oases, grew out of city leaders' concerns for Brooklynites' health as the city's population and industry rapidly increased. Parks became important refuges from the noise, bad air, and stresses of urban life; large and small, these beautifully designed public spaces appealed to wealthy Brooklynites who dwelled in elegant spacious homes and especially to poorer residents who lived in cramped tenements.

And Brooklynites spend a lot of leisure time in their homes and neighborhoods entertaining themselves and following their own ethnic, cultural, or religious traditions. In every neighborhood, people transform streets, sidewalks, and rooftops into playgrounds and spaces where neighbors and families mingle.

Only recently have historians paid much attention to the ways that people spent leisure time, so the surviving records of Brooklyn's amusements are often fleeting images or ephemeral objects: a photograph of intrepid Parachute Jump riders at Coney Island; a program from a vaudeville matinee at the Orpheum, saved some seventy-five years; or a spaldeen (a street pronunciation of the company's name, Spalding) ball that once bounced off Brooklyn stoops and curbs. Through the lens of the camera, the public-relations posturing of amusement entrepreneurs, and the eyes of participants themselves, Brooklynites have preserved a record (however fragmented) of their city at play.

Early Coney: Three-card Monte, Educated Pigs, and Lucy the Elephant

Long before the screams and laughter of the Cyclone's riders pierced the air, long before anyone ever ate a Nathan's hot dog, long before bathers crowded sandy beaches, Coney was the summer settlement of Native Americans. They called it Narriockh, "the place without shadows." Dutch colonists who used it as grazing land for their cattle and horses called it Conyne Eylant for the "conies," or rabbits, that darted among its sandy dunes. Today part of the borough of Brooklyn, during the colonial period Coney Island was part of the township of Gravesend. Recounting a harrowing tale of arriving in a "low, decayed and small boat, with rotten sails, and an inexperienced skipper," European traveler Jasper Danckaerts in 1679 described Coney's wild state: "This island, on the sea side, is a meadow or marsh intersected by several kils or creeks. It is not large, being about half an hour or three quarters long, and stretching nearly east and west. It is sandy and uninhabited. . . . We found good oysters in the creek inside, and [ate] some of them."

Coney *was* an island when Danckaerts saw it, with a creek separating it from mainland Brooklyn (the creek was later bridged and then largely filled in). A desolate parcel of land along the sea, Coney remained largely undeveloped until the first half of the nineteenth century, when a few hardy entrepreneurs improved transportation, and exploited the island's proximity to Brooklyn and New York to make Coney the quintessential resort.

The word resort conjured up different images in the early nineteenth century than it does today. Instead of the enormous hotels of the Catskills or the glitzy cabarets of Las Vegas, a resort in the 1800s was simply a place of amusement or leisure. French traveler Moreau de St. Méry in 1794 described such a place, a "house for sea bathing . . . built close to the water's edge" in New Utrecht. "As it was also planned as a pleasure resort, it has a dining room forty-five feet long by eighteen feet wide, in which one can dine for half a gourde [French money] a person. The owner makes his greatest profits from certain picnics at which the palm is awarded to the one who drinks the most." It was thirty years before the Coney Island House, a hotel, opened in 1824, eventually followed by a plethora of resorts.

An 1820s promotional piece described the Coney Island House as a resort with safe bathing, grand vistas, gently rolling waves, and eminent grandeur. The Gravesend and Coney Island Bridge and Road Company built the resort at the end of a private toll road, a clever and commonly used strategy to get people to pay to reach their destination and to exclude ordinary people. Explicitly appealing to a well-to-do clientele, the promotional circular noted the place was for "merchants and men of business"—people who had the luxury of time, control over their work schedule, and money necessary to travel by ferry or by slow stages over miles of

The Beach

Throughout Coney's colorful history, one constant remained: the lure of the beach, whether for a sedate picnic lunch or a rollicking good time. Walt Whitman, who boarded a stage for the beach one hot July day in 1847, wrote of the pleasures of bathing at Coney "in the salt water; ah, that was good indeed! Divers marvellous feats were performed in the water, in the way of splashing, ducking and sousing, and one gentleman had seri-ous thoughts of a sortie out upon some porpoises who were lazily rolling a short distance off. The beautiful, pure, sparkling, seawater!" Coney's beach *was* beautiful. And except when garbage scows dumped their loads off its shore later in the century, digging for clams and enjoying the view and the salt air on its broad, open expanse were welcome diversions for thousands of visitors and families—even though as development peaked in the late nineteenth century, operators carved up shorefront lots and charged visitors beach fees.

In the same way that neighborhoods had informal boundaries, twentieth-century visitors to Coney developed their own informal patterns of usage. Tessie Gordon, who went to Coney Island in the 1940s, recalled an Italian section near Stillwell Avenue, a Jewish section from around Twenty-seventh Street to Thirty-sixth Street, and an Irish section beyond, all of which roughly corresponded to neighborhoods inland from the beach and boardwalk. Former Midwood resident Anne Marie Barba Palone recalled that when she went to Coney with her family in the 1950s, specific bays were informally known as hangouts for certain neighborhoods. "If you lived on Avenue O and East Twelfth Street," she recalls, you would say "Meet you at Bay 7" to your friends, since that was where the teenagers in that parish went.

"Negro Family, Coney Island," silver gelatin print, ca. 1880. Photograph by George B. Brainerd. Courtesy of The Brooklyn Museum X892.6. Gift of The Brooklyn Museum Collection.

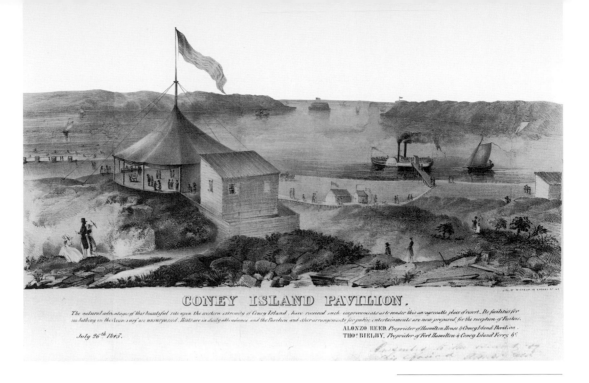

CONEY ISLAND PAVILION.

The natural advantages of this beautiful site upon the western extremity of Coney Island, have received such improvements as to render this an agreeable place of resort. Its facilities for sea bathing in the ocean surf are unsurpassed. Boats are in daily attendance, and the Pavilion and other arrangements for public entertainments are now prepared for the reception of Visitors.

ALONZO REED, Proprietor of Hamilton House & Coney Island Pavilion.
THOs. BIELBY, Proprietor of Fort Hamilton & Coney Island Ferry &c.

July 26th 1845.

Coney Island Pavilion, **lithograph, July 26, 1845.**
Pictured larger than life, the 1840s Pavilion was a huge tent anchored by ropes; its canvas walls could be let down in case of rain to protect dancers.

rutted dirt roads. The Coney Island House eventually became enormously popular, visited by writers Washington Irving, Walt Whitman, and Herman Melville; famous pre–Civil War statesmen Daniel Webster, Henry Clay, and John C. Calhoun; and, in 1850, acclaimed Swedish singer Jenny Lind.

In 1844, Coney Island got its first real amusement—not a hotel, but a place to play: the Pavilion, located at what would come to be known as Norton's Point. Little more than a wooden platform sheltered by a huge tent, it served as a dance floor, and proprietor Alonzo Reed and Thomas Bielby, whose ferry carried pleasure seekers to the island, list it among Coney's amenities on an 1845 print of the site:

> The natural advantages of this beautiful site upon the western extremity of Coney Island, have received such improvements as to render this an agreeable place of resort. Its facilities for sea bathing in the ocean surf are unsurpassed. Boats are in daily attendance, and the Pavilion and other arrangements for public entertainments are now prepared for the reception of Visitors.
> ALONZO REED, Proprietor of Hamilton House & Coney Island Pavilion
> THOs. Bielby, Proprietor of Fort Hamilton & Coney Island Ferry &c
> July 26th 1845

The promotional print captures the essential ingredients that would make Coney a nationally known resort: a fabulous beach, beautiful ocean views, amusements and amenities for public enjoyment, and the transportation to get people there.

When the Pavilion was erected, the only habitations on the island besides the Coney Island House and the newer Wyckoff's Hotel, erected by Gravesend farmer and schoolmaster John Wyckoff, Sr., were the Van Sicklen and the Voorhies farmhouses. Two hotels and two farmhouses. In 1847, Allen Clarke, a physician, purchased land from Court Van Sicklen for a hotel just north of the Coney Island House. The Oceanic, marketed as a resort for respectable businessmen and their families, burned down after one summer and was replaced by another hotel that also burned, a fate many Coney Island attractions would share. When a Brooklyn mill owner built the Brooklyn, Bath and Coney Island Railroad from Coney Island, through the villages of Bath and New Utrecht, to Green-Wood Cemetery's Fifth Avenue entrance (a nexus of various transportation routes), Stephen H. Bogart put up an elegant hotel, the Tivoli, at its Coney Island terminus. It burned down soon after.

As entrepreneurs made sporadic attempts to develop Coney Island, the place was gaining an unsavory reputation, particularly at the West End, or Norton's Point, where by the 1860s gamblers, pickpockets, pimps and prostitutes flourished under the protection of crooked New York politician Mike "Thunderbolt" Norton. A visitor in 1863 later reminisced in an 1883 guidebook, *Coney Island. An Illustrated Guide to The Sea*, about the honky-tonk scene that greeted him:

> We sailed down the bay in an antiquated steamer, mid scenes of confusion and hilarity. At the landing there was a barn-like bar-room, more conspicuous than the dingy dining-room with two barrels at either end supporting boards used as a lunch or dining counter. Chops, chowder, steaks, etc., of a very inferior quality, were purveyed at the prices of fashionable restaurants in the metropolis.
>
> Three-card monte-men and swindlers occupied tables along the beach, which either for bathing purposes or promenade could not be surpassed. It is no exaggeration to say that respectable citizens, and especially ladies, could not visit this Island then without danger of robbery or violence.

An illustration in the September 8, 1866 issue of *Harper's Weekly* shows the Coney Island beach on a hot summer's day, including a three-card-monte man practicing his trade on unsuspecting passersby. Noting how he first chose a card,

"The 'Three-Card Monte'—A Scene on Coney Island" by Stanley Fox, 1866.

With a movable stand stuck into the sand, a cardsharp woos the unwary with three-card monte in this illustration from *Harper's Weekly* for September 8, 1866: "The scene presented . . . is one frequently seen at Coney Island. The sharper who performs the trick, having gathered about him a crowd, selects from the pack a figured card."

Brooklyn! *An Illustrated History*

"say the Queen of Diamonds, which he facetiously nick-names 'Polly Berdyne'," *Harper*'s described the trickery of the three-card monte man: "He shuffles the cards in such a way that is perfectly easy for the spectators to follow the card in all its wanderings; and, as if to aid the eye, the card usually bears upon the back some mark which gives the spectator unusual confidence as to the accuracy of the vision. 'I'll bet you five dollars,' he says, 'you can't follow Miss Polly.'" After the audience grows confident that they can follow the card, betting increasingly larger amounts, "By some sleight of hand [the "sharper"] slips in another card, similar in appearance. . . . The spectators follow this curiously and confidently as on the previous occasions, but upon pointing out the card find to their astonishment that Miss Polly has vanished—and likewise their money!"

Historian Peter Ross's 1902 chronicle of Long Island history describes Coney's haphazard development in these years: "Every year from 1847 witnessed

Coney Island

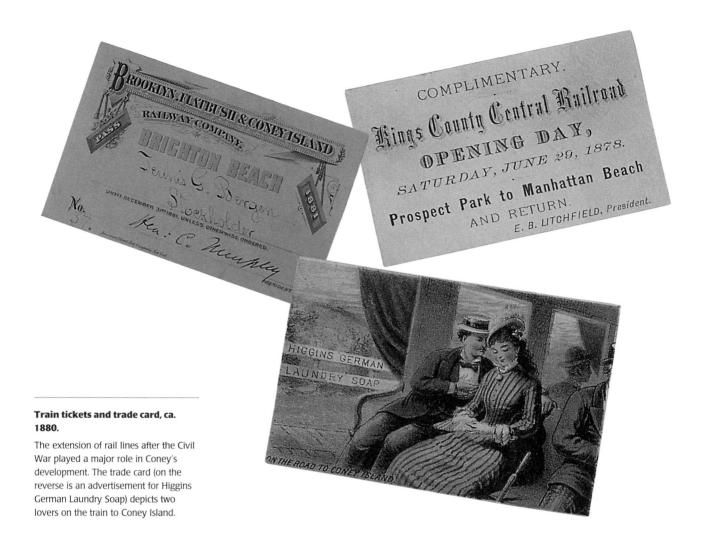

Train tickets and trade card, ca. 1880.

The extension of rail lines after the Civil War played a major role in Coney's development. The trade card (on the reverse is an advertisement for Higgins German Laundry Soap) depicts two lovers on the train to Coney Island.

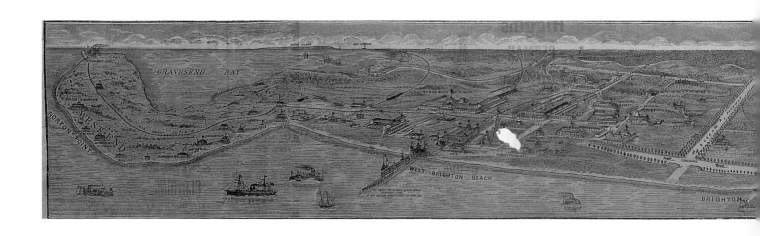

some improvement, some new bathing-houses run up with unplaned lumber and primitive appointments, some roughly constructed hotel or restaurant, cheap saloon, democratic eating-houses where you could bring your own luncheon or eat what was produced on the premises, lager-beer bars, and a show or two, generally of a startling character, such as . . . educated pigs . . . and the like."

As the crowds grew, so did the island's reputation for roughness. The new breed of investors that saw Coney's potential after the Civil War realized they would have to redo Coney—both in image and reality—if they were to attract the large, well-to-do crowds that would make their venture profitable. So these railroad owners, entrepreneurs and businesspeople began to piece together a new vision for Coney in the 1870s. In a gesture worthy of twentieth-century Madison Avenue, much of Coney was renamed, and so remade. The result was four major divisions: to the west, the West End (formerly Norton's Point) and West Brighton; to the east, Manhattan Beach (formerly the Sedge Bank) and Brighton Beach (named for the popular English resort), which essentially divided the more egalitarian west from the tonier east.

Brighton Beach was largely developed by William Engeman, who around 1868 began to track down the hundreds of heirs to thirty-nine lots in the middle part of Coney Island. Locating some heirs as far away as the Sandwich Islands, Engeman bought up a huge tract of marsh land and sand dunes, considered quite undesirable, and transformed it into fairgrounds, hotels, and a bathing pavilion. As it developed into a transit hub that also offered excellent bathing facilities, Brighton Beach attracted a broad cross section of classes: "Brighton Beach is a resort for Brooklyn people, and differs from Manhattan Beach much as Brooklyn does from New York, slightly less elegant but more family," commented *Appleton's Dictionary of New York and Vicinity* in 1884. A June 16, 1890 *Brooklyn Times* article approved of the area's patrons, who were "chiefly good middle-class Brooklynites—people who brought books and babies and light luncheons with them and sat on the smooth sand, or occupied seats around the paths or walked

Overview of Coney Island, lithograph, 1879.

While most of the island is colored green on this 1879 overview, indicating undeveloped land, by this date the island's main subdivisions were set, and there was an impressive jumble of hotels, piers, racetracks, a few homes, and railroad lines and depots. The maze of railroad lines laid the groundwork for much of the transportation in place in southern Brooklyn today.

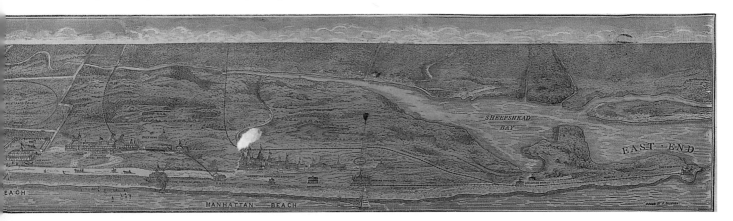

Coney Island

BROOKLYN, FLATBUSH & CONEY ISLAND RAILWAY

Hotel Brighton, **lithograph by the Graphic Co., ca. 1880s.**

The imposing Hotel Brighton, a.k.a. the Brighton Beach Hotel was topped with ornate Victorian cast-iron cresting and surrounded by fountains and a verdant lawn. The vignettes highlight horsecar and rail connections and picture popular activities on the grounds—and in the ocean.

around the magnificent lawns or listened to the babble of the wavelets and enjoyed themselves in a quiet, orderly, and thorough fashion." There was a reason for the great number of Brooklyn (vs. Manhattan) visitors at Brighton Beach; rail service to the area was targeted specifically at Brooklyn, with depots at Bedford, the Long Island Railroad Terminal, and other sites accessible to the city's middle-class residents.

Brighton Beach's two largest hotels were the Ocean Hotel, a family-oriented establishment, and the Hotel Brighton (a.k.a. Brighton Beach Hotel). Which was built by Brooklynite Henry C. Murphy (see Brooklyn Bridge chapter) and a group of businessmen and opened to the public in July 1878 as a 3-story, 174-room hotel. The wood-frame Brighton achieved a certain notoriety not just for its fine accommodations but for its relocation after ocean waves began washing under the building. For the project—a feat of astonishing proportions at the time—the Brooklyn and Brighton Beach Rail Road Company laid twenty-four tracks under the enormous structure and planned to load the hotel on 112 cars to move it back from the oceanfront. Work began in the winter of 1887. To a population that had seen the Brooklyn Bridge completed on the shores of the East River just several years earlier, moving the gargantuan hotel must have seemed just one more example of the march of progress. An eyewitness, Robert Foster, quoted the April 4, 1888 *World* description of the event in a pamphlet titled *The Brighton Beach Hotel and the March from the Sea.*

> Simultaneously six throttles were thrown open—first gradually, then to their full. The music of the guy ropes and tackle was weird and Wagner-

176   Brooklyn! *An Illustrated History*

ian; then the tug of war began. Panting and puffing, the iron horses strained every fibre of their mechanical muscle. For a moment, and a moment only, they tugged in vain; their immense drive wheels revolved with perceptible swiftness; then, as if with a mighty effort, they forged ahead. Slowly but surely the mammoth structure followed. The puzzling problem as to what was to be the fate of Brighton Beach Hotel had been solved. Shouts of joyous approval and triumph arose from the small army of workmen and spectators which was caught up and echoed by six brazen throats in shrill and prolonged blasts.

And so the magnificent hotel was saved from drowning.

To the east of Brighton Beach and its "movable" hotel lay Manhattan Beach, which had developed into a somewhat ritzier neighborhood. Combining pleasure with exclusivity, it offered great hotels, firework displays, and music. Famed American author Theodore Dreiser visited there around the turn of the century and observed in his account of New York as it was between 1900 and 1915, *The Color of a Great City,* that it was "a world of politicians and merchants, and dramatic and commercial life," and that he had never seen "so many prosperous-looking people in one place, more with better and smarter clothes, even though they were a little showy. The straw hat with its blue or striped ribbon, the flannel suit, with its accompanying white shoes, light cane, the pearl-gray derby, the check suit, the diamond and pearl pin in necktie, the silk shirt. What a cool, summery, airy-fairy realm!"

Moving Brighton Beach Hotel, 1888.

Could it be done? With six locomotive engines pulling—and the skill and experience of B. C. Miller & Sons, House Movers, whose advertisement can be seen toward the rear of the photograph—the Brighton was saved from the sea. Photograph by J. H. Beal.

MOVING BRIGHTON BEACH HOTEL, CONEY ISLAND, WITH LOCOMOTIVES.

LENGTH, 460 FEET. DEPTH, 210 FEET. WEIGHT, 5,000 TONS. J. H. BEAL, Photographer, 870 Pearl St., New York.

By B. C. MILLER & SONS, House Movers, 979 and 998 Bergen Street, Brooklyn, N. Y.

Coney Island

Porcelain nameplate from the Manhattan Beach Hotel, ca. 1877.

This tiny decorative fragment of the imposing Manhattan Beach Hotel was saved by Dorothy Dick, a Brooklyn resident whose uncle, John Nagle, was a hotel official. The nameplate most likely hung on or above the door to the room.

Austin Corbin, a wealthy New York banker, developed Manhattan Beach as a resort in hopes of creating a rival to Newport, Rhode Island. He had scouted out land for sale at Coney Island while visiting there with his infant daughter. She was sickly, and doctors had recommended that she partake of Coney's pure, salt air for its restorative powers. Corbin was shown what was to become Manhattan Beach and decided to buy. As Engeman had built private rail connections to attract people to Brighton Beach, Corbin built the New York and Manhattan Beach Railway between 1876 and 1877. He built depots in Manhattan and provided ferry service via the east Twenty-third Street ferry in order to attract more of a New York audience. Manhattanites could now travel from midtown straight to Corbin's two new hotels, the Manhattan Beach and the Oriental, in an hour.

The hotels catered to slightly different crowds. The Manhattan Beach, ceremoniously opened by popular former president Ulysses S. Grant in 1877, accommodated both day and seasonal guests. "This hotel is particularly adapted to the wants of transient guests, for whose convenience two spacious piazzas, commodious parlors, and extensive rooms on the first floor are offered," claimed an 1883 guide of the hotel. "All above the first floor is reserved for the permanent sojourners, who can have all the enjoyments of the place, without mingling with the crowd." The establishment catered to Manhattan society types, politicians, and well-known men about town, who made it their families' summer home, joining them on weekends. In the Gold Room, a private buffet, aspiring comics tried out their routines on business leaders and professionals.

Corbin did not welcome everyone to his Coney Island properties. To insure a "select" clientele, Corbin installed a high fence around the grounds. He hired Pinkerton detectives to oversee arriving trains and remove any "undesirable" guests. And an incident in July 1879 revealed that the prejudices of the city never took a vacation: Corbin banned Jews from the Manhattan Beach Hotel. The July 23rd *New York Times* reported that "Mr. Austin Corbin, President of the Manhattan Beach Railway Company, says that Jews, as a class, have made themselves offensive to those who patronize his road and hotel on Coney Island . . . and that he will leave nothing undone to get rid of them. Prominent Jews, while disinclined to discuss the matter, because, they fear . . . that by discussion it will gain a dignity it does not merit, condemn Mr. Corbin's action most heartily . . . and call Mr. Corbin a narrow-minded bigot."

In 1880, Corbin opened the Oriental Hotel, as large as the Manhattan Beach but designed with a Moorish feel and catering to a wealthy but more settled audience. "In building the 'Oriental,' particular reference was had to the needs of families, the aim being to have it as retired as possible, where a household could live in a body, be quiet and secluded, and yet be within reach of the livelier attractions if desired," noted a contemporary source. One of the few remnants of this spacious hotel, an alphabet plate, evokes images of a child of one of these households, clamoring for a parent to buy the souvenir plate with the picture of the "big hotel" as a reminder of a special summer.

While each of Coney's major hotels was distinctive, all were huge, their size a product of their owners' desire for big crowds and bigger profits, and of plenty of available land. And all conducted business on a scale to match, claiming to serve thousands at one sitting and offering dramatic extravaganzas with enormous casts of characters. The Manhattan Beach Hotel boasted "panoramas" that featured hundreds of actors, clowns, and dancers. Taking their cue from the attractions of the popular world expositions of the time, panorama themes frequently focused on famous scenes from history, such as the storming of the Bastille, or current events, such as the Spanish-American War. For an extravaganza about Pompeii's destruction, spectators sat on rickety chairs while toga-clad performers raced around as "Mt. Vesuvius" erupted. It was quintessentially Victorian: a fascination with large-scale spectacle, and an interest in the exotic, the foreign, and the historic. Fabled events and places were brought to life before the audience's eyes.

Along with the hotels and their attractions, among the amusements that sprang up in the post–Civil War period were great racetracks, the first of which was built by William Engeman at Brighton Beach in 1879. It was followed by the

Child's alphabet plate, Oriental Hotel, ca. 1890.

Given the Oriental Hotel's air of exclusivity, this mass-produced souvenir seems incongruous. The water is bright green, the beach pink, and the sky a sickly shade of brown.

Coney Island

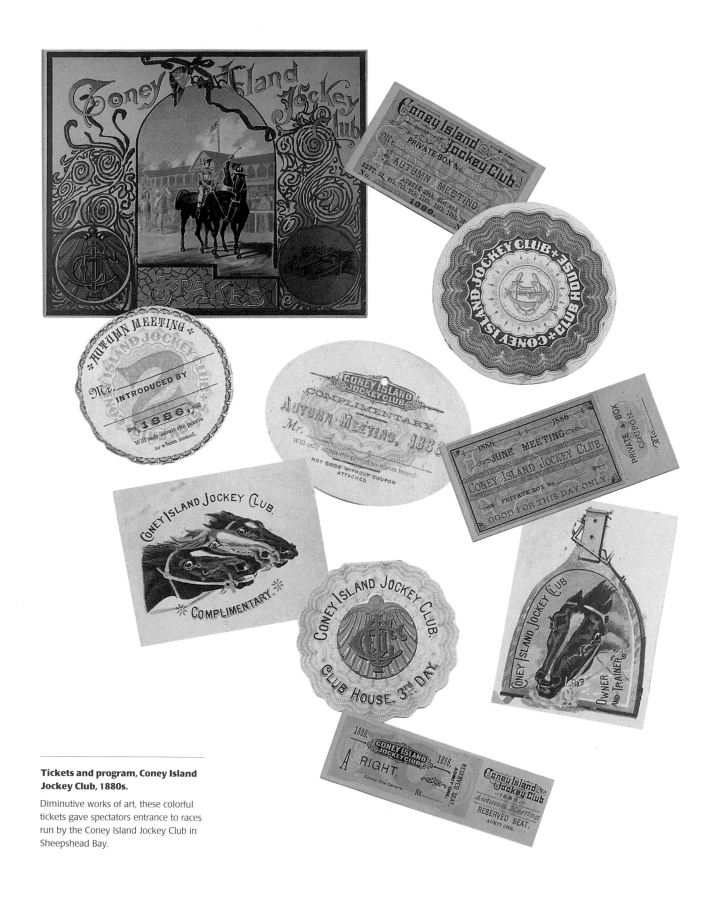

Tickets and program, Coney Island Jockey Club, 1880s.

Diminutive works of art, these colorful tickets gave spectators entrance to races run by the Coney Island Jockey Club in Sheepshead Bay.

MAKING BETS AT THE BOOKMAKERS' STANDS—EXCITING SCENES AT THE CLOSE OF A RACE.

"Making Bets at the Bookmakers' Stands," 1888.

This illustration from *Frank Leslie's Illustrated Newspaper* shows men waving cash at the course of the Coney Island Jockey Club, trying to place bets near the close of a race.

Gravesend Race Track, run by the Brooklyn Jockey Club, and the Sheepshead Bay Race Track, operated by the Coney Island Jockey Club. Within walking distance of each other, all three achieved national reputations. Races from May through October not only attracted countless well-to-do spectators and bettors but transformed the surrounding neighborhoods, as track patrons built fine homes in nearby Sheepshead Bay and track hands either moved in locally or boarded for the season. By 1900 the tracks employed hundreds of workers, many of them Irish Americans and Southerners, both white and African American.

By 1900 Brooklyn was the horse-racing capital of America. The Sheepshead Bay Race Track, founded by Leonard Jerome, William Vanderbilt, and August Belmont, hosted the Suburban Handicap and the Futurity races; the Gravesend Race Track organized the Preakness and the Brooklyn Handicap, all of which attracted tens of thousands. Many famous thoroughbreds streaked down the tracks bearing the leading jockeys of the day: Tod Sloan, Snapper Garrison, George Odom, Marty Miles, Winnie O'Connor, Arthur Redfern, Isaac Murphy. Some of the jockeys were African Americans, many of whom traveled north from southern horse farms to compete on the racing circuit. But Black people were increasingly excluded from the sport as horse racing gained in prestige and profitability after the Civil War.

While the fancy hotels and racetracks of Brighton and Manhattan Beaches had given Coney a degree of respectability, some people still considered the western part of the island disreputable, reflecting the divisions of the island that owed as much to economic class and social status as to geography. In this sense, Coney was a microcosm of Brooklyn, whose neighborhoods were often divided along similar lines. Entrepreneurs had hoped to separate Brighton and Manhattan

Coney Island

Beach from Coney's West End (synonymous with "Coney Island" to many at the time) in the minds of prospective patrons and to some extent succeeded. "The regular visitors to the Oriental Hotel, or Manhattan Beach, or Brighton Beach . . . would hardly care to admit that they had any connection with Coney Island," wrote historian Peter Ross in his 1902 volume, *A History of Long Island.*

> That good old name has become somewhat demoralized, too much associated with "the great unwashed," with cheap shows, bawling photographers, Sunday beer and vulgar frankfurters to be congenial to ears polite. So at all three the name of Coney Island is tabooed, and when in these modern days the island is referred to we are supposed to speak of the long stretch of sand lying still further to the westward. Here, however, the island retains all the many peculiarities and types which won for it its first popularity. Its manners are free and easy, its crowds have assembled to have a good time according to their individual ideas, and they have it.

The patrons of the island's western area knew they were having a good time. True, the West End—Norton's Point—was home to prizefighting, gambling, and prostitution, legacies of the reign of local political boss John Y. McKane, successor to Mike Norton. (They continued even after McKane went to Sing Sing in 1894, a victim of the reform movement of the early 1890s.) Yet it was a popular destination for day trippers with lunch baskets, many of whom were not well-to-do—factory workers, clerks, and domestic servants. Many were enjoying the fruits of the summer Saturday half holiday movement which had spread through retail and manufacturing businesses in the 1880s. Yet others were undoubtedly on the forced, unpaid vacations imposed by many industries—such as iron foundries and glass works—where blazing fires and blistering summer temperatures made it too hot to work. A June 4, 1893 *Eagle* article described the crowd headed for West Brighton on a hot Sunday as "a bustling, cursing, squeezing, perspiring crowd of men, women and children from the tenements." And while its bathing houses tended to be crudely built—far from elegant hotels—they were affordable and practical. West Brighton was viewed as tainted only by an elite uncomfortable with the area's appeal to a more democratic crowd. It was Coney's *true* entertainment district, attracting the lion's share of the island's visitors.

Those who arrived at West Brighton via the Prospect Park and Coney Island Rail Road alighted at the depot, facing a broad, grassy piazza planted with flowers. The piazza and a three-hundred-foot Iron Tower transplanted from the Philadelphia Centennial Exposition of 1876 were the handiwork of Andrew R. Culver, who built the railroad line and wanted attractions at its terminus. And attractions there were: piers, restaurants, bathhouses, a concourse with rustic pavilions, bands playing day and night, saloons, variety shows, games, and food vendors.

Two of the most famous attractions were Feltman's and Lucy the Elephant. A combination restaurant and theme park, Feltman's epitomized the grand scale of West Brighton attractions. Entrepreneur Charles Feltman, a German immigrant, began his Coney career in the early 1870s by converting a rented shanty into a shelter where he sold lunches—frankfurters, clam roasts, ice cream, and lager—at lower prices than his competitors. He parlayed his lunch-counter success into a huge establishment along West Tenth Street from Surf Avenue to the shore, where he offered shore dinners, a roller coaster, and later other attractions, all with a German theme. He claimed to serve an astounding number of diners:

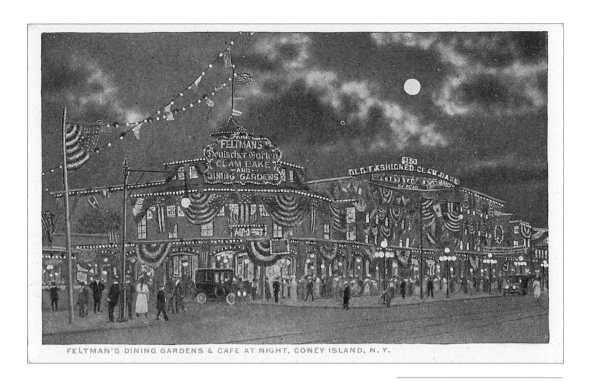

FELTMAN'S DINING GARDENS & CAFE AT NIGHT, CONEY ISLAND, N. Y.

200,000 people over the course of an 1880s season. By the second decade of the twentieth century, Feltman's reportedly accommodated ten times that number. To attract the ever larger crowds that excursion groups of unions, employers, ethnic organizations, and social groups offered, Feltman's continuously renovated and expanded. According to the 1883 publication, *Coney Island. An Illustrated Guide to the Sea,*

> Since the improvements made, better facilities are offered for the purpose of festivals for large societies, lodges and clubs. Already arrangements have been made with the following: July 10, the "Norddeutschen Bruder" (North German Brothers), with 2,500 admission tickets; July 11, the "Lamstedter Society," with 2,500 admission tickets . . . the "Bremervoerder Society," . . . the United Lodges of the "German Order of Haragari," with 8,000 admission tickets; July 30, the "Scandinavian Singing Society," with 2,500 admission tickets; . . . August 16, the Grand Lodge of the "A.O. of G.F.," under the auspices of 19 lodges, with 8,000 admission tickets; August 23, "South Brooklyn Turners and Thalia Singing Society," with 3,500 tickets . . . besides other smaller festivals held every night during the season.

On nearby Surf Avenue, Coney's main thoroughfare, Lucy the Elephant towered over visitors, her sheer physical size reflecting the humor and fantasy that would come to characterize the area. Standing 150 feet to the top of the crescent on the flagpole, the tin-skinned Lucy housed 34 rooms, including "the stomach room . . . owing to its special location in the body of the beast," as well as a "thigh room, brain room, hip room, etc." according to the *Scientific American's* July 11, 1885 issue. The elephant also carried a howdah, a covered seat, on her back. Lucy's "colossalness" made her kin to other architectural feats of the day. As a

SCIENTIFIC AMERICAN

[Entered at the Post Office of New York, N. Y., as Second Class Matter.]

A WEEKLY JOURNAL OF PRACTICAL INFORMATION, ART, SCIENCE, MECHANICS, CHEMISTRY, AND MANUFACTURES.

Vol. LIII.—No. 2.
[NEW SERIES.]

NEW YORK, JULY 11, 1885.

[$3.20 per Annum.
[POSTAGE PREPAID.]

THE COLOSSAL ELEPHANT OF CONEY ISLAND.

The reputation that the American people have long had of always doing everything on the grandest possible scale, has received lately a very substantial confirmation in the two monuments that have recently been bestowed upon this country. The Washington Monument and the statue of Liberty are the greatest works of art in height and magnitude that have been raised by the hands of man since the Tower of Babel. In addition to these, there is a third monument, facetiously styled the eighth wonder of the world, that has recently been raised in the neighborhood of New York, that for one reason deserves to be, named in the same connection with the foregoing, namely, on account of its size. The Colossal Elephant at Coney Island has not been favored with much serious public attention, owing to the fact principally that it is not an artistic work, and secondly, because it is the project and property of a stock company, whose unexalted aim was to rear a structure that would serve, not so much to elevate the public mind artistically, nor to stand as a monument to some of our noted forefathers, but rather to abstract the unwary dime from the inquisitive sightseer. This fact, and the grotesque nature and enormous size of the colossus, has deprived it, up to this time, of much consideration, but this should not deter us from inquiring how a building of such unique design and original construction was called into being.

It was designed and built under the personal supervision of the architect, Mr. J. Mason Kirby, of Atlantic City, N. J. It was first intended to make it a hotel, but later this idea was abandoned, and it was decided to construct the interior with the purpose of using it as an auditorium for concerts, etc., while the platform on the top, or the howdah, as it is termed, would serve as

(Continued on page 21.)

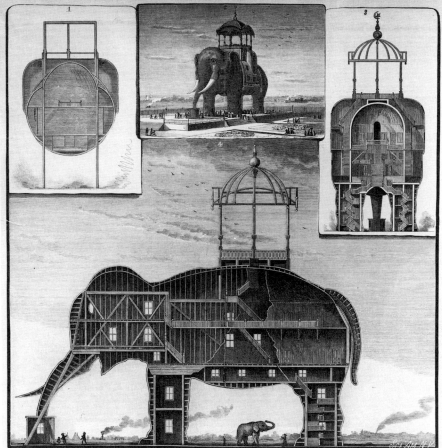

THE COLOSSAL ELEPHANT OF CONEY ISLAND.

"The Colossal Elephant of Coney Island," 1885.

Lucy may have been inspired by Jumbo, the elephant showman P. T. Barnum brought from London to New York in 1882, an immediate hit with New Yorkers (she stands, for comparison, beneath Lucy in the illustration). Coney's Lucy was wood with skin made of tin and stood seven stories high, as this illustration in *Scientific American,* July 11, 1885, indicates. Essentially a huge indoor bazaar, she weighed an estimated 100,000 tons. Visitors entered through a door at the foot of the right hind leg.

writer for *Scientific American* theorized in the same issue, she was part of a national trend, a cult of bigness, an "American" way of doing things:

> The reputation that the American people have long had of always doing everything on the grandest possible scale, has received lately a very substantial confirmation in the two monuments that have recently been bestowed upon this country. The Washington Monument and the statue of Liberty are the greatest works of art in height and magnitude that have been raised by the hands of man since the Tower of Babel. In addition to these there is a third monument, facetiously styled the eighth wonder of the world, that has recently been raised in the neighborhood of New York, that for one reason deserves to be named in the same connection with the foregoing, namely, on account of its size.

Because Lucy's conception was "tainted" with money-making motives, the writer was reluctant to consider Lucy in the same league as her fellow, more permanent monuments:

> The Colossal Elephant at Coney Island has not been favored with much serious public attention, owing to the fact principally that it is not an artistic work, and secondly, because it is the project and property of a stock company, whose unexalted aim was to rear a structure that would serve, not so much to elevate the public mind artistically, nor to stand as a monument to some of our noted forefathers, but rather to abstract the unwary dime from the inquisitive sightseer.

For a strictly male crowd, West Brighton also housed a huge wooden arena, where the Coney Island Athletic Club, in particular, staged boxing matches. Great early African American fighters like George Dixon, Joe Gans, and "Jersey" Joe Walcott drew huge crowds. In 1890, West Brighton hosted the first annual Black boxing championship of America.

More than any other area on the island, West Brighton—home to Feltman's, Lucy, and a host of other amusements—appealed to a working-class crowd, bringing together established groups and recent immigrants who in everyday life were often segregated into separate neighborhoods and work places. Along with the hotels, horse tracks, and numerous attractions of the areas to the east, Coney had become the famous resort post–Civil War entrepreneurs had dreamed of. "Within the last few years," wrote Henry Stiles in his 1884 history of Kings County, Coney Island "has become celebrated as THE watering place of New York and Brooklyn."

New Coney: Steeplechase, Luna, and Dreamland

By the close of the nineteenth century, Coney, like Brooklyn, had become a landscape of distinctive areas with distinct personalities: fancy Manhattan Beach, the tainted West End, fun-packed West Brighton, family Brighton Beach. Of them all, West Brighton, long Coney's entertainment heart, drew the attention of amusement entrepreneurs whose money and imagination would transform it into one of the most famous spots on earth.

In 1893 and 1895 fire destroyed much of West Brighton's entertainment facilities and opened up a large amount of land for development at a time when

View of Brooklyn and Staten Island from Coney Island by August Laux, oil on canvas, ca. 1890s.

Laux's scene suggests that even as a large and well-known resort, Coney retained much of its natural windswept beauty. Day trippers alight from a steamer.

the potential market for mass entertainment was already huge and growing. Hundreds of thousands of southern and eastern European immigrants were streaming into Brooklyn and New York, along with the Irish and Germans who had been arriving in large numbers since midcentury. Brooklyn's population swelled. New trolley lines to Coney Island in 1895 made day excursions relatively quick and inexpensive for working-class families and individuals. The commercial potential was enormous.

"A Holiday Crowd Bound for Coney Island, Ulmer Park and Bath Beach," 1899.

Holiday revelers could catch the trolley to any of a number of resorts along the Brooklyn shore: Coney Island at the farthest end, Ulmer Park (in Unionville—today part of Bensonhurst/Gravesend), or Bath Beach, just south of Dyker Heights. From E. Idell Zeisloft, ed., *The New Metropolis,* New York: D. Appleton & Co., 1899.

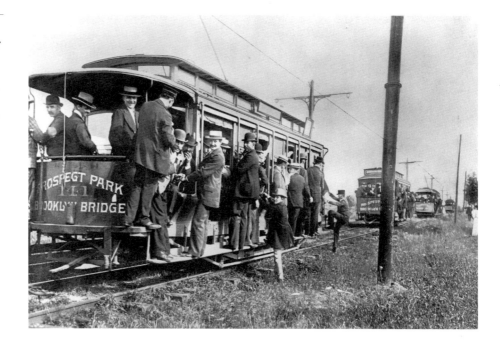

Shrewd, perceptive, and eager to make money, a few entrepreneurs decided to rebuild West Brighton after the fires. Paul Boyton (who built Sea Lion Park) and Elmer "Skip" Dundy (who years later would build Luna) were among the creative individuals who descended on Coney's old, odd mix of buildings and planned the "New Coney" as consolidated amusements within enormous parks, each with its own character or theme.

Local businessman George C. Tilyou was the leading force in the movement to create enclosed parks. At first, Tilyou was merely competing with Paul Boyton, who in 1895 opened Sea Lion Park, which featured sea lions, a water circus, and Shoot the Chutes. It differed from earlier parks by charging one price for multiple attractions, but it was short-lived. Before long Tilyou's was the only show in town.

Tilyou's family had been at Coney Island since 1865, when he was just a toddler, and he seems to have inherited an urge to attract a paying audience. Believing that the western end's reputation for rowdiness kept away the more "respectable" workingman and his family, who had money and time to spend, he created an enclosed park where he could have some control over who would be admitted.

Tilyou bought up fourteen acres in West Brighton and in 1897 opened what would prove one of the most enduring amusement parks in history—Steeplechase. Named after a ride he had imported from England—mechanical horses that visitors mounted and rode around a simulated steeplechase route—Steeplechase was big, brassy, and brazen. "The Funny Place" embodied fun at its most raucous, with mechanical devices, sideshow attractions, and shocking rides like the Hoopla, which threw male and female riders together in a manner strictly taboo in genteel Victorian circles. Steeplechase reveled in jostling and jerking its patrons. "The Isle of Idiocy" is what *Munsey's Magazine* called it in its September 1901 issue, noting Coney's true and essential character: "That, above all, is Coney Island's specialty; to toss, tumble, flop, jerk, jounce, jolt, and jostle you by means of a variety of mechanical contrivances, until your digestion is where your reason ought to be, and your reason has gone none knows whither. For the privilege you pay the appreciable sum of ten cents. If the same thing happened to you the next day on a trolley car, you would in all probability sue the company for a thousand dollars." Visitors loved it.

Tilyou advertised the park in working-class newspapers such as the Socialist *New York Call*, offering "10 hours of fun for 10 cents." He wanted to attract a cross section of men, women, and children—in short, the biggest audience possible. In "cleaning up" West Brighton and consolidating his attractions within an enclosed area with a single admission charge, Tilyou created a model that would be imitated again and again.

Steeplechase's opening coincided with a drop in the postage rate for commercially printed postcards from two cents to one cent in 1898, which helped spread its image far and wide. As companies churned out printed cards of every imaginable scene—and some quite fantastic ones—Coney Island appeared in thousands of views that captured the marvels of the new parks.

In 1903, six years after Steeplechase opened, Fred Thompson and Elmer "Skip" Dundy opened Luna Park, named after Dundy's sister in New Jersey. When George C. Tilyou had seen the two showmen's Trip to the Moon ride while visiting the Pan-American Exposition in Buffalo in 1901, he had invited them to Coney Island. They liked what they saw, bought the old Sea Lion Park, razed

LUNA PARK

THE HEART OF
CONEY ISLAND

LUNA PARK
THOMPSON & DUNDY

Entrance to Luna Park,
by night, Coney Island, N.Y.

ENTRANCE TO
DREAMLAND,
CONEY ISLAND.

DREAMLAND

COPYRIGHT 1904 BY LUNA PARK CO.
Japanese Roof Garden by night.—LUNA PARK, NEW YORK.

Greetings from Coney Island

Postcards from Coney Island, ca. 1905.

Both missive and souvenir, these cards capture the diversity of Coney Island's great parks in the early years of the twentieth century, from Luna's delightful Japanese Garden to Steeplechase's zaniness and Dreamland's promise of exoticism, as well as risqué hugging on the beach by bathers clad only in swimsuits!

everything on its twenty-two acres except Shoot the Chutes, and erected a fantasy realm of far-off lands, even evoking exotic Baghdad in a rainbow of dazzling colors. Luna featured a circus, the ever popular Trip to the Moon, Helter Skelter (a bamboo slide for adults), Shoot the Chutes, circus elephants performing on a platform in the middle of a lagoon, historical extravaganzas, restaurants, gardens, lemonade stands, and more. But the most spectacular attraction was Luna itself, a fairy-tale fantasy lit at night by thousands of electric lights—an "Electric Eden," Thompson called it. For turn-of-the-century visitors electricity was still a novelty (not until about 1920 did most houses have it). The nearly forty-five thousand people who amassed for opening night on May 16, 1903, "rubbed their eyes, and stood in wonder and pinched themselves," wrote one reporter. Another remarked that once inside the massive gates, they found "an enchanted, story book land of trellises, columns, domes, minarets, lagoons, and lofty aerial flights. And everywhere was life—a pageant of happy people; . . . It was a world removed—shut away from the sordid clatter and turmoil of the streets." For those early visitors, Luna must have been unforgettable.

Luna departed from Steeplechase's jostling, bumping notions of fun. Its developers deliberately emphasized the educational aspects of its attractions to appeal to a middle-class audience. The park was entertaining but also supposedly instructional by bringing to life places Luna's visitors had only heard or read about. Luna featured Middle Eastern architecture, historical re-creations such as "War Is Hell," as well as numerous "re-created" communities—like an Eskimo village, a Venetian city and an Irish village. Such "villages" were also popular features of the international expositions mounted in major U.S. cities between 1876

Luna Park, 1906.

In many ways, Luna's spectacular landscape was a cityscape, cleaned up and fantasized and packed with visitors who found it sublime.

Brooklyn! *An Illustrated History*

and World War I. Whether in "world's fairs" or Coney, these villages were presented as realistic re-creations and intended to satisfy a middle-class desire for scientific and historical information. A century later they seem exploitative and decidedly racist. "Exhibits" showing how cultures and peoples fit into a racial hierarchy, with non-whites as the most "savage" or "simple," had little to do with science and much more to do with reinforcing biased views.

"Fighting the Flames," a disaster-based amusement, titillated audiences with spectacle and the vicarious experience of danger. A four-story building was repeatedly set ablaze. Heroic firemen fought the flames (successfully, of course) as "residents" jumped from windows into safety nets below. In creating the exhibition, Luna developers chose a clearly urban scene—a tenement was on fire, not a barn or farmhouse—something familiar to Coney's visitors, most of whom were city dwellers. Major fires were commonplace in cities. For instance, three hundred people died in the horrific Brooklyn Theater fire of 1876, the nation's worst theater fire up to that time. "Fighting the Flames" did not seem like a reenactment of some far off, historical event, but like an everyday possibility. The sense of real danger relieved by a safe, happy ending surely struck a deeply responsive chord in viewers; it was one of Luna's most popular attractions.

Just one year after Luna's debut, Dreamland, the last of Coney's huge fantasy parks, went up in 1904 on the other side of Surf Avenue. Unlike Steeplechase and Luna, both created by veteran showmen, Dreamland was developed by a consortium of investors led by William H. Reynolds, a former New York state senator, real-estate promoter (he developed Borough Park), and theater manager. In an effort to outdo Luna, Dreamland's developers installed in their fifteen-acre park four times as many electric lights and two Shoot the Chutes instead of one. At Dreamland's center a 375-foot central tower (substantially taller than Luna's) modeled on the Giralda (a minaret surviving from the period of Moorish rule in Seville, Spain) presided over Venetian villages, miniature locomotives, concert halls, a circus, a Lilliputian village inhabited by three-hundred Little People, and more. And, as in the case of Feltman's, Lucy the Elephant, and the grand hotels, "bigness" was a major draw. At the park's entrance stood a monumental sculpture that one guidebook identified as Eve, although her enormous wings suggested she might be the Angel of Creation. She towered over visitors who walked beneath her outstretched wings to enter the world of Genesis, traveling along in little boats to view scenes of the Creation. The notion of Dreamland as sanctified space was almost comical. Despite its religious veneer, Dreamland was unmistakably elevating spectacle and titillation over biblical instruction.

Like Luna, Dreamland was largely patterned after Chicago's world's fair of 1893. In what was probably the most concerted effort to date among the parks to reach a more middle-class audience, Dreamland concentrated less on the physical experience of jostling, jarring rides than on more "educational" or "genteel" attractions, such as European cities, historic re-creations like the Fall of Pompeii, and pure white buildings inspired by the World's Columbian Exposition and signifying deference to the classical past. Pretentious and moralistic, it was probably too cultivated for fun-seekers; it never generated the popularity of its neighboring parks. Perhaps because the developers were politicians and venture capitalists, not entertainment impresarios, Dreamland lacked the panache of Luna and Steeplechase.

With the advent of Steeplechase, Luna, and Dreamland, West Brighton shook off much of its earlier reputation. "Time was when the place was shunned by

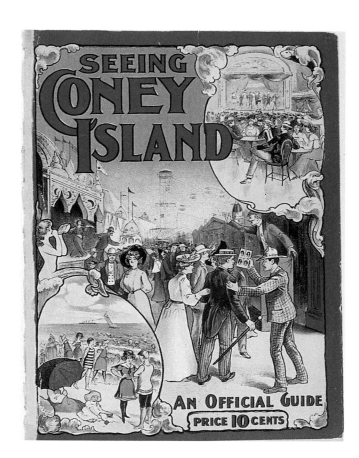

ultra-respectable New Yorkers, who went instead to Manhattan Beach, but nowadays Coney is visited by all classes," reported *Harper's Weekly* on July 8, 1905. "The character of the crowds showed a great change," added *Munsey's Magazine* the same year. "The man who formerly came with a gang of fellows from his office or shop to enjoy a relapse into rowdyism now brought his womenfolk and was decent."

Promoters played to the hilt "New Coney" as a bastion of respectability. Guidebooks especially went out of their way to promote it. *Seeing Coney Island,* published in 1904, featured pictures of well-dressed, happy visitors and rhapsodized:

> There was a Coney Island, not many yesterdays ago. There *is* a Coney Island of to-day, which differs as widely from the sandy and unsavory Coney of the past as the uptown avenues and palatial buildings differ from the Harlem goat pastures and shanties of recent memory.
>
> Brains, enterprise and capital and the purifying effects of a sweeping conflagration have contributed to make a new Coney, and the result is a marvelous transformation almost incredible and quite impossible fully to describe.

The audiences were in fact mixed, and the risqué character of many of the attractions was exactly what drew many visitors, who were anxious to cut loose from the restrictions of everyday Victorian life. The survival of the Bowery, a seedy lane of amusements squeezed into West Brighton between West Sixteenth Street and Jones Walk proves the point. Its namesake was Manhattan's Bowery, a neighborhood that even by the 1830s was a center for amusements and cheap theater for the working classes. Brooklyn's Bowery, with its raucous Silver Dollar Hotel, palmists, saloons, photo galleries, dance halls, and a cacophony of pianos, calliopes, hand organs, whistles, and gongs, represented the old West Brighton,

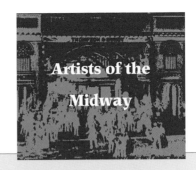

From Marcus Illions's Coney Island shop emerged some of the most fantastic steeds ever to grace carousels—strong, energetic animals who chafed at the bit and tossed their manes angrily. Born in Poland in 1866, Illions started his shop in 1909, one of a small group of carvers who practiced their craft in Brooklyn around the turn of the century. Largely German and Russian immigrants, they created the distinctive "Coney Island style" of carousel horse—flashy, fanciful, often be-jewelled, even romantic. In 1912 a photographer captured Illions in his shop, holding a chisel to cut

a flowing horse's mane. His son Philip is at left, his son Rudy at right. Mr. Gudke, a carver and upholsterer stands at the band saw. Another craftsman stands in the doorway.

In small workshops similar to Illions's, banner makers created huge, painted canvases that heralded attractions at Coney and elsewhere. A handful of local banner artists at the turn of the century included Robert F. Wicks, initially a sign painter; Algernon W. Millar, who opened his first shop in 1909; and August Wolfinger, called by the *Brooklyn Daily Eagle* "The Michelangelo of the Midway." This canvas banner, made by Edward Hayden at his shop at 108 Broadway in Brooklyn around the turn of the century, is typical of those made and used at Coney.

Circus banner made by E. J. Hayden & Company, ca. 1900.

M. C. Illion's shop, 1912. Photograph courtesy of Barney and Bette Illions.

the Coney before the new parks. Originally laid out by George C. Tilyou, the area survived Coney's "cleansing" and remained popular even after the glittering parks were erected, because the crowds liked it. Directly next door lay Henderson's Walk, which, as the *Brooklyn Times* pointed out in an August 31, 1906, article, shared the Bowery's exotic, roguish flavor, with fortune tellers, smoking parlors, and, according to a contemporary source, "a pool and billiard parlor . . . filled with the cheap crooks of the island."

Henderson's Walk and the Bowery were at odds with the promoters' vision of a sanitized Coney. But they were fun, as even civic reformer Belle Israels Moskowitz admitted in 1909 when she described why their dance houses and concert halls attracted young working women on weekends. "They know the bad reputation of some of them, but the dancing floor is good, there are always plenty of men and there are laughter and liberty galore."

But beneath the laughter, liberty, and glitter of the parks and the Bowery lay not only imagination and the desire to make a buck but the ordinary people making a living who undergird any grand scheme. For the factory workers who printed tickets or made chocolate and taffy, the workers who ran amusement booths, the families who took in boarders and the thousands who staffed the great parks, Coney was as much demanding employer as amusing diversion. Like those who had come a generation earlier to man the great hotels—bartenders, cooks, waiters, servants, musicians, many of them newly arrived immigrants—their fortunes were often tied directly to the resorts' successes and failures.

"Working Girls' Life at Coney Island," published in the November 1911 *Yearbook of the Women's Municipal League,* offers a rare glimpse behind the scenes at Coney. Beatrice L. Stevenson, a volunteer with the league, went undercover to document the world of "girls working as cashiers, salesgirls, or manufacturing hands." She found that "Germans and German Jews are very numerous as property holders, but not among girl workers, where the Southern Europeans far outnumber the others," not surprising given the numbers of Italians that had immigrated at the turn of the century. "Italians and Greeks hold most of the positions at stands," she observed. "They are quick to seize any employment which is open to inexperienced help. They readily accept low wages and they very soon become experienced." In an observation that reminds us that the working woman is not a late twentieth-century phenomenon, she reported that "a good many workers are married women, some assisting their husbands at the latters' own stands, others . . . tide over a period of unemployment on their husbands' part, and some being widows."

Wages averaged "about $1.00 to $1.50 per day," but ran "from $3.00 per week (toilet tending), to $15.00 per week (experienced cashiering)." In both booths and factories, workers put in seven days a week, although factories had better hours. "In some instances," she noted, "money is deducted for rainy and unproductive days." Almost all workers had to stand: "Seats are provided in cashier boxes, but behind booths there is often very little room for them, while in factories the work cannot be accomplished sitting down. Toilets are provided in all the larger amusement places. Running water and sometimes pails of ice are provided for drinking."

Stevenson concluded that "on the whole, life at the Island is gay and noisy, from the outside. . . . Behind all the noise and glitter, however, there is a good deal of hard work done, and the people who do the work have very little time or inclination for the garish attractions of the place."

Nathan's, ca. 1960s.

Nathan and Ida Handwerker opened
Nathan's at Coney Island in 1916, and
sold their hotdogs for a nickel—five
cents cheaper than those of Charles
Feltman, who is credited with the origin
of the frankfurter in the United States.
The crowds still show up at Nathan's
every summer.

The Nickel Empire: The 1920s and Beyond

Like its flimsy architecture of wood and painted papier-mâché, the glittering city that was Coney Island in the early twentieth century was in many ways impermanent and ephemeral. In 1911 Dreamland burned to the ground. Luna creator Skip Dundy died in 1907, and five years later his partner, Fred Thompson, went into bankruptcy.

To the east, the racetracks and great hotels of the post–Civil War era were fading. The Brighton Beach track closed to racing in 1907, and in 1910, antigambling fervor and a state ban on racetrack betting by New York's reform governor Charles Evans Hughes closed the rest of them. The sport never revived in Brooklyn. Harry S. Harkness bought the Sheepshead Bay Race Track in 1917, renamed it the Harkness Motor Speedway, and eventually sold it for real estate, opening the way for large-scale residential development in Sheepshead Bay. The hotels' exclusivity was disrupted by the presence of the tens of thousands of people who poured into the new parks; by the 1920s they were gone.

What was the death throes for the hotels and tracks was merely a brief decline for Coney Island. In 1920, the subway arrived, bringing nearly every New Yorker within a rapid, five-cent ride of its amusements. In 1900, a nice Sunday in the summer might draw 100,000 to Coney's beach, restaurants, hotels, and attractions; in 1920 Sunday attendance sometimes soared over one million. This was the final democratizing touch for Coney Island and earned the area the nickname the "Nickel Empire." Subway fare, an amusement-park ride, and a hotdog at Nathan's, conveniently located across from the subway terminal, each cost a

The Parachute Jump, 1950s.

Sitting two abreast, high above the beach, riders on the Parachute Jump dropped with heart-stopping speed until the parachute filled—fifteen seconds of fun.

nickel. Visitors thronged to such rides as the Cyclone, built in 1927, with its hundred-second ride up and down nine hills, and the 1920 Wonder Wheel. In 1923, the boardwalk opened, eighty feet wide and nearly two miles long (it later doubled in length).

With the subway's arrival, Dreamland gone, and Luna barely limping along, Steeplechase continued to thrive by combining George C. Tilyou's emphasis on rides and mechanical fun and an ability to change with the times, recognizing what new generations wanted and giving it to them. (When the park burned down in 1907, Tilyou charged admission to the smoldering ruins. He eventually built upon the grounds between Surf Avenue and the ocean a Pavilion of Fun, an enclosed five-acre amusement area unique in being roofed.) After Tilyou died in 1914, his descendants kept up his formula for success through the Depression, and then through World War II.

Attendance rose as visitors were drawn by new rides like the Parachute Jump, built for the 1939 World's Fair and brought to Steeplechase by Tilyou's heirs. During World War II, single women often ventured with their friends to Coney, known as a safe place to go with—or meet—sailors and soldiers on leave. Virginia Grant Cobb, who was about eighteen at the start of the war and had been working in a war plant at Bush Terminal, recalled that "we met sailors and soldiers all over Brooklyn and New York, and sometimes we would go with them to Coney Island. We brought the boys home for dinner—my dad called our house 'Grand Central Station' because we were always bringing some boys from the services over for a meal. After dinner, we all went to Coney and walked along Surf Avenue singing 'Yankee Doodle Dandy' and went on the rides. When we got to the Tunnel of Love my sister Wynn instructed all the boys to behave—no shenanigans. Most of the young men I met were all nice guys and most had never been away from home before. They were all homesick."

The 1940s was a pivotal time for Coney. Luna by the 1940s was in trouble. On top of huge bills for such attractions as John Philip Sousa's band and other extravagant shows and outdated rides, the park had experienced a series of fires and in August 1944 was almost completely destroyed. In 1946, it closed for good. After World War II, government incentives for home ownership lured large numbers of city dwellers to the suburbs, and a rising car culture and the new Belt Parkway drew people away to places like Jones Beach—accessible only by highway, limiting visitors to more middle-class car owners. Coney Island was not designed for car owners; parking space was nearly nonexistent. More and more televisions meant less and less need to go to Coney for entertainment and vicarious visits to foreign lands. Steeplechase, in a desperate effort to compete with television's growing popularity, installed a hall of TVs, all tuned to different channels.

New generations, weaned on Hollywood movies, TV, travel, and Disneyland, felt Coney Island's pull less strongly than had their parents, although mass transit continued to take urbanites to the beach every summer weekend. "This is Coney Island," wrote the *New York Mirror* on July 23, 1961, "tired, worn, tawdry, but a fairyland to those who follow the sun by subway." Or, as Irish playwright Brendan Behan put it in his 1964 book, *Brendan Behan's New York*, Coney Island "is a terrific, fabulous and an extremely proletarian institution . . . where thousands upon thousands of ordinary folk get out on the subway for fifteen cents and thoroughly enjoy themselves." Then came the final blow. In 1965 the Coney Island of the turn of the century died when Steeplechase, the last of the great parks, closed. Rising property taxes and skyrocketing operating expenses had made it a losing business proposition.

Around the amusement-park area, the neighborhood itself was changing. Since the early twentieth century, Coney had become increasingly residential. Italian and Jewish immigrants, among others, were attracted by low rents, the ocean, and an expanding employment market. When the subway was extended to Coney, apartment houses went up, followed in the late 1920s and 1930s by a large colony of summer bungalows. The outside world was encroaching on the amusement area.

Following World War II, many of the summer bungalows were winterized and eventually replaced in the 1960s by large, public high-rise projects on Coney's western end. At the same time, lower-income people displaced from urban-renewal projects elsewhere in the city arrived, straining community resources. Middle- and upper-income families settled in new high-rises like Luna Park and Trump Village at Coney's eastern end, but the area never achieved the mix of residents intended. In the 1980s single-family low-rise homes built on city-owned land began what has been a continuing process of rejuvenating the residential districts.

Today, Coney's landscape differs from its heyday as a resort and amusement center. At the far western end of the island is the private neighborhood of Sea Gate. Brighton Beach is largely residential, filled with rows of apartment buildings and home to long-time Jewish residents as well as thousands of recent Soviet emigrés. Manhattan Beach, once the site of the exclusive Manhattan Beach and Oriental Hotels, is now a neighborhood of expensive homes. At the far eastern end of the island is Kingsborough Community College. Sheepshead Bay, formerly home to a horse racetrack turned speedway is now a residential area of one- and two-family homes, former summer cottages transformed to year-round use, and apartment buildings. On the site of Dreamland stands the Aquarium for Wildlife Conservation.

Although Coney's twenty oceanfront blocks of amusements have shrunk to three, the old Coney spirit lives on. According to the Chamber of Commerce, over five million people come each season by public transportation alone to visit Coney's remaining amusement area, the beaches, and such events as the Great Irish Fair and the annual Mermaid Parade, which every June snakes its way along the boardwalk. Each winter, the Polar Bear Club plunges into ice-cold seas for a brisk unseasonal swim. Above all, the same beach that drew the first resort users

Lilly Santangelo and Changing Times

Lilly Santangelo and her husband opened the World in Wax in the 1920s (she later ran it on her own). Like its Coney Island rival, the Eden Musee, the World in Wax featured figures from history, famous entertainers, athletes, and gory scenes. Lilly Santangelo chose the figures, ran the operation, and served as barker, pitching the attractions of the World in Wax to entice passersby on the boardwalk to buy tickets, adapting her pitch to the audience.

A shrewd businesswoman, Lilly Santangelo responded to changing audience tastes with new wax figures. Besides the perennial favorites—what she called "killers" and "crazies," mass murderers and others—she "usually got the ones that were popular," she explained in a 1987 interview. "They cost a lot of money, and I didn't want to spend a lot of money for nothing, so I had to make sure." Clark Gable and murderers of the 1930s gave way to John Kennedy and sensational killers of the 1960s. As her audience became increasingly African American and Latino, reflecting Brooklyn's changing population, Santangelo added figures like baseball great Roberto Clemente, boxing champion Muhammad Ali, and vocalist Nat King Cole.

When an especially vicious heat wave hit one year, "I saw my beloved Marilyn [Monroe] had melted and I started to cry," she recalled in a 1985 *Village Voice* interview. "So much tragedy, I said to myself, so much sadness. Even in wax I loved her." Rising costs and dwindling crowds made it impossible to buy the one last figure Santangelo thought would really draw crowds. If she hadn't been forced to close the World of Wax in 1984, she would have added him to her collection—entertainer Michael Jackson.

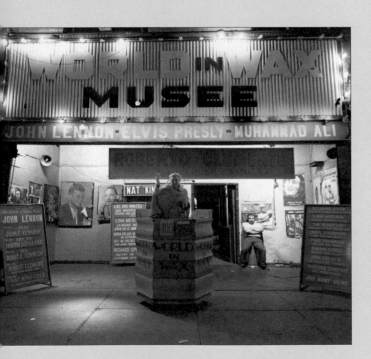

Lilly Santangelo and the World in Wax, 1984. Photograph © Susan Wides, all rights reserved.

and entrepreneurs to Coney Island continues to attract hordes of people. An easily accessible resort for city dwellers, Coney continues to sing its summer siren song to visitors who seek a cool respite from New York for the price of a subway token. Along the boardwalk, the air is thick with the aroma of hotdogs, popcorn, and pizza, as they stroll, sun themselves, listen to music, and make this most public of urban spaces their own.

Diversions for a Growing City

When Coney Island was still just windswept dunes, for entertainment Brooklynites practiced a form of recreation that they still enjoy today—socializing, with and without food and drink. In his 1679 journal, Jasper Danckaerts described visits with local people. "We went on, up the hill, along open roads and a little woods, through the first village, called Breukelen, which has a small and ugly little church standing in the middle of the road. Having passed through here, we struck off to the right, in order to go to *Gouanes*. We went upon several plantations where Gerrit [his local guide] was acquainted with most of all the people, who made us very welcome, sharing with us bountifully whatever they had, whether it was milk, cider, fruit or tobacco, and especially, and first and most of all, miserable rum or brandy which had been brought from Barbadoes and other islands, and which is called by the Dutch *kill-devil*."

Socializing was an important part of Pinkster, a holiday festival celebrated on the first Monday in June by Dutch arrivals from the early days of settlement. In his 1875 publication, *Antiquities of Long Island*, Brooklynite Gabriel Furman described how colonists in the eighteenth century observed the day by "treating their friends to an abundance of good cheer," and "riding in parties about the country making visits." The festival had religious Christian ties as well as seasonal ones, marking both Pentecost and the renewal of life in springtime. It was also a celebration that Brooklyn slaves made their own, combining African traditions of singing and dancing with the European festival at gatherings held in the marketplace near the Brooklyn ferry or across the river in Manhattan. By the 1820s, the Dutch in Brooklyn no longer marked Pinkster, but Furman wrote how Brooklyn's Black citizens continued to celebrate the festival, coming into New York days before the event "with their sassafras and swingled tow for sale, in order to raise money with which to keep this day."

Early taverns, largely for men, provided drink, food, and often lodging—as well as a more communal place to socialize. As early as 1700 a "publick house of Entertainment" was required by the ferryman's franchise at the Brooklyn ferry landing. Taverns multiplied as Brooklyn developed and increasing numbers of travelers passed through. Particularly classy was the Kings Head, where Loyalists Loosley and Elms had set up business in 1779 to cater to British officers and Brooklynites loyal to the Crown during the British occupation of Brooklyn and New York. Among its amenities were dining and card tables, expensive paintings and prints on the walls, fancy sets of china, and a billiard table. A British officer, Lieutenant Anbury, mentioned the tavern in a letter to a friend in England on October 30, 1781. "On crossing the East River from New York, you land at Brooklyn, which is a scattered village, consisting of a few houses. At this place is an excellent tavern, where parties are made to go and eat fish." The tavern also sponsored fox hunts, cricket, and bull baitings, promising that "the bull is remarkably strong and active; the best dogs in the country expected, and they that afford the best diversion will be rewarded with silver collars." On Monday, September 27, 1779, for instance, Brooklyn battled the Greenwich [Village] cricket club for fifty guineas, and in 1781 Loosley advertised a horse race at Ascot Heath (formerly Flatlands Plains).

While taverns served as informal gathering places, Brooklyn's open spaces were a perennial draw for pleasure seekers. In 1794, Moreau de St. Méry wrote that "on Sunday afternoons . . . thousands of people from New York go for walks in Brooklyn, where they eat and destroy all the fruit, even green, that they can reach. The owners don't dare to stop them, and the waste is deplorable. Everyone carries away as much as he wishes." So popular were Brooklyn's rural charms, noted St. Méry, that "at one time the ferries on Sunday carried on every trip and in both directions as many persons as could be loaded aboard."

In the early 1820s, Gabriel Furman kept an extensive, detailed diary over the course of two years that provides some rare glimpses of how people amused themselves in Brooklyn, particularly outdoors. With Brooklyn on the edge of great commercial and industrial development, the open landscape Furman so enjoyed would begin disappearing within a decade.

Some of Furman's leisure time was spent visiting Manhattan. On March 11, 1822, Furman wrote, "In the afternoon went with my cousin Joseph Week to New York—went to see Francis Guy's paintings—Guy was certainly a great landscape painter." Guy, who had recently painted *Summer View of Brooklyn* (see Brooklyln Bridge chapter), was a well-known Brooklyn figure. More often, Furman wrote of spending spare time simply walking, and his accounts are punctuated by detailed descriptions of the nature he encountered. On May 15, 1822, he described a walk that took him from South Brooklyn to a road in what is today the downtown area: "A very warm day. In the afternoon took a walk to Gowannes—the road very

Brooklyn! *An Illustrated History*

***Gray's Baths* by unknown artist, watercolor on board, ca. 1850s.**

Poet and *Brooklyn Eagle* editor Walt Whitman was known to patronize Gray's Baths, a floating covered barge just north of the Brooklyn Heights waterfront.

dusty—the country looks beautiful—saw a patch of peas in the blossom on Mr. John Reid's place near Red Hook Lane."

That summer, he had little desire to pursue his usual activities, for "the alarm of the [yellow] fever is very great in the City of New York," he wrote on August 23, and "almost every person who can afford it is leaving the city." On September 23, he wrote that "the yellow fever has made its appearance in the Village of Brooklyn—there are now three cases of it in Poplar Street, one of whom has had the black vomit all day, and is expected to die before tomorrow morning."

On October 15, 1822, Furman marked "The first day of the Union Races," horse races that were enormously popular spectator sports at the time. "There was an abundance of passing at the Catherine Street, Jefferson Street and Williamsburgh ferries this morning; the boats went as full as they could carry—at the Fulton Ferry the passing was greater than I expected, but by reason of the fever it is nothing to compare with the crossing at the last races." He added that "this afternoon has been all bustle with the people returning from the race, which was easily won by the Long Island horse 'Eclipse.'"

As the fever subsided and winter came, Furman described sleighing parties. "February 15, 1823: . . . Everything in the shape of a sleigh is put in requisition, and parties are fast driving out to Tuckers, the Halfway house, and to Jamaica; at all of which places, dancing and suppers, as well as sleigh riding, are the order of the night—It is really surprising to see how full all these public houses are of the young men and women from all the surrounding country every night while the sleighing continues—The black fiddlers, musicians I suppose they must be styled, make a good business of it, they receive a shilling from each gentleman dancing for every dance—the ladies of course pay nothing."

In the summer of 1823, a novelty appeared on the Brooklyn waterfront—a bathhouse. "This evening I walked on Clover Hill, Brooklyn Heights, for recreation," Furman wrote, and "in the course of my walk met my friends Cooper, and Webb—We descended the hill to the shore, to view a Bathing house lately erected, the first in Brooklyn." The bathing house may well have been Gray's Baths (or a similar one), which an artist depicted in the 1850s. A kind of floating, covered platform, Gray's Baths had separate entrances for women and men.

Holiday celebrations figure prominently in Furman's description of Brooklyn life. On July 3, 1823, he wrote of the "bustle and preparation to celebrate the birth day of our nation on the morrow—In our Village, Brooklyn, on Clover Hill a tent is spread with five tables under it, each of which is sixty two feet long—at which our citizens are to take their fourth of July dinner. . . . At the corner of Washington and York Streets, Brooklyn, [workmen are] erecting a large wheel 35 feet in diameter, with eight swinging seats to hang perpendicular in any position of the wheel—The wheel is turned around by means of a rope attached to its outer edge, and 'Here we go up, up, up and Here we go down, down, down' taking our fourth of July ride to settle our fourth of July dinner." The celebration the next day "closed as usual with the burning of tar barrels in bonfires in a row upon the edge of Brooklyn heights, overlooking the harbour of New York—throwing of rockets, Concerts, illuminations of Gardens, &c. Rockets were seen streaming through the air in every direction like fiery meteors."

As the year ended, Furman seemed pleased on the day after Christmas, reflecting that the holiday had "not been so generally observed in our Village for many years past, as it was yesterday—all business seemed to be at a stand—the Streets in that respect wore the aspect of the Sabbath—In the morning most of inhabitants attended public worship in the different churches; the afternoon and evening were spent in convivial parties." Finally, he saw the year 1824 in with a traditional evening with friends. "This evening I passed very agreeably at the house of my friend Rodman Bowne in keeping *New Year's Eve*—The time passed very agreeably in conversation for about an hour, when the music made its appearance, consisting of a Violin, Clarionette, and tambourine; upon which the party separated into couples, and prepared for the 'mazy dance'—I remained until midnight when I took French leave of them, while they were dancing Scotch reels, and French cotillions—as I passed the gate into the Street, the Clock struck 12 midnight, announcing that the old year had ceased to exist, and that the new one had just then come into being—and which was welcomed by huzzas, firing of guns, and playing of music."

Gabriel Furman's diary, with its tales of walks through Brooklyn Heights, Gowanus, and the ferry district provides a view into a way of life that was on the wane. For Brooklyn's largely rural demeanor was beginning to change. In 1824, the *Long Island Star* noted that "Brooklyn is . . . a rising city, and it behooves us to lay the foundation of certain improvements which are indispensable to economy and comfort," for example, a park. In 1839, a state-appointed commission provided for Brooklyn's future growth by planning streets and roads and urging that public squares be laid out throughout the city. Probably because urbanization did not concern residents who could still walk in a matter of minutes to outlying fields, the report was ignored. By the 1840s and 1850s, though, as the gridiron claimed more and more of the rural landscape, a park seemed more "indispensable." By 1850 the city's population was 97,000. By 1860, with the annexation of Williamsburg, it reached 267,000, as thousands of immigrants arrived. With the unspoken subtext that a park could improve surrounding real-estate values, in 1866 Brooklyn Park Commission president James S. T. Stranahan (a significant figure in the creation of the Atlantic Docks and later the Brooklyn Bridge) prophesied in the commission's sixth annual report that the yet unbuilt park would become a "favorite resort for all classes of our community, enabling thousands to enjoy pure air, with healthful exercise, at all seasons of the year; while its magnificent bay and ocean views, with the beautiful drives through its

Brooklyn! *An Illustrated History*

broad meadows and shady groves, free from the dust and confusion inseparable from crowded thoroughfares, will hold out strong inducements to the affluent to remain in our city, who are now too often induced to change their residences by the seductive influences of the New York [Central] park."

Park planners chose a site west of Gowanus in central Brooklyn because they wanted both high elevations and trees, features considered especially healthful to nineteenth-century urban dwellers vulnerable to diseases like yellow fever. The design was modeled on the American rural cemetery, with its winding paths, clusters of trees and plants, and carefully planned vistas. Brooklyn's Green-Wood Cemetery, incorporated in 1838, was one of the earliest, finest rural cemeteries in the United States; like other Victorian cemeteries, it was built on the city's outskirts and, particularly in its early years, was used not just as a burial site but as a park. In the years before Prospect Park was built, Brooklynites who could afford to travel to Green-Wood were drawn to its verdant spaces, the architecture of its ornate monuments, and the spiritual quality of the grounds. Visitors strolled the grounds and even lounged on the grass and raced carriages along its

Paper sign, ca. 1860s.

Green-Wood Cemetery management frowned on behavior that interrupted the tranquility and contemplative character of the cemetery, including fast horses, lolling on the grass, and picnics. This sign admonished Sunday pleasure seekers driving carriages, delivery people, and even departing funeral processions. Nevertheless, visitors often ignored the rules.

roads, distressing cemetery management, who saw Green-Wood as a place that deserved greater respect.

To create a beautiful pleasure ground for Brooklyn, the city's park commissioners selected landscape architects Frederick Law Olmsted and English-born Calvert Vaux, codesigners of Central Park. On high, rocky land that was home to squatters, who were summarily ejected, the two designed a plan that covered 526 acres with miles of paved drives and walks, a region of open meadow with trees, hilly areas with groves and shrubbery, and "a lake district . . . with picturesque shores and islands," as the *Sixth Annual Report of the Commissioners of Prospect Park* described it. The "natural" look of the park would be achieved through modern technology, and the "rural" landscape would stand in sharp contrast to the city's angular grid plan and stacked buildings as well as to the surrounding farms' plowed and muddy fields.

Olmsted and Vaux's meticulous plans for Prospect Park, recorded in annual reports of the Brooklyn Park Commissioners, reveal that every plant, bridge, shelter, and seat was designed to fit their guiding vision of the park as a celebration of nature. Believing that "modern civilized men . . . find more refreshment and

---

Design for Prospect Park by Olmsted, Vaux & Co., 1866–1867.

Olmsted and Vaux wanted the park kept free of reminders of city traffic, and so designed it without the major thoroughfare included in earlier plans by engineer Egbert L. Víele. They also gave it an irregular outline to further give a feeling of separateness from the city. This design was included in the *Sixth Annual Report of the Commissioners of Prospect Park, 1866.*

Brooklyn! *An Illustrated History*

more lasting pleasure in . . . natural landscape," they strove to fashion one that would provide refuge during the sweltering summer months. For Brooklyn's poor, who had few alternatives to places like the East River docks for cool breezes and respite at the end of long, hot days, Prospect Park would offer a visit to the "country" in their own backyard. The final product was an unqualified success; according to park statistics, 2,136,792 people visited the park in 1868 (a year after it was partially opened), 6,684,645 in 1873, and 10,464,225 in 1888.

The pacific, landscaped grounds that Olmsted and Vaux designed immediately provided a stage for both celebration and conflict. Rustic and natural in appearance, Prospect Park became the scene of highly metropolitan quarrels over its role. Olmsted and Vaux's idea of the park as a rural retreat was upended by turn-of-the-century city planners who envisioned Prospect Park as a civic space with busts of famous men and neoclassical pavilions and buildings. Individualized activities like skating gave way to more active, organized sports, and the once tranquil park hosted parades and celebrations that drew huge crowds.

In 1908 a series of incidents in the park illustrates how concepts of its use clashed. By then one could ride from Manhattan to downtown Brooklyn for an affordable five cents over the Williamsburg Bridge via the Coney Island and Brooklyn Railroad. Many Lower East Side immigrants seeking temporary relief from overcrowded tenements came to Prospect Park—somewhat closer and more accessible by subway than Central Park—for a little fresh air and pretty country scenery. Over several successive summer Sundays, park police arrested groups of these immigrant visitors. Olmsted's idea of a democratic park obviously was not shared by those charged with "protecting" it. The first Sunday they arrested thirty-eight immigrants—thirty-two from Russia, four born in Austria and two born in the United States who bore "names that were typically foreign," reported the

Prospect Park, Brooklyn. Thatched Cottage and Long Meadow from Eastdale Arch by Lyman W. Atwater, watercolor, 1886.

These activities typify those park founders advocated; the thatched cottage is one of the rustic structures designed for this "rural" landscape. Such early images of the park rarely record the huge crowds, focusing instead on scenes of nature and individual activities.

Brooklyn Daily Eagle. The next Sunday, fifty-eight were arrested. The number rose the week after that. Brooklyn magistrate Steers slapped the arrested with heavy fines for breaking rules that were satirized in the following excerpt from the June 29, 1908, *Brooklyn Daily Times*, titled "The Seven Prospect Park Commandments":

> Thou should not throw papers on the walks or lawns.
> Thou shalt not play with a ball.
> Thou shalt not walk on forbidden grass.
> Thou shalt not pick flowers nor shrubs nor break branches from the trees.
> Thou shalt not bring thy luncheon nor even bags of fruit.
> Thou shalt not loll about on the lawns or benches in unseemly attitudes.
> Thou shalt not be boisterous nor hilarious nor interfere with thy neighbor's peaceful enjoyment of the pleasures of the park.

Most of the arrested immigrants could neither read the signs that told them to stay off the grass nor understand why the police were taking them into custody. Only when a rabbi went to the park and translated warnings into Yiddish, and volunteers from the United Jewish League of Brooklyn and other social-service organizations handed out copies of the park ordinances printed in Yiddish did the arrests abate.

The conflict on those summer days seems to have had its roots in prejudice and the police's fear that the "moral" tone of the park reserved for middle- and upper-middle-class users was being threatened. A June 22 article in the *Brooklyn Daily Times* noted that, "though Prospect Park was set aside and laid out by Brooklyn officials as a pleasure ground and breathing spot for Brooklynites, there are few residents of this borough who now go there on Sundays or holidays." It complained that "There is really little or no room for them. They have been crowded out by the denizens of the [Lower] East Side of Manhattan, who have turned this beauty spot, which was once the pride of all Brooklynites, into a place where self-respecting citizens hesitate to go, especially in the company of women." And, according to a June 29 article a week later in the paper, Magistrate Steers at the Flatbush police headquarters said that "these people are ruining our beautiful parks . . . and making it so that a native born American can't go to the park on Sunday." Steers complained that "these foreigners come over from the East Side," and they "look upon Prospect Park somewhat as a wilderness, I guess, in which they can do what they please."

But the Lower East Side residents trying to escape the city heat wanted to use Prospect Park actively, for ball playing, walking on the cool grass, and if they were captured by the beauty of a flower or branch, picking it to take home with them. Their differing concept of the park only pointed out that the place some saw as an oasis was anything but a retreat from the urban scene. It was instead a vital link to the city, a place where the value of Olmsted and Vaux's legacy was continually being tested against changing ideas of how to best use the park.

Prospect Park continued to draw hundreds of thousands of people to its verdant pastures. Today, mammoth efforts by park, citizen, city, and government

Scene of a Section on the Meadow on a Sunday Afternoon, 1925.

In a welcome respite from the city in high summer, families enjoy the huge Prospect Park meadows. It is a scene still common today.

Program from the New Brighton Theatre, 1910.

This New Brighton Theatre program includes a small photograph showcasing the establishment's new, huge size.

groups, spearheaded by the Prospect Park Alliance, are restoring the park to the original splendor created in the nineteenth century while celebrating the many changes that have taken place over the years. Through these efforts, Brooklyn's diverse population continues to enjoy one of New York's most monumental and beautiful attractions.

While Prospect Park was originally created to look distinctly different from the growing city, vaudeville—which emerged as what was perhaps the most popular form of commercial entertainment from the late 1880s to the early 1910s—was embracing city life, appearing in neighborhoods all over Brooklyn. From the diversity of popular entertainments available at the turn of the century—including theatrical offerings, "serious theater," music, and ethnic-related entertainments—vaudeville proved to have the most wide-ranging appeal. It was fun, had a variety of acts, and spoke directly to the audience. Part of a nationally successful, flourishing entertainment industry, it was carefully packaged to attract women and families and became a favorite pastime for a growing working- and middle-class crowd. Its routines and skits often included characters and scenarios that reflected life in ethnic and working-class neighborhoods.

By the 1880s, vaudeville was featured in theaters as far away as Brighton Beach. "The New Brighton Opens With a Good Vaudeville Bill and a Big Audience," headlined a May 17, 1910 *Eagle* article, noting that manager David Robinson "must have found the big audience strong support for his favorite contention that there is population enough south of Kings Highway to support a good vaudeville theater permanently." Vaudeville theaters were also centered in downtown Brooklyn, and neighborhoods like Bushwick, Bedford-Stuyvesant, and Flatbush, which offered popular entertainment close to home and were open, unlike Coney, year round. Because convenience often determined whether such ventures failed or flourished, in the same way that Coney's development was directly linked to transportation's availability, vaudeville entrepreneurs competed for locations near transit lines and shopping districts. Stores, public buildings, and offices helped provide patrons for their theaters. Downtown Brooklyn, by the late 1800s home to numerous department stores and the center of municipal government, was such an area. There vaudeville impressario Percy Williams built the Orpheum on Fulton Street in 1899, part of a chain of Williams theaters in New York City. With 1,700 seats, the Orpheum (razed for a parking lot in 1957) was big-time vaudeville and featured major stars. A week before escape artist and magician Harry Houdini appeared there in April 1907, the *Eagle* wrote that "The Handcuff King" would "perform some entirely new feats . . . one of the principal ones being that of releasing himself after being handcuffed and shackled to the four wheels of a large automobile." Lesser performers worked for smaller neighborhood houses, giving four or five shows throughout the day.

B. S. Moss Flatbush Vaudeville, ca. 1920s.

On Church Avenue near Flatbush Avenue, B. S. Moss's location on a trolley line (see the car pulling into view at right) enabled it to draw audiences from outside the immediate area.

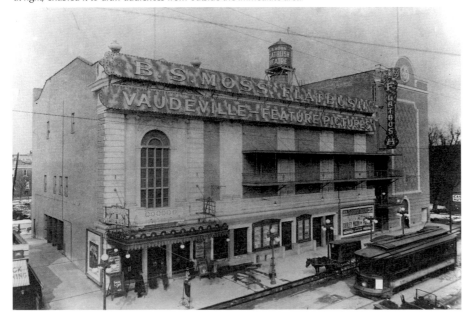

THE ORPHEUM

PERCY G. WILLIAMS, PRES'T & MANAGER.

FULTON STREET NEAR FLATBUSH AVE.

BROOKLYN.

THE CAST PUBLISHING CO. NEW YORK AND BROOKLYN.

Program from the Orpheum, 1901.

Lights beckoned audiences into the enormous, magnificently decorated interiors of the Orpheum, in downtown Brooklyn on Fulton Street near Flatbush Avenue.

Among the true vaudevillians was John W. Cooper, an African American ventriloquist who sometimes worked alongside his wife and was always accompanied by his dummy, Sam. Talented African Americans like Cooper were welcome on the vaudeville stage, even though African American patrons were barred from many Brooklyn playhouses and relegated to the galleries of others. Cooper performed at Brooklyn theaters as well as the Labor Lyceum, the Hotel St. George, and local churches. In 1897, a letter from the pastor of a Canarsie church mentioned that "Professor John Cooper, the well known colored ventriloquist, vocalist and Dialectician, gave one of his entertainments at our lunch on September 30, 1897 which was a grand success. He kept the audience in laughter from beginning to end." As did many other vaudevillians, Cooper used stock characters which would have been recognizable to his audience to represent large ethnic, social, and racial groups: A broadside dated February 16, 1898, for a benefit at the Central Baptist Mission of the Concord Baptist Church of Christ at Gates and Nostrand Avenues in Brooklyn announced that "Professor Cooper will furnish the audience with German, Irish, Italian and Yankee recitations." One of Cooper's most popular acts was "Fun in a Barber Shop," which created a sensation with audiences everywhere. Cooper appeared as a barber in a shop occupied by five cus-

THE GREAT COOPERS

Are offered as real artists—they amuse, entertain and mystify. For pleasing, refined and astonishing novelties they cannot be equaled. Mr. Cooper tells stories in dialect, tears beautiful designs from paper and does free-hand drawing. Not to hear Mr. Cooper and his mischievous boy "Sam" is to miss one of the greatest treats in the amusement world. He is an artist of natural talent and gained his high standing after years of success before the public.

Mrs. Cooper, while blindfolded, will tell the numbers placed on the blackboard, the kind of watch you carry, also the exact time of the same and many other wonderful feats.

Broadside, 1910s.

The Great Coopers' poster reveals the range of talent a vaudeville performer needed to be successful. Courtesy of Joan Cooper Maynard.

Sam, made by Theodore Mack, Chicago, ca. 1920s.

This ventriloquist's dummy once used by Brooklyn vaudevillian John W. Cooper is a different version of the Sam pictured in the Great Coopers' poster. Courtesy of Joan Cooper Maynard.

tomers, actually dummies he had rigged with wire and operated using five different voices.

Vaudeville was not the only show in town. By 1890, Brooklyn's many legitimate theaters, offering more strictly dramatic fare and mostly located near City Hall, offered musicals and drama to its middle- and upper-class patrons. The Park Theater, Brooklyn's first regular commercial playhouse, opened in 1863. Under the management of Col. William E. Sinn, who took over in 1875, it featured such celebrated tragedians of the day as Edwin Booth, Blanche Walsh, and Maurice Barrymore. The Majestic, now part of the Brooklyn Academy of Music, opened on Fulton Street in 1904 and gained a reputation as the most important "try-out" house for theatrical productions heading to Broadway. Immigrant theaters also sprang up throughout Brooklyn. They provided a link with native languages and cultures, like the traditional marionette theaters imported by immigrants from Italy. A writer for *Frank Leslie's Illustrated Newspaper* described attending such a theater at 35 Union Street (now West Carroll Gardens) in the October 25, 1890 issue: "Paying the sum of 5 cents, we pass through a small door . . . the sons of Italy crowd each other upon the narrow benches . . . the clientele of this house is . . . regular in attendance [since] one play runs for many nights." Brownsville, by the 1890s a neighborhood of largely Eastern European Jewish immigrants, had four concert halls that doubled as Yiddish theaters; all flourished into the 1940s.

Souvenir of Colonel Sinn's Park Theater, 1885.

In the heyday of Brooklyn theaters, manager-impresarios were personalities themselves. In 1875 the colorful Colonel Sinn took over the management of the Park Theater downtown, where traffic from busy department stores and city offices offered a good prospect for audiences. One of the city's legitimate theaters, its features included Shakespearean productions.

Vaudeville was finally eclipsed in the 1930s by the movie house, its rival even a decade before, although for a time vaudeville theaters also featured movies, and vice versa. Among the many movie theaters built across the country between World War I and the late 1920s, an exciting array appeared in Flatbush—in the early decades of the twentieth century a growing commercial and residential center—the Albermarle, Farragut, Flatbush, Linden, Rialto, Parkside, and Patio, all (except the Patio) built between 1915 and 1920. When Loew's Kings Theater opened there in 1929, the movie palace had arrived on Flatbush Avenue. Unlike more neighborhood theaters like the Albermarle or Farragut, the movie palaces were elaborate architectural affairs, some seating more than 1,500 people, and were designed to look extravagant and provide an environment that suggested opulence, all for a relatively low admission fee. Loew's—with its two lobby levels, promenades featuring art, and special sitting rooms—was grand.

In the 1950s, movie theaters fell on hard times, both in Brooklyn and across the United States, as everyone stayed home and watched television. Brooklyn also lost some of its population to the suburbs. In the 1950s and 1960s, many Brooklyn movie theaters adapted by hosting rock-and-roll shows. Anne Marie Barba Palone, the granddaughter of Rocco Yulo, who emigrated from Italy at the turn of the century (see Brooklynites chapter), remembers rock-and-roll shows at the Brooklyn Paramount in the 1950s, introduced by famous DJ Alan Freed. And

"The Smallest Theatre in the World—An Italian Play-House in Brooklyn," 1890.

In contrast to the elaborate buildings erected by big entertainment entrepreneurs, there were locally oriented immigrant theaters like this one at 35 Union Street near the waterfront in South Brooklyn, a working-class neighborhood. From *Frank Leslie's Illustrated Newspaper*, October 25, 1890.

Loew's Kings Theater, Flatbush, ca. 1920s.

Ostentation reached new levels in the interior of movie palaces like Loew's, which was far more plush than ordinary local movie houses.

The Paramount, ca. 1940s.

Rock-and-roll rang out from the Brooklyn Paramount when groups like the Platters and Bill Haley and the Comets played Brooklyn. When teens were out of school, the theater offered five performances a day. At Flatbush Avenue Extension and DeKalb Avenue, the Paramount was converted into a gymnasium, part of the Long Island University's Brooklyn campus.

Program, *Alan Freed Easter Jubilee,* 1957, and *Sid Bernstein Presents the Easter Parade of Stars,* 1961.

Held at the Brooklyn Paramount, pioneering disc jockey and concert promoter Alan Freed's Easter Jubilee featured such stars as the Cleftones, Bo Diddley, the G Clefs, the Harptones, and the Solitaires. The *New York Daily Mirror* claimed 90,000 teenagers a week "jam the Brooklyn Paramount" for one of Freed's shows.

she recalls trips to the theater from her home in Midwood: "On Saturday mornings we would take the train to DeKalb Avenue and line up on Flatbush Avenue with our sandwiches in hand waiting for tickets to the next show while police on horseback would keep the crowds of loud teenagers from becoming too unruly. Once inside the theater I was like all the other screaming fans watching my favorite rock-and-roll singers. We saw the most popular groups like the Penguins sing their hit song 'Earth Angel' or the Moonglows' 'Sincerely' or the Cadillacs with hits like 'Down the Road' and 'Speedoo' and singer LaVern Baker sing 'Tweedle-Dee.'" The Bedford, the Fox, and the Paramount featured acts like Little Anthony and the Imperials, Bo Diddley, and the Shirelles. For Palone's generation these Brooklyn theaters hold a special place in their memories of growing up.

While commercial entertainments enjoyed a huge and wide following, one of the most appealing things about Brooklyn is the way Brooklynites have fashioned forms of entertainment from the urban fabric—streets, buildings, and stoops. Children often are the most creative. In April 1846, *Brooklyn Daily Eagle* editor Walt Whitman wrote that "toward sundown of a pleasant day, in the streets adjacent to the Heights, hundreds of these boys and girls come forth to play on the walks in front." Especially in densely packed residential areas, where stuffy tenements lacked privacy, the street offered a sense of release and freedom. In 1891, folklorist Stewart Culin's "Street Games of Boys in Brooklyn, N.Y." in the *Journal of American Folk-Lore* suggested that children had made the city itself an integral part of their games: "The games of which I shall give an account are all boys' games or games in which both boys and girls participate, and were all described to me by a lad of ten years, residing in the city of Brooklyn, N.Y., as games in which he himself had taken part. They are all games played in the streets, and some of them may be recognized as having been modified to suit the circumstances of city life, where paved streets and iron lamp-posts and telegraph poles take the place of the village common, fringed with forest trees, and Nature, trampled on and suppressed, most vividly reasserts herself in the shouts of the children."

Culin described games in which the players needed no money and creatively incorporated elements of street life (including the weather). They played arrow chase "on a cold morning, when boys wish to play some game in order to keep warm;" the "side that starts first" had to mark on the pavement the direction of the course, and the other side followed after "five minutes have elapsed," promising a brisk run. In "I Spy," or "hide-and-seek," the block became the boundary, and players hid behind its stoops and other architectural features. Using vacant lots for ball games, a lamppost as home base, discarded items like old rubber hose as wickets, or stoops as hiding places, the children whom Culin described in 1891 made the city into a fantastic playground. Street games still are an important part of children's life in the city. Stickball, stoop ball, double dutch, skateboarding, hopscotch, or skelly require little planning or equipment. And everything is

The Saloon

Through much of the nineteenth century, the neighborhood saloon was the Brooklyn workingman's club, offering freedom from both workplace constraints and crowded tenements along with fellowship, gossip, and tips on new job opportunities or places to live. In this photograph of Charles Schindler's saloon from around 1890, beer-truck men stand at the bar. As the handwritten scrawl on the back of the photograph notes, "Drinks for them, no doubt, 'on the house.'" Notedly, these largely male preserves were frequently under attack from the temperance movement, which was largely staffed by women.

Saloons played an important role in Brooklyn's nineteenth-century Irish community, where they often served as gathering places for political discussions and events. Though many Brooklyn Irish Americans have long since moved on to Queens and the suburbs, pockets of residents remain in places like Gerritsen Beach, Flatbush, Windsor Terrace, and Park Slope—where Farrell's flourishes, one of the last great Irish saloons. Opened in 1933, it has kept the aura of an old-time bar: polished brass,

polished wood, and a general spit-and-polish cleanliness. In the morning, as retired men stop in to chat with friends, Farrell's takes on the ambience of a social club. In the evening, it attracts mostly police, fire fighters, and some Park Slope professionals.

Schindler's Saloon, ca. 1890.

Street scene, Clinton Hill, ca. 1920s.

On a hot city street in the summer, a gushing pipe becomes a private sprinkler.

Children playing skelly, 1982.

Also called skelsies or skellycaps, depending on the neighborhood and even the block, skelly can be played almost anytime, anywhere, with few supplies—the quintessential city game. Any number of kids can play, shooting markers (an old bottle cap, for instance) around a numbered court drawn onto a sidewalk or street. © Martha Cooper/CityLore.

portable, should other games or traffic compete for space. The city has always provided unique materials for children's games—manhole covers, fire escapes, stoops, vacant lots—and derives some of its character and vitality from their play.

Residents have adapted Brooklyn to their own needs in hundreds of ways that take advantage of the city's verticality, architecture, and abandoned infrastructure. High above the crowded streets, city roofs become private refuges for those who enjoy the urban sport of pigeon flying, especially popular among Italian and Puerto Rican residents. The hundreds of birds that spread out across the city from rooftop coops seem to enlarge their keepers' worlds, as they watch the birds fly into an open, expansive sky high above crowded urban streets and neighborhoods. Sometimes, discarded spaces are recycled, like the abandoned railroad tracks in Bensonhurst that have become a boccie court for elderly men or the abandoned lot on Columbia Street in South Brooklyn that serves as a kind of urban front yard for *casitas*, the small wooden structures that mimic Puerto Rican country cottages and serve here as informal clubhouses. Vacant lots, piers, bridges, promenades, rooftops, stoops, and sidewalks become places to relax and socialize. The perennial stage for block parties, community celebrations, and religious festivals, the streets themselves can be the liveliest places in the borough as Brooklynites make their own fun and make Brooklyn uniquely their own.

1947
WORLD SERIES

Dodgers Yankees

LON KELLER

World Series program, 1947.

This Dodgers-Yankees program pictures many of the institutions and aspects of Brooklyn life that, like the Dodgers, had their roots in nineteenth-century urbanization: from Borough Hall, *top right*, to industrial growth, represented by the Gowanus Canal, *center right*, and the Navy Yard, *top left*. (As for the series, the Dodgers lost.)

The Brooklyn Dodgers

W hen the Brooklyn Dodgers faced the New York Yankees in the 1947 World Series, the cover of the home team's program deployed the rich imagery of its borough. Here were the icons of Brooklyn's illustrious history: the massive Brooklyn Navy Yard; the elegant Grand Army Plaza; Henry Ward Beecher's Plymouth Church; Coney Island's world of pleasure; and—of course—a trolley. At dead center, a baseball bat pierced an arch of the Brooklyn Bridge, and of course "Dodgers" in bold letters dominated "Yankees." (Every fan knows, though, that their "Bums" didn't emerge as series winners that year.)

By identifying the Dodgers with Brooklyn's most visible symbols, promoters recognized that the team was something of an icon itself. By the time the team won the 1955 World Series, more than a century after baseball had its beginnings in Brooklyn and neighboring Manhattan, Ebbets Field had become a shrine of concrete and steel in central Brooklyn. In their "golden years," the 1940s and 1950s, players like Jackie Robinson, Duke Snider, Gil Hodges, Pee Wee Reese, Ralph Branca, Carl Erksine, Clem Labine, Johnny Podres, and Roy Campanella generated an extraordinary level of adoration and identification. To many minds, the Dodgers and Brooklyn were inseparable.

The phenomenon known as the Brooklyn Dodgers seemed to have an impact on every aspect of city life. Stories of Dodger feats appeared in all the city papers, distributed on newsstands from Crown Heights to Dyker Heights, from Carroll Gardens to Coney Island. And a Dodger win was especially good for business. Former Brooklyn resident Charles Hummel recalls that at his in-laws' stationery store and ice cream parlor in Bensonhurst, they "sold twice, sometimes three times as many papers in the morning when the Dodgers won." With the advent of radio broadcasting of games in 1939, accounts of the team's exploits reached with a new immediacy into the homes of thousands of Brooklynites. Tuning their kitchen radios to a night game at Ebbets Field, fans heard Red Barber's familiar drawl and colorful play-by-play commentary. And in neighborhoods throughout Brooklyn, youngsters played stickball—essentially baseball of the streets—and imagined they were Dodger players.

The Dodgers drew people together, whether it was a crowd of thirty thousand on an August night at Ebbets Field or subway straphangers discussing a recent game as they barreled along on the IND. As the October 13, 1941 issue of

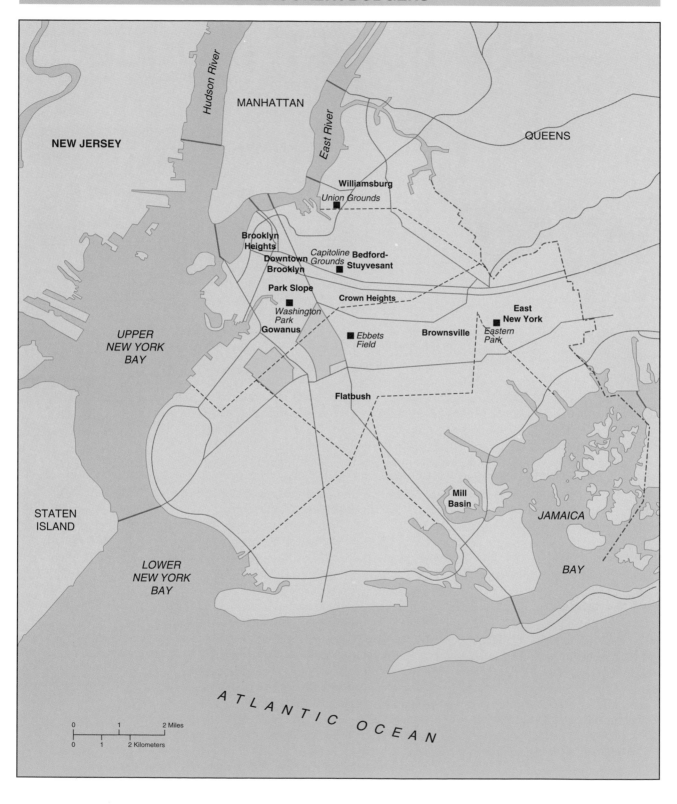

NEW JERSEY

MANHATTAN

QUEENS

Hudson River

East River

Williamsburg

Union Grounds

Brooklyn Heights

Capitoline Grounds

Bedford-Stuyvesant

Downtown Brooklyn

Park Slope

Crown Heights

Washington Park

Gowanus

Ebbets Field

East New York

Brownsville

Eastern Park

UPPER NEW YORK BAY

Flatbush

Mill Basin

JAMAICA

BAY

STATEN ISLAND

LOWER NEW YORK BAY

ATLANTIC OCEAN

0   1   2 Miles
0   1   2 Kilometers

Life Magazine put it, love of the Dodgers conquered all. "As the World Series with the American League's Champion [New York] Yankees progressed, it became evident that loyalty to the Dodgers is perhaps the most powerful emotion man can experience," *Life* observed. "It is an emotion that blurs all political, racial, and geographical lines." A bombastic statement—the team was still segregated in 1941—but it conveys the level of team spirit that united so many.

The metropolis may have lost its independence in 1898, but the presence of a professional baseball team meant that Brooklyn still enjoyed some of the formal trappings of citydom. The very evolution of baseball in nineteenth-century Brooklyn was connected to its growth as a city. As the pace of urbanization picked up at midcentury, the intense preoccupation with business that characterized rising commercial life in the city was, some feared, creating a sedentary population. As a healthy form of outdoor exercise, baseball seemed the perfect antidote. And so it flourished, first as an amateur sport, later increasingly professionalized, but prospering in nineteenth-century Brooklyn precisely because it *was* a city, with a large population that could consistently draw enough players and audiences. Baseball was also tied to the city's infrastructure. Influenced by real-estate moguls and transit-company owners, teams played and ballparks were built close to transportation networks and centers of population. Ultimately, these very elements played a major role in the Dodgers' departure.

As popular as the team was, some Brooklynites were not fans, and the team's relationship with the borough was not always tension-free. Nonetheless, the Dodgers did come to symbolize an aspect of Brooklyn, so when the team left for Los Angeles in 1957, at the very heart of its departure lay issues of identity and loyalty. To legions of Brooklynites, the move symbolized the apparently troubled state of their borough. Brooklyn was beginning to experience wrenching changes as people and businesses left. Borough residents had been deeply shaken when longtime Brooklyn institutions such as the *Brooklyn Daily Eagle* and the Brooklyn Navy Yard folded, the paper in 1955, the yard in 1966. Their city seemed to be falling apart.

In recent years a new generation of Brooklynites has pulled the borough out of the downward spiral that was driven by the postwar exodus to the suburbs and the decline of industry in America's older, northern cities. Today's Brooklyn is different from the one where the Dodgers flourished, but its residents have no less vitality and creativity. This strong, diverse community is responsible for the residential, economic, and cultural revival that is taking place.

Brooklyn may no longer have a major-league baseball team, but it has a proud history that lives in people's memories and in things left behind—souvenirs and echoes of ways of life long gone . . . the stirring monument to James Creighton, baseball's first superstar, that stands in Green-Wood Cemetery . . . a Jackie Robinson baseball card that speaks silently of a childhood spent rooting for the Dodgers . . . a lone base from Ebbets Field that brings back the crack of the bat and the roar of the fans.

Baseball's Roots in Brooklyn

Caleb Sniffen, third base. William Bliss, left field. A. Gildersleeves, right field. William Babcock, pitcher. Members of Brooklyn's Atlantic Base Ball Club whose names few would recognize today. But throughout the 1850s and 1860s, baseball players like these were personalities whose actions on the field were chronicled by the local and national press. They were present at the birth of baseball.

Sporting-goods magnate Albert G. Spalding was wrong when he claimed in 1907 that baseball was invented by General Abner Doubleday in Cooperstown, New York, in 1839. Spalding hoped to prove that baseball was an all-American sport without foreign influences. Not only was baseball not born in rural America, but its roots lay outside the country in the English game of rounders. In Brooklyn very early teams played cricket—cricket had been played in the eighteenth century and by 1855 was more popular than baseball—but it eventually died out in part because baseball was easier to play and because cricket was seen as an English, not an American, game.

A growing interest in sports began to emerge around the middle of the century. The industrial revolution improved standards of living and more clearly demarcated work time and other time; simultaneously, the fast-growing commercial sector in cities created a growing sedentary population of office workers and professionals—that is, circumstances perfectly combined to nurture both an audience for spectator sports and men eager to get out on the field. In 1858, the *Brooklyn Daily Eagle* explained the rise of baseball on similar grounds:

> The newspapers lamented the physical degeneracy of the people and generally attributed it to the over-exertion of the intellect and the disuse of the muscular system . . . leading to innumerable diseases of body and mind. . . .
>
> Something of the truth of these homilies seemed to impress itself on the popular mind; and all at once the rage—for it can hardly be called by a more sober term—for field sports seized on the male portion of the community; and base ball clubs sprang up with marvellous rapidity all over the city. Their games have been attended by large crowds of spectators and it became evident that a great popular want was being supplied by these clubs.

Baseball emerged as an organized American sport in Brooklyn and Manhattan through the numerous amateur clubs that sprang up in the decade or so after 1845, teams like the Atlantics of Bedford, the Excelsiors of South Brooklyn, and Williamsburg's Eckfords. By 1858 more than 125 teams had formed in the metropolitan area, 71 in Brooklyn and 25 in Manhattan, up from only a dozen in 1855.

At first, these early Brooklyn athletes were men who played for sociability (some ball clubs emerged out of existing men's social clubs) and exercise and had jobs flexible enough to permit a game of ball on a workday afternoon. Manhattan's players tended to be lawyers, doctors, and merchants—men occupying the higher rungs on the social ladder—as well as shopkeepers and clerks. Players for Manhattan's Knickerbockers, baseball's first team, were largely prosperous, middle-class New Yorkers, some well-to-do. Brooklyn players, on the other hand, were a mixture of craftsmen and a variety of white collar workers—certainly a more democratic lot than their New York counterparts. The Eckfords, a Brooklyn team that organized about 1854, consisted of shipwrights and mechanics.

The Eckfords' team name poses an interesting view into the team's sense of its own identity. The name referred to Henry Eckford (1775–1832), a Scottish immigrant famous as a shipbuilder and as one of the richest men in New York City. Eckford had strong Brooklyn connections. His shipyards near the Brooklyn Navy

Yard built vessels for the navy during the War of 1812. Appointed naval constructor at the Brooklyn Navy Yard in 1817, he built half a dozen line-of-battle ships based on models he had devised. Back in his own yards, Eckford gained more renown as the builder of the *Robert Fulton,* whose pioneering steam voyage (in 1822) from New York to New Orleans and Havana was a widely celebrated technical achievement.

But what endeared Eckford to baseball players establishing a team some twenty years after his death? Was it the neighborhood tie? The Eckfords played in Williamsburg, even though some of the team lived in New York City. Did the shipwrights identify with him as their most successful colleague? Perhaps it was all of these.

If the Eckfords suggest the class makeup of Brooklyn baseball, the Excelsiors, also founded in 1854 and Brooklyn's first organized team, reflect baseball's shift from an amateur to a professional sport during the late 1850s and 1860s, which was accompanied by a new emphasis on winning and a surge in the game's popularity. As the Excelsiors increasingly focused on winning games and fans, between 1857 and 1860 the team revamped itself, adding new, better players. Though still considered largely a social club (whose rowhouse headquarters at 133 Clinton Street still stands), the team paid more attention to talent during player selection. In a formal studio portrait made about this time, players clutch their equipment—a bat, a ball, a cap—in much the same way industrial workers held the tools of their trade in similar photographs.

That talent was becoming a major criterion for membership was apparent in the Excelsiors' selection of James Creighton, brought on the team in 1860 to make an already good squad more competitive. The club either paid him or found him a job as a way of compensating him for his efforts. Creighton became baseball's first professional player, and this unprecedented arrangement changed the nature of the game.

Excelsior Club of Brooklyn, 1860.

At midcentury one of the best teams in the metropolitan area, the Excelsiors sport dark pants, bowties and fancy E's on their white shirts, a look patterned after Manhattan's Knickerbockers, baseball's pioneer team. Courtesy of the Brooklyn Public Library—Brooklyn Collection.

GREAT BASE BALL MATCH BETWEEN THE ATLANTIC AND ECKFORD CLUBS OF BROOKLYN, AT THE UNION BASE BALL GROUNDS, BROOKLYN, E. D., OCT. 21, WITH PORTRAITS OF THE LEADING PLAYERS OF THE PRINCIPAL CLUBS OF NEW YORK, BROOKLYN AND NEWARK.

"Great Base Ball Match," 1865.

This spread from *Frank Leslie's Illustrated Newspaper,* November 4, 1865, draws together numerous elements of baseball. *Around the perimeter,* leading players strike poses; *right,* newspaper mastheads and a portrait of Brooklyn's Henry Chadwick pay homage to sportswriters; *top,* a shrouded, deceased baseball star Jim Creighton. On the field, the Atlantics beat the Eckfords in the world's championship, thirty-eight to eight.

Creighton quickly rose to star status. The nineteen-year-old fired a mean curve ball and was "celebrated," according to the *Brooklyn Daily Eagle* on July 28, 1862, "for his great speed and the perfect command of the ball in delivery." Later that year, the young pitcher collapsed during a game—the *Eagle* surmised he ruptured his bladder taking a powerful swing at a ball—and died a few days later. Enshrined as a hero in the popular press and illustrated newspapers of the time, Creighton was buried in Green-Wood Cemetery, his monument crowned by a giant baseball and adorned with crossed bats, a baseball cap, base, and scorebook.

Besides hiring baseball's first professional player and superstar, the Excelsiors started another trend that shaped baseball's course. In 1860, they made the game's first road trip, a two-week tour to western New York where they were paired with less experienced teams and won all six games. They returned to a major event, a championship game against Bedford's Atlantics in the era's forerunner of the World Series (which didn't start until 1903). In a two-out-of-three contest, the first game was a rout. The Atlantics lost, twenty-three to four, before a crowd of about seven thousand.

The Excelsiors then ventured as far south as Baltimore, beating hometown teams along the way. On their return they suited up against the Atlantics again: The Atlantics won the second game, and the third was called off in midgame when the Excelsior captain pulled his team from the field to protest unruly behavior by the Atlantics and their fans—even though the Excelsiors were leading eight to six. In the midst of this championship play in which no one emerged a victor, the Excelsiors' tours launched the sport toward becoming national, rather than purely local, contests, and set baseball's direction. In 1862, the *Brooklyn Daily Eagle* noted that "nowhere has the National game of Baseball taken a firmer hold than in Brooklyn and nowhere are there better ballplayers." Even discounting the *Eagle's* boosterism, Brooklyn in fact had the best teams during the 1850s and 1860s. Here was an area in which Brooklyn was not the underdog in its longstanding competition with Manhattan. The local paper crowed, "If we are ahead of the big city [Manhattan] in nothing else, we can beat her in baseball."

With better teams and more intense competition, baseball was developing into an enormously popular spectator sport. The earliest contests were played on open multipurpose fields. William Babcock, one-time pitcher for the Atlantics, reminisced in 1884 that the team used to play on "old lots on York Street," a location not far from the Brooklyn Navy Yard. As a regular feature, the *Brooklyn Evening Star* printed lists of contests in Williamsburg, Greenpoint, and Bedford, suggesting the extensive activity and diverse locations of games on any given summer day. As baseball's popularity continued to grow and crowds swelled, fields were often converted into enclosed wooden ballparks. These enclosed parks were commercial endeavors, built and owned by business entrepreneurs who rented to the teams and often took a share of the gate receipts as well.

Brooklyn's first ballpark was Williamsburg's Union Grounds, bounded by Marcy Avenue, Rutledge Street, Lynch Street, and Harrison Avenue, just east of Lee Avenue. (The site today is part of the neighborhood that is home to the Satmarer Hasidic community.) Originally a skating rink, the "Union Base Ball Grounds" opened in 1862 with a ten-cent admission fee. Owner William Cammeyer allowed three clubs to play there rent-free as long as he pocketed the profits. *Frank Leslie's Illustrated Newspaper* printed a view of the grounds during an October 13 championship game between the Atlantic and Eckford clubs in a November 1865 article. Located near residential buildings and tenements, it was a spacious area surrounded by a wooden fence, over which throngs of people managed to peer at the players. The success of the Union Grounds inspired the 1864 conversion of the Capitoline Skating Grounds in what is today Bedford–Stuyvesant into a ball field.

Tickets to the Capitoline Skating Pond, 1864–65.

These tickets gave bearers admittance to the Capitoline Skating Pond, used as a ball field in warmer months beginning in 1864.

Carnival of the Washington Skating Club, lithograph by G. E. Jones, 1862.

On a site that later became the Dodgers' first ball field, members of the Washington Skating Club twirl and spin at a rink in what is today considered the lower section of Park Slope. Baseball on ice, a short-lived fad of the 1860s and 1870s, was also enjoyed at the skating pond. The Vechte-Cortelyou House is at right.

(The land had once been part of the huge Lefferts family farm.) By August 1865, the *New York Herald* was calling the Capitoline Grounds the "most extensive and complete ball grounds in the United States." Others soon followed. In the off-season the parks often reverted to ice-skating rinks or race courses. The Union Grounds, for instance, continued to be used by the Union Skating club as a rink through the 1870s.

Given that none of the ballparks were covered over, Nature frequently intervened, threatening spectators' comfort and disrupting play. In many early ballparks, fans who could pay extra sat in pavilions and were somewhat sheltered from sun and rain. Most patrons sat or stood in an open grandstand area, where, like the players on the field, they were exposed to the elements. At a match at the Union Grounds on July 9, 1867, a crowd of more than three thousand turned out for the first game of the series between the champion Atlantics and the Eckford club. At the start of the fifth inning "a dark and threatening cloud was observed rising in the west," which, noted the *Brooklyn Daily Times*, "admonished players and spectators to be on their guard, or they would get a wet jacket." The ensuing panic over the weather ruined the game. "In order to make it a game before the shower," recounted the paper, "play was pushed, and by over-eagerness on the part of the Eckfords, they indulged in some wild throwing." The game continued, but as the Eckfords took the field for the seventh inning, "it was found impossible to play from the wind and dust, so the game was called by the umpire."

In its early years, baseball was a hitter's game. There was no ball-strike count and no gloves, and batters could virtually call their pitches. Forty runs in one game were not uncommon, and many players could not resist gambling on an apparent sure thing. When the second game of the 1860 championship series between the Atlantics and Excelsiors ended in a close final score, fifteen to twelve, the *Brooklyn Evening Star* "hoped that the score will frighten the Base Ball players from betting any more," less on moral than on practical grounds. The practice "should be discountenanced because if this very popular game is ever to lose its favor in the eyes of the public it will be by betting alone." The public was not in a moral position to cast the first stone, though. In the case of the third game of the series—when the Excelsior captain pulled his team off the field in protest of unruliness—much of the problem came from the fans, who harassed the umpires and Excelsior players after close calls. The police at the game could barely keep the crowd under control.

An artist who attended an 1866 championship game between Brooklyn's Atlantics and the Athletics of Philadelphia captured some of the typical antics in the stands. The scene is one of constant motion—a young boy carrying a basket of cakes and drinks for sale, which a fan upsets as he staggers by; a top-hatted gentleman choking a fellow spectator; a stumbling drunk; and two sports exchanging money—no doubt a bet on the game's outcome.

As rowdy as it was, by the 1860s, baseball was booming. As the number of games, teams, and players increased, so did spectatorship and newspaper coverage. People were eager to read about what was happening on the fields of Brooklyn and elsewhere. Taking advantage of new technology that quickly relayed scores and betting odds from city to city by telegraph, newspapers became home to a new breed of sportswriters. These writers developed a colorful baseball jargon to describe the action, kept box scores and statistics, and published a checkerboard of weekly team standings. At a time when all the games were played in daylight and there was no other source of news, next-day reporting on the games became an important dimension of the sport. Baseball reportage appeared not only in local papers like the *Brooklyn Daily Eagle* and the *New York Times*, but also in national illustrated publications such as *Harper's Weekly* and *Frank Leslie's Illustrated Newspaper*. Reporters thus played an important role in popularizing the game and the players; they brought paying fans to the ballparks as well as to the newsstands.

Detail of *The Second Grand Match Game for the Championship between the Athletic Base Ball Club of Philadelphia and the Atlantics of Brooklyn . . . October 22, 1866* by J. L. Magee, lithograph, 1867.

The wooden chairs at this championship match are a sign of the impermanence of early games. Considered too boisterous for women, club owners later made attempts to clean up games so that they could create an atmosphere "suitable" for women and draw bigger gate receipts. Courtesy of the Racquet and Tennis Club, New York.

Constitution and By-Laws of the National Association of Base Ball Players, with the Rules and Regulations of the Game of Base Ball; Beadle's Dime Base-Ball Player; 1903 photograph of Henry Chadwick; and Spalding's umpire's counter.

"The Father of Baseball," Brooklyn sportswriter Henry Chadwick edited *Beadle's Dime Base-Ball Player,* which helped regulate a fledgling American sport. The umpire's counter, which counted balls and strikes and belonged to Chadwick, was another in a series of efforts to regulate the game. Chadwick also chaired the rules committee of the National Association of Base Ball Players. Chadwick photograph and umpire's counter courtesy of the Family of Henry Chadwick.

Brooklyn's own Henry Chadwick, an English-born writer for dailies and journals and an editor of leading baseball guides, became the game's first celebrity writer. His name and baseball's evolution, particularly its rules, are practically synonymous. Chadwick influenced the professionalization of baseball, heading the committee of the National Association of Base Ball Players that formulated rules to standardize the game. A mix of delegates from Brooklyn and New York, the NABBP was formed in 1858 and met annually for thirteen years to revise rules, settle disputes, and control the game's development. Chadwick also wrote and edited *Beadle's Dime Base-Ball Player,* an annual guide, in the early 1860s; edited *Spalding's Official Base Ball Guide* from 1881 to 1908; invented the box score; and developed the batting average.

Baseball's popularity continued during the Civil War, although no aspect of life could be unaffected by such a terrible and bloody conflict. When Confederates fired on Fort Sumter in 1861, people expected the war to last only weeks; instead it dragged on for four years. On the battlefield 140,414 men lost their lives, and another 224,097 died from wounds and disease. But even at the height of the hostilities, the *Brooklyn Daily Eagle* on March 17, 1864 professed that it saw no reason to believe that baseball's appeal was on the wane—although it did note a slight decline in attendance. "To outsiders such a result would imply a sad falling off in the popularity of the game, but when it is considered that at no time since the game became a national pastime were there greater crowds of spectators present at matches than last season, thereby showing that the game is just as popular as ever and also, that for the past three seasons, base ball has had to contend with obstacles resulting from the war, that would have entirely destroyed any less . . . popular sport." Baseball fans even helped to support the war effort. Reporting on a game at the Union Grounds between the Atlantics and the Eckfords, the *Sunday Mercury* noted that "a small entrance fee for the privilege of entering the ground was charged, for the benefit of the Sanitary Commission [the organization that helped sick or wounded Union soldiers] and perhaps a couple of thousand persons contributed their might to this patriotic purpose."

The famed Atlantics were one of the teams that hung on through the war years; in November 1865, just seven months after war's end, *Harper's Weekly* ran

Champion Nine of the Atlantics, 1865.

Marking the growing national interest in baseball, *Harper's Weekly* devoted almost a full page of its November 25, 1865 issue to "the nine members of the Atlantic Base-Ball Club in Brooklyn who were engaged in the recent contest for the championship with the members of the Athletic Club of Philadelphia." The Atlantics, who had on their roster quite a few Irish immigrants, won two matches in a row.

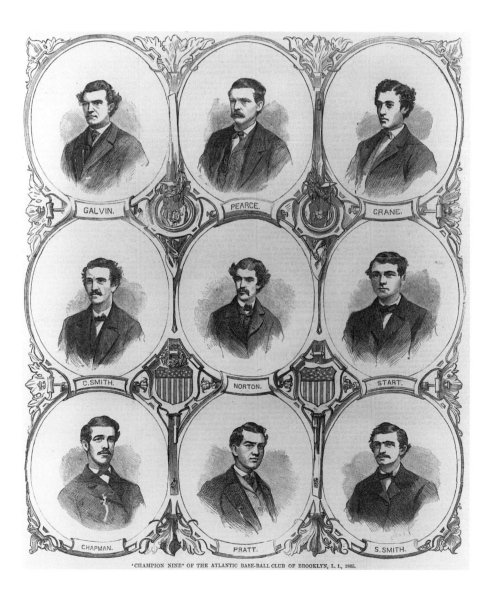

"CHAMPION NINE" OF THE ATLANTIC BASE-BALL CLUB OF BROOKLYN, L. I., 1865.

The Brooklyn Dodgers

individual pictures of team members in formal attire. Fresh from trouncing the Philadelphia Athletics in a championship game, the team also received a gentle roasting in "Corry O'Lanus' Epistle," a regular column in the *Eagle,* on September 4, 1865:

> Dear Eagle:
>
> > I am beginning to take an interest in our national game.
> > Which is base ball.
> > Our noble city, third in population and first in Base Ball, has been glorified in field sports by the Atlantic Club, who have whipped everything in the Ball line.
> > As a Brooklynite, I am proud of the Altantics.
> > There are nine of them.
> > They are wonderfully smart fellows. Stand six feet two in their stockings, can run two miles a minute, jump over a forty foot fence, or through a knot hole, turn a somersault and catch anything from a base ball to the measles.
> > They are an honor to Brooklyn.

After the war, the Atlantics added a few paid players; there was also a split between the ballplayers and the social club that sponsored the team. Nevertheless, the Atlantics went on to great renown for ending the sixty-nine-game winning streak of the Cincinnati Red Stockings, baseball's first entirely professional team, at the Union Grounds in 1870.

Highly competitive and commercialized, baseball by the end of the 1860s was dominated by paid professional players earning good salaries. Audiences were paying to watch games and expected players to take competition seriously. On June 19, 1869, an *Eagle* writer, after attending a game at which a country team slaughtered Brooklyn, lodged a complaint on behalf of paying customers.

> The time has gone by when late hours can be kept by the players and stimulating liquors indulged in to within a few hours of the match with the expectation of winning. . . . Those who would excel, or who would be at the top, must train for it. . . . Will our ball players accept the lesson they have learned within the last week? . . . Our ball players—the professionals—will have to do it in order to please the public. It may be asked, "What have the public to do with it?" It has just this—inasmuch as the money which they pay to obtain admittance to the ball-grounds goes to the support of the players and puts them in the light of men purchasing amusement, and the players in the light of exhibitors of their skill, they have a right to demand the best exhibition that can be afforded them.

Just when baseball was established as a paying, potentially lucrative sport, African Americans were formally excluded from it. Racial discrimination and economics lay behind the move, for the practice occurred in other sports, too, as a way to protect job opportunities. In the early years of horse racing, for instance, many Black people were jockeys, but they were increasingly excluded after the Civil War as the sport became more profitable. In 1867, the National Association of Base Ball Players (NABBP) voted to bar the admission of any club with one or more African American members from participating in its new professional league, using the highly prejudiced and spurious argument that "if colored clubs were admitted there would be in all probability some division of feelings, whereas by excluding them no injury could result to anybody, and the possibility of any rupture being created on political grounds, would be avoided." By this time, the clubs were already unofficially segregated, as the *Brooklyn Standard Union* indicated on October 4, 1867: "The contest for the championship of the colored clubs, played yesterday on the Satellite Grounds, attracted the largest crowd this season, half of whom were white people." Even though the NABBP folded several years later, most of its successors continued to exclude Black players through tacit consent. By 1887, when the International League banned any new contracts with African Americans, the color line was firmly drawn. It would be over three decades before Black players had a flourishing league of their own, the Negro National League, and sixty years before Jackie Robinson would cross the line that had been drawn so many years before in a blatant act of bigotry.

Brooklyn and New York dominated professional ball until 1869, when the Cincinnati Red Stockings went undefeated and won baseball's championship, cementing the sport's national scope and appeal. Baseball's amateur era came to a close with the formation of the National Association of Professional Base Ball Players in 1871, and its successor, the National League of Professional Ball Clubs in 1876. Baseball as business was the name of the game, and the overall aim was to make it pay.

The Bushwicks

As baseball turned pro during the late nineteenth century, dozens of Brooklyn semiprofessional teams made up of "part-time" paid players also came into being. Among the greatest were the Bushwicks, considered the finest semipro team in the country during the 1930s.

They played at the 17,000-seat Dexter Park (also known as Bushwick Park and Sterling Oval), right across the Brooklyn/Queens border on Bushwick Avenue in Woodhaven, almost every weekend the site of games between the Bushwicks and Negro League teams. The park also was home to the Brooklyn Royal Giants for a time in the 1920s; the team's owner, Nat Strong, was also an owner in the Bushwicks. In one Bushwick–Royal Giants game in 1924, thirty-eight-year-old pitcher Joe Williams struck out twenty-five Bushwicks in twelve innings.

While the Bushwicks were well-known and even employed several future major leaguers, several factors probably led to the decline of theirs and similar clubs by the end of the 1940s, among them the advent of television and the expanded interest in intercollegiate baseball.

Bushwick manager Overton Tremper, who played briefly for the Dodgers in the 1920s, strikes a classic pose in this 1934 photograph. Photograph courtesy of the Brooklyn Public Library–Brooklyn Collection.

The Birth of the Dodgers

In 1883, the same year that Brooklynites gathered to cheer the completion of the Brooklyn Bridge, the Dodger club was born as a minor-league team. Largely a financial venture, the "Brooklyns," as the team was first known, were backed by New York realtor Charles Byrne; George J. Taylor, night editor of the *New York Herald*; Joseph Doyle, Byrne's brother-in-law; and Rhode Island gambling emporium owner Ferdinand Abell. Doyle hired Charles Ebbets, a young printer, to sell tickets, print score cards, and keep the books. The group leased land from Edwin Litchfield, the driving force behind Park Slope's large-scale residential development, and created the club's first home in Washington Park.

Located in Gowanus, near Third Street and Fourth Avenue, the site had historic associations. Where players tossed baseballs and lined up for batting practice, muskets had once sounded as soldiers fought the Revolutionary War's Battle of Long Island. Byrne's group commandeered the wooden addition to the late seventeenth-century Vechte-Cortelyou House nearby for a clubhouse; the farmhouse had at one point been occupied by British general Charles Cornwallis (see Brooklynites chapter).

Abell, Doyle, Byrne, and Taylor put the considerable sum of $30,000 into fixing up the promising site, which had the prime advantage of easy access—horse-car routes ran along Third and Fifth Avenues, for one—as well as a potential audience in an Irish community close by (many of the ball players were Irish). In its first year the team attracted a large following and won the pennant. Fired with enthusiasm, in 1884 the owners bought into one of the numerous fledgling major leagues with a franchise in the American Association, created in 1882 by beer barons who knew a captive audience when they saw one. Where the National League targeted a more middle-class audience, the American Association appealed to a working-class crowd which had less discretionary income and worked Saturdays by offering cheap tickets (twenty-five cents), Sunday games (the only full day off for most working-class people), and alcoholic beverages.

In their six seasons with the American Association, the team first became the Trolley Dodgers, the jibe Manhattanites used for Brooklynites, and later simply the Dodgers. (Among other nicknames, they were for a brief time also called the Bridegrooms, because six players were married during the 1888 season.) In 1890, the Dodgers switched to the National League and won the league pennant. In a move that pointed up the extent of economic war between early franchises, the Players, or Brotherhood, League, organized in Manhattan as a third major league in 1889. It was headed by businessmen and athletes whose intent was to both manage (a new concept—players as managers) and pull in profits; the new league raided National League and American Association teams for players. In Brooklyn, Flatbush businessman George Chauncey financed a Players League team for Brooklyn and built as its home Eastern Park in a sparsely populated Brownsville, where he had extensive real-estate holdings. Now there were three leagues, all pretending to be major, with a Brooklyn team in each. Even in the fourth-largest city in America, it was a bit too much. Interleague jumping and raiding was disastrous and one year later, the Players League folded.

In 1891, the American Association merged with the National League, and Players' owner George Chauncey arranged a merger of his team with the Dodgers. As part of the deal, the Dodgers (a.k.a. the Bridegrooms) left Washington Park for Eastern Park. The team's 1891 scorebook reflects its new location:

Eastern Parkway and Vesta Avenue (now Van Sinderen Avenue), as well as another permutation of the team's name.

Brownsville may not have been the best choice for an entertainment site. The local residents, mostly new immigrants, were not fans; rent was high; transportation to the park was poor; and many saw it as too far away. In a January 23, 1897 article the *Eagle* blasted owners for not offering more cheap seats, which would not only attract more people from the local community (many of whom were out of work, it noted) but increase profits and help the park compete with popular attractions, such as vaudeville. Twenty-five cents should be the price to see a game, they argued—"as much as baseball is worth to a good many citizens." Why would anyone choose baseball? queried the paper. Not only does it cost more but the "ball game is held on the outskirts of the town, the seats are hard, the stand is open to the wind and snow and rain, there are no reliefs of scenery or music—nothing but sandwiches and frankfurters—and no legal guarantee that a poor, spiritless show may not be given." In spite of such helpful advice, the team stayed in East New York for eight undistinguished years, struggling under three different managers as business fell.

In 1898 Charles Ebbets, who had risen to president and stockholder in the club, took his team back to a new Washington Park across the street from the old grounds. Demonstrating the interdependence of transportation interests, ball fields, and entertainment, the relocation was financed by several local transportation moguls, who saw the potential profit in having a popular destination like a baseball park along their streetcar lines. One of the major supporters was Cleveland's Al Johnson, who along with his brother Tom (the Ohio city's mayor) had already financed the development of trolley routes to Coney Island in the early to mid 1890s. Witnessing the masses of people who rode streetcars to games in Cleveland, where he had streetcar interests, had converted Johnson to the financial possibilities of such a move.

A year later, the whole team was reshuffled as a result of one of the idiosyncracies of late nineteenth-century ball—owners with stock in more than one ball club. Baltimore Oriole ball-club owner Harry B. Von der Horst, whose team was in decline, invested money and players in Brooklyn while retaining control of the Orioles. Von der Horst also transferred Orioles manager Edward "Ned" Hanlon, one of the most brilliant managers of late nineteenth-century ball, to Brooklyn, and Hanlon brought along some of his better players. The scheme paid off: The Brooklyn club won pennants in 1899 and (over the New York Giants) in 1900, the highest honors at the time.

Hanlon's successes earned the team a new nickname, the "Superbas," after a popular vaudeville act, "Hanlon's Superbas," a name that stuck well into the teens. In a set of 208 gold-bordered baseball cards issued in 1911 by ten cigarette companies as promotional giveaways, a large B for Brooklyn shares billing with the name "Superbas."

Flying the pennant, 1900.

Brooklyn wins the pennant over New York in 1900, celebrated on the cover of *Golden Hours* magazine for July 14. The small portraits include players which former Orioles manager Ned Hanlon had transferred up—slugger Joe Kelly, batting champion Wee Willie Keeler, and shortstop Hughie Jennings. Hanlon himself, *lower left,* shakes hands across home plate with Giants manager Buck Ewing, who sports a tremendous walrus moustache.

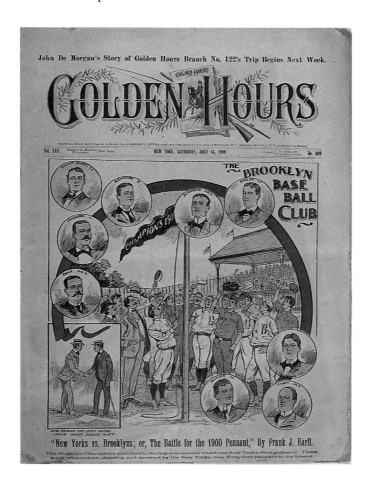

Brooklyn Superbas tobacco cards, 1910s.

Tobacco companies distributed the first baseball cards in cigarette packs. One company—Allen and Gintner—used them to replace the pictures of young women that were the usual promotional giveaway. Beautifully printed in rich color, these bits of ephemera helped spread the cult of personality that surrounded such baseball players as those on Ned Hanlon's Brooklyn Superbas.

Charles Byrne had died in 1898, and in 1902, Charles Ebbets bought out the rest of his partners and became the Dodgers' principal owner. That year the Brooklyn roster was looted by the upstart American League, and for the next thirteen years, the Dodgers never finished in the first division. The great teams of Brooklyn's nemesis, New York, helped keep the Dodgers alive. Attracted by the long-simmering interborough rivalry, fans filled the park, and those without tickets lined the tops of tenement roofs beyond the outfield fences.

As the Dodgers foundered, one of the most brilliant teams in the country was born—the Brooklyn Royal Giants. The team was founded in 1904 by John W. Connor, the Black proprietor of the Royal Cafe at 176 Myrtle Avenue in Brooklyn, who thought a Black team would be good for business and for the borough. To create a foundation for the fledgling team, he hired greats like shortstop Grant Johnson and catcher Bruce Petway, who had been attending college in Nashville. The team operated primarily as a traveling team until July 1912, when Connor announced that the team would play as the home team on Sunday afternoons at Brooklyn's Washington Park. In 1913 Connor sold the team to Nat Strong, a white booking agent. The club continued to thrive, adding pitching ace "Cannonball" Dick Redding and others in the 1920s. Another famous Negro League team, the Brooklyn Eagles (who rented Ebbets Field for home games), played for only one season in the borough before leaving for Newark, New Jersey, in 1935.

The Brooklyn Dodgers

The Brooklyn Royal Giants, 1917.

In a photograph taken at Washington Park—where the team played on Sundays—members of the Brooklyn Royal Giants pose with owner Nat Strong (*top left*) and Max Rosner (*top right*), an associate of Strong in ownership of the semipro Bushwicks. Seated in the front row, *left*, is famous catcher and slugger Louis Santop. His uniform, which reads "World's Colored Champions," is probably a leftover from the team he played with in 1916. Photograph courtesy of the Bennett Rosner Collection.

Meanwhile, the Dodgers were still playing in Washington Park, which was too small, in the opinion of owner Charles Ebbets. To realize his dream of a solid, permanent home for the team, though, he needed land. In 1908, to avoid driving real-estate prices up he bought lots in an underdeveloped section of Flatbush through a dummy company. By 1912 he announced the purchase of the site, just east of Prospect Park, for $100,000 and his plans to build a new "fireproof" park. Many greeted the announcement with guffaws, but Ebbets gambled on the location being a good one; the site was just several miles from the Brooklyn Bridge and near over a dozen transit lines. He also counted on the populations of Flatbush and Bedford expanding toward each other, with the hopes that they would eventually envelop the new ballfield and provide an easy, paying crowd. Even though city officials helped him out to some degree, seeing the construction project as important for the borough, its $750,000 cost forced Ebbets to take his contractors, the McKeever Brothers, as partners. In March 1912, they broke ground for the stadium, kin to places like Forbes Field in Pittsburgh and Comiskey Park in Chicago which were made possible by the development of poured concrete. Increased fan interest across the nation suggested that these new, larger stadiums would be sound financial ventures, given that from 1901 to 1908, the total attendance for the two major leagues doubled, from 3.5 million to 7 million.

A New Era: Ebbets Field Opens

In a photograph taken shortly after Ebbets Field opened in 1913, the stadium looms in the foreground like a modern-day Roman coliseum, combining concrete, brick, glass, and steel with such classical architectural details as pilasters and ornate capitals. The size alone must have impressed both Brooklynites and fans of opposing teams. Not only did it break visually with the scale of its surroundings, but this new, substantial stadium contrasted with visitors' experiences of earlier fields—Washington Park, for instance, was all wood and, not incidentally, a firetrap. Ebbets Field was also elaborate, no doubt a conscious effort to compete with other attractions that vied for consumers' leisure dollars, like Coney Island or new movie houses. In the ticket lobby, an ornate marble rotunda with a stucco ceiling, patrons could line up at twelve ticket booths, as opposed to the four or five at Washington Park. And Ebbets Field was a permanent home for the team, a neighborhood commitment, and a major capital investment on the part of the club owners.

On April 5, 1913, opening day, borough dignitaries poured into the stadium for formal ceremonies and an exhibition game between the New York Yankees

Ebbets Field, ca. 1914.

Fans gather outside Ebbets Field in this early view of the new ballpark at Bedford Avenue and Montgomery Street in Flatbush (in an area today thought of as Crown Heights). Finally, the Dodgers had a permanent home.

and the Dodgers, who were going by the name "Superbas." The Twenty-third Regiment played. Genevieve Ebbets threw out the first ball ever used in a game at the new field, and Mrs. Edward J. McKeever raised the flag. The *Brooklyn Daily Eagle* captured the excitement and glory of the "day of days":

> Twenty-five thousand hearts thumped with joy, twenty-five thousand pairs of feet pounded the concrete floor and twenty-five thousand voices roared with delight—the day of days had at last arrived. [Manager] Bill Dahlen's Superbas made their debut in Ebbets Field this afternoon, crossing bats with [manager] Frank Chance's Yankee Americanas in an exhibition game, and the baseball season of 1913 was ushered in. . . .
>
> From all parts of the Greater City the fans moved on, like an army of allies, to storm the Ebbets citadel and roar a welcome to Bill Dahlen's ball tossers and Frank Chance's Yanks, and incidentally to baptize the new ball park in a manner befitting such a combination of notable events—the return of the Brooklyns, the first game of the season and the opening of the great field.

For Brooklyn, it was a glorious moment. The borough had joined the select club of major U.S. cities with brand new stadiums: Chicago, Pittsburgh, Cincinnati, and New York (ravaged in a fire in 1911, Manhattan's Polo Grounds had to be rebuilt). For Charles Ebbets, who had risked everything to achieve his dream, it was a day of triumph.

While small by today's standards, in 1913 Ebbets Field seemed spacious although not overwhelming, with its 24,000 grandstand seats. It measured just under three hundred feet down the right-field line, and about four hundred feet to straightaway center field. Over time, left-field stands, double-deck stands in left and center field, and the famous scoreboard in right field were added. Outfield walls transformed into advertising space helped pay the enormous overhead. Perhaps the most famous advertisement was Abe Stark's sign, which proclaimed "HIT SIGN WIN SUIT." Essentially it was an offer of a free suit at Stark's store at 1514 Pitkin Avenue, Brownsville, to any batter whose ball hit the sign—mounted at the base of the right field scoreboard—on a fly. Although rarely hit, the sign helped Stark, the son of Russian immigrants, achieve a certain renown, and he went on to become president of the City Council in 1954 and later Brooklyn borough president. After World War II, the famous Schaefer Beer sign was erected on top of the right-center scoreboard. An H in the name lit up for a hit, and an E for an error. Score cards carried advertisements as well.

With a new ballpark, and under the new management of Wilbert "Uncle Robbie" Robinson, the team finally achieved some stability, although it was alternately known as the Dodgers and the Robins. While the team rallied to win the pennant in 1916, it seemed unable to win consistently. The Dodgers went to the 1920 World Series but lost to Cleveland, and for most of the 1920s, the team languished in fifth or sixth place. In general, business was slow, and people were staying away.

When Charles Ebbets died in 1925, he was succeeded as president by Robinson, whose six-year reign was tainted by a bitter feud with owner "Judge" McKeever. In spite of stars like slugger and fan favorite Zach Wheat and the 1924 National League Most Valuable Player, Dazzy Vance, the club played some of the worst games in its history. It continued to make a profit mainly because atten-

At Ebbets Field for the World Series, October 6, 1920.

In 1920 Brooklyn's great pitchers put the team in a World Series showdown with the American League Cleveland Indians. In the second game, on October 6, the final score was Brooklyn, three, Cleveland, zero. Cleveland won the Series, five games to two. Courtesy of the Library of Congress, Bain Collection, LC–USZ6Z–92826.

dance had risen for most teams with the addition of Sunday games, and because under Robinson's casual management, the Dodgers had an engaging and amusing charm that led New York columnist Westbrook Pegler to dub them the "Daffiness Boys." A classic example of Dodger daffiness occurred in a game against the Braves in 1926–three Dodgers contrived to reach third base at the same time. For years, it was a Brooklyn joke: When a game announcer said, "The Dodgers have three men on base," the proper response was "Which base?"

In 1931 Robinson left, and the Dodgers spent the next half dozen years under the stern, no-nonsense management of Max Carey, a one-time crack base stealer, playing baseball but not having much fun. Casey Stengel, a former Giants outfielder, replaced Carey in 1934. Except for a spectacular showing against the Giants in 1935 that ruined the New Yorkers' chance for the pennant, the Dodgers spent most of the 1930s in the league cellar, a condition that matched the despair of the Depression years. During these down-and-out seasons, one particularly vocal fan made it a practice of pointing out the team's deficiencies by shouting "Ya bum, ya!" from his seat behind the home-plate screen. Sportswriter Sid Mercer dubbed him "the Spirit of Brooklyn" and made him a regular feature in his columns. Soon headlines labeled the team "Bums" as often as "Dodgers," and the Flatbush bum created by cartoonist Willard Mullin became a nationally known symbol not only of the Dodgers but of Brooklyn as well.

By 1938, the team had lost public support, was deeply in debt, and Ebbets Field was in a state of disrepair. George McLaughlin, president of the Brooklyn Trust Company (to whom the Dodgers owed $500,000), warned that the club's credit would be severely limited unless some new, vital leadership turned the team around. It appeared in the person of Larry MacPhail, and the golden age of the Brooklyn Dodgers began.

The Golden Age

Leland Stanford MacPhail came to Brooklyn from Ohio, where he had rebuilt the Columbus team in the Cardinal chain. Faced with staggering problems—first and foremost a team on the verge of going out of business—MacPhail rejuvenated the Dodger franchise on and off the field by borrowing thousands and making some savvy choices. A firm believer in the philosophy that you had to spend money to make money, in his first year he gave twenty-five-year-old Ebbets Field a much needed face-lift. It included a new paint job and renovated bathrooms, the latter an improvement especially popular with the patrons. On June 15, 1938, the team played Ebbets Field's first night game under artificial lights to a sellout crowd. The Dodgers hired Babe Ruth, whose playing career was over, as first-base coach for the last half of the season, another drawing card for fans. With these improvements, attendance doubled to 800,000 for the season.

MacPhail made other changes as well, moving Dodger headquarters to 215 Montague Street in Brooklyn Heights and after the 1938 season replacing manager Burleigh Grimes with one of his players, Leo Durocher. Brash and quick-tempered, Leo "the Lip" Durocher liked a good time. In Brooklyn, he frequented the rooftop garden of the elegant Bossert Hotel on Montague Street, which was done up like a yacht, and had a reputation for mixing with a somewhat unsavory crowd of hustlers, gamblers, and low-level mob figures. But on the field, he was exactly what the Dodgers needed.

The winter of 1938-39 MacPhail lured broadcaster Walter "Red" Barber from Cincinnati to New York to give the city its first radio coverage of big-league baseball from Ebbets Field. With his smooth voice and engaging personality, his warm radio signature—"This is the ol' redhead"—and his slight southern drawl, Barber made radio announcing an art. For a *New York Knickerbocker* story on March 3, 1968, he reminisced about his first day on the job in New York:

> I look back some twenty-nine years—back to Opening Day at Ebbets field in 1939. That was my first ball game in Brooklyn.
> The Giants were at Ebbets Field that Opening Day in '39. It was also Opening Day for radio play-by-play in New York. Until then the Yankees and the Giants had blacked out radio—they were terribly afraid of it—and the hapless Dodgers had been forced to follow suit. But Larry MacPhail . . . killed the anti-radio ban. Now it was the two big clubs over the river that followed—both had to broadcast.
> Before that game began, Bill Terry and Leo Durocher, the two managers, went on the air, which is pretty good booking; that is, if you like talent.

Barber—and radio—changed the nature of the game. Now you could hear play-by-play in your armchair, in your own backyard in Carnarsie, on a Bedford-Stuyvesant stoop, or in a downtown office. Charles Hummel, who lived with his family in a cold-water flat in Ridgewood, recalled that his father took him to his first ball game at Ebbets Field in 1940. But with money tight, you could choose to skip the trip to the stadium and "listen everywhere, wherever you were," Hummel remembers. "If somebody had a radio on you'd stop to catch the score or find out how the team was doing, especially during World Series time. In the warm weather people who had radios would pipe the sound into the street." Television coverage at Ebbets Field, which also debuted in 1939 (a time when only several

Night-game ticket, ca. 1940s.

In 1938 the Dodgers became the second professional baseball team to play under artificial light. The first was the Cincinnati Reds at Crosley Field, in 1935. Photograph courtesy of the National Baseball Library and Archive, Cooperstown, New York.

hundred people in the Greater New York area had television sets), stopped during World War II and was revived at war's end. Hummel remembers those days too, when people would "stop to look at televisions in a storefront."

Determined to create a winning team, MacPhail signed such Dodger greats as first baseman Dolph Camilli, outfielder and slugger "Pistol Pete" Reiser, slugger Joe Medwick, and pitchers Kirby Higbe and Whitlow Wyatt. Pee Wee Reese

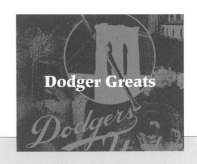

Dodger Greats

The 1940s and 1950s were the Dodgers' golden age, when the roster listed great players like Whit Wyatt, Dolph Camilli, Roy Campanella, Carl Erskine, and Jackie Robinson. Today their gloves or uniforms, and baseball trading cards with their images evoke the personalities who brought the Dodgers fame. Johnny Podres wore this shirt (later accidentally cut in half by one of his young children) in the second game of the 1955 World Series. Considering that Podres went on to shut out the Yankees in the last game of the series with a stretch of spectacular pitching, it could indeed rank, as one Dodger fan pointed out, "as the most important garment in Brooklyn Dodger history."

Baseball cards, ca. 1950s: Johnny Podres, Dodgers' Sluggers, Ralph Branca, Sandy Amoros, Carl Furillo.

Uniforms and equipment of Dodger stars, 1930s to 1950s, as seen in Brooklyn's History Museum (*left to right*): Whit Wyatt's glove; Dolph Camilli's cap; Carl Erskine's spikes; Johnny Podres's shirt; Roy Campanella's home uniform; manager Casey Stengel's uniform. Campanella uniform courtesy of the Fields family; other items courtesy of Marty Adler, Brooklyn Dodgers Baseball Hall of Fame.

The Brooklyn Dodgers

Dodger stars in dugout at Ebbets Field, September 1941.

This lineup includes some of the most brilliant Dodger players of the era. *From left*: Joe Medwick, Billy Herman, Pee Wee Reese, Pete Reiser, Mickey Owen, and Whit Wyatt. In October, the team went to the World Series against the Yankees—and lost. Photograph by Barney Stein.

came in as a trade from the Boston Red Sox farm team in Louisville. MacPhail's efforts paid off. The Dodgers finished third in 1939 and won their first pennant in twenty-one years in 1941. In September of that year, six team stars—all players MacPhail had brought onto the team in the previous two years—posed for a dugout portrait: Whit Wyatt, Joe Medwick, Billy Herman, Pee Wee Reese, Pete Reiser, and Mickey Owen.

That year, the Dodgers went on to face the Yankees in the first of their many runs for the world title. Behind by one game as they entered the fourth game, by the ninth inning they led four to three. And then came one of the worst moments in Dodger World Series history. With two outs and no one on base, Dodger pitcher Hugh Casey threw a curve and struck out Tommy Heinrich, apparently ending the game in a Brooklyn win. But the ball got away from catcher Mickey Owen. When he went after the ball, the police who were trying to keep back fans now that the game was "over" got in the way. Heinrich proceeded to first, and the door was open for a Yankee win. Four runs were batted in, and the Dodgers lost.

Two months later, Japanese war planes screamed over Pearl Harbor, Guam, and the Philippines. The U.S. declared war on Japan, then on Germany and Italy. Several players left for the front—as they did from almost every major league team—but baseball carried on, accommodating whenever possible Washington's request that games be scheduled to be as convenient as possible for fans who worked in war-related industries. Shortly afterwards, Larry MacPhail resigned. The man who had rejuvenated a dying team was the victim of stockholders who thought their dividend checks were too small and, perhaps, of his own irascibility. The next year, Branch Rickey came from the St. Louis Cardinals to take over as president. A one-quarter owner of the Dodgers, Rickey shared ownership with Walter O'Malley, a Brooklyn Trust Company lawyer; the heirs of former owner Steven McKeever; and John L. Smith, Pfizer's vice-president. (Smith would make history at the company's Williamsburg plant, devising the means to mass produce penicillin for the first-time—a savior for Americans at home and at the fighting front.) Rickey changed the team makeup, releasing such veterans as Whit Wyatt, Dolph Camilli, and Joe Medwick and recruiting new players—pitcher Ralph Branca and, at the start of the 1946 season, batting ace Carl Furillo, and outfielder Gene Hermanski. Burt Shotton replaced Leo Durocher as manager.

The astuteness of Rickey's choices paled next to his announcement in 1945 that he had signed Jackie Robinson to the Dodgers' top farm club in Montreal. A former UCLA star, Robinson had played one season with the Kansas City Monarchs, a team in the Negro National League. When he walked onto Ebbets Field in his Dodger uniform on April 15, 1947, before 26,623 fans, more than half of whom were Black, he marked the end of a ban against African Americans in the major leagues that dated back to 1867. Total attendance at Dodger games in Robinson's first year broke all National League records—1,807,526 fans at Ebbets Field games and 1,863,542 spectators on the road.

A range of human reactions from wild enthusiasm to blatant racism greeted Robinson's debut. A group of his teammates signed a petition saying they refused to play with him. When they were offered the opportunity to leave the team, they

The mitt that lost the 1941 Series.

Dodger catcher Mickey Owen was wearing this mitt on October 5, 1941, where he let a third-strike pitch get past him in the ninth inning. The Dodgers went on to lose the World Series to the New York Yankees. Loan courtesy of Marty Adler, Brooklyn Dodgers Baseball Hall of Fame.

Branch Rickey signs Jackie Robinson, 1947.

Dodger president Branch Rickey challenged segregated baseball when he brought Jackie Robinson up from the Montreal farm team and signed him as a Dodger. Robinson had lettered in four sports at UCLA and played one year in the Negro Leagues, and Rickey thought he had character stoic enough to survive the racist firestorm that was sure to follow his major league debut. Photograph courtesy of the Bettmann Archives.

The Brooklyn Dodgers

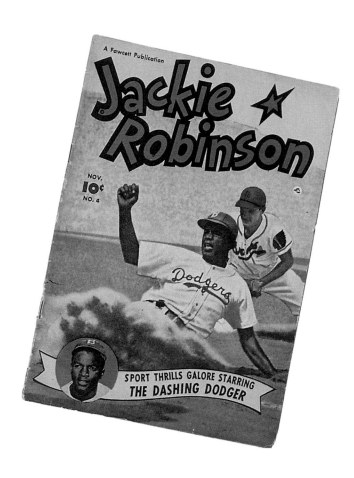

Jackie Robinson comic book, 1950.

Robinson's appeal crossed most boundaries, including age. This 1950 comic book captures a familiar pose for the master of the slide.

backed down, and many came to respect Robinson for his superb athletic skills. Some reached out to him, like southern-born Pee Wee Reese, who became a friend. Not only did local fans wait hours to see him after games, but fans all over the country idolized him, particularly African Americans. Jackie Robinson became a phenomenon. His image appeared on the covers of comic books and he played himself in a movie of his life with Ruby Dee as his wife, Rachel. The hatred leveled at Robinson on the field came mainly from opposing players who taunted him with racial slurs, aimed brushback pitches at him, and tried to grind their spikes into him as they rounded second base. Baseball in this case hardly lived up to its billing as a clean-cut, all-American sport.

The animosity aimed at Jackie Robinson may have resulted in part from fear by some that the country in general was becoming more integrated—and he made an obvious target. For years before Robinson joined the Dodgers, baseball commissioner Judge Kenesaw Mountain Landis had blocked integration of the major leagues. His death in 1944, and his replacement, Albert B. "Happy" Chandler, a former U.S. senator, marked the beginning of the end of segregation in baseball. On a national scale, too, cracks appeared in segregation policies. CIO labor organizations had begun to admit Black people. In 1941 African Americans had won access to defense jobs. And the 1948 desegregation of the military was just over the horizon. In addition, the wartime migration of African Americans from the rural South was changing the makeup of many northern cities.

Brooklyn! *An Illustrated History*

African Americans who followed Robinson onto the Dodgers' roster included Don Newcombe, who had pitched for the Negro League Newark Eagles, and catcher Roy Campanella, who had played for the Negro League Baltimore Elite Giants. Predictably, the slow but steady integration of the major leagues was a death sentence for the Black leagues throughout the United States; attendance at games fell, and the leagues slid into an irreversible decline.

In Robinson's first year with the Dodgers, 1947, his batting average was .297 and he led the league in bases stolen—29. And he helped the Dodgers win the pennant over the Cardinals. It was a joyous occasion. On September 26, a 17-car motorcade—including players riding in "flashy, open cars donated for the occasion by admiring fans," said the *Eagle*—progressed from Grand Army Plaza down Flatbush Avenue, one of Brooklyn's main thoroughfares. The procession was headed for Borough Hall. Once there, at Brooklyn's political center, an enormous crowd let go a "roaring Niagra of cheers." On the front of the building hung square silk banners combining two major Brooklyn icons, the Brooklyn Bridge and Ebbets Field. Borough president John Cashmore awarded a watch to each of the Dodgers, Dixie Walker and Jackie Robinson spoke, and Robinson was presented the newly instituted Baseball Writers Association of America's Rookie of the Year Award, sponsored by *Sporting News.* (Arguably the major U.S. magazine on baseball, *Sporting News* had neglected to cover Black games, scores, and standings for many years.) Ultimately, the cheering stopped when the Dodgers met the Yankees in the World Series and lost.

The following year, the Dodgers were in the race for the pennant until September; in 1949, they fielded an even better squad. That year the team hosted the only All Star Game held at Ebbets Field, and the first in which African American athletes participated. Three were Dodgers: Jackie Robinson, Roy Campanella, and Don Newcombe. Outfielder Larry Doby of the Cleveland Indians was

Pennant welcoming the National League champions, 1947.

To hail the pennant-winning Dodgers, this banner was hung along the front of Borough Hall when the team won in 1947 and again in 1949, where it can be seen in the photograph (*following page*) of Dodgers and dignitaries on Borough Hall steps. Dates of later pennant wins against the Yankees were subsequently glued on by a Dodger enthusiast, who left out 1949.

The reception for pennant winners at Borough Hall, 1949.

Note the presence of the pennant on Borough Hall steps.

the fourth. Robinson scored three runs in the eleven to seven defeat. When the Dodgers again won the pennant that year, the team returned to Borough Hall for a victory celebration. Against this backdrop of civic pride, the team gathered with a crush of dignitaries under an enormous welcoming sign and amid bunting and American flags. And once again, the team played in the World Series against the Yankees—and lost.

Repeated trips to the World Series and repeated losses did not dim the magnificence of the Dodgers of the 1940s and 1950s for its audience, which streamed back to Ebbets Field now that their team was on a winning course. Many fans became minor celebrities themselves. One of them was Hilda Chester, whose raspy voice and clanging brass cowbell, presented to her by Dodger players in the 1930s, could be heard throughout the park. The Dodger Sym-Phony, a five-piece band, consisted of fanatic fans from Greenpoint, where they also participated in the annual giglio festival. They came to Dodger games dressed like bums and serenaded fans with a repertoire that included "The Worms Crawl in, the Worms Crawl Out" when an opposing pitcher was knocked out and "Three Blind Mice" when the umpires came onto the field before a game (until the National League added a fourth umpire). When opposing players complained about unfair calls, they harassed them by throwing the official crying towel at them, taunting, "Here, ya cry baby!"

Brooklyn! *An Illustrated History*

Dodgers Sym-Phony and welcoming fans, 1949.

The Dodgers Sym-Phony from Green-point greets the team, returning from a victory over St. Louis in the National League race. The loosely organized group of fans began playing at Ebbets Field before World War II but achieved its greatest fame in the 1946 and 1947 seasons. Photograph from the *World Telegram,* September 30, 1949, courtesy of the National Baseball Library and Archive, Cooperstown, New York.

Apart from these few well-known fans, thousands of the faithful over the years crowded the rails to shake the players' hands, or sent birthday cakes to the locker room, or simply filled the stands in clamorous support of their Bums. Many remember a sense of intimacy at Ebbets Field during those decades. Compared to modern stadiums, it was small; its size gave fans easy access to players. And it was part of the surrounding cityscape, rather than being set apart from it by acres of parking lots.

That accessibility enabled a Brooklyn teenager, Leslie Sachs Sherman, to ful-fill her dream of embroidering the Dodgers' signatures on an old shirt of her fa-

Official crying towel of the Dodgers Sym-Phony, 1940s.

Tossed to complaining players on op-posing teams, this crying towel be-longed to Sym-Phony founder Shorty Laurice and was first used by the band in the war years. It is covered with "in" references for fans, including the name of Dodger organist Gladys Goodding and "Three Blind Mice," one of the band's mainstay songs. Loan courtesy of Marty Adler, Brooklyn Dodgers Baseball Hall of Fame.

The Brooklyn Dodgers

Pee Wee Reese Night

Pee Wee Reese Night at Ebbets Field, 1955. Photograph by Barney Stein. T-shirt worn on Pee Wee Reese Night by seven-year-old fan Jack Daly.

One summer night at Ebbets Field was so special to seven-year-old Jack Daly that he saved the T-shirt he wore to that game—and the memory—into his adulthood.

The celebration of Pee Wee Reese's birthday on July 23, 1955, was a publicity stunt cooked up by Dodger public-relations director Irving Rudd. Thirty-five thousand fans were handed candles and matches, and when the lights went out as the team ran out onto the field in the bottom of the fifth, everyone lit up and sang. As Jack Daly remembers it:

It was the summer of 1955. My Uncle Jack and Aunt Julia took the subway all the way from Jackson Heights to go to a night game at Ebbets Field with my father and me. We had great seats, field level, off first base, up close to my favorite player, Gil Hodges.

It was Pee Wee Reese Night and in the middle of the game the house lights went out and all the fans lit candles and sang Happy Birthday to Pee Wee. It was the greatest sight my seven-year-old eyes had ever seen.

A lot of gifts were brought out including a set of golf clubs, which I though was an odd present for a baseball player. Why didn't they give him bats?

For the finale five cars were driven onto the field. Four ordinary ones and one two-toned beauty. It was pink and black or pink and dark grey, I'm not sure, but it was clearly the best-looking car out there and I really wanted to see Pee Wee win that one.

The keys for all the cars were put into a fish bowl and someone picked one set out and which ever car they started Pee Wee would drive home in. He went down the line of cars trying each until he got to the last one, the beauty. I had my fingers crossed as Pee Wee got into the car, put the key in, turned it, the engine started, and the crowd groaned with disappointment. I said to my father, "What's wrong?" My father said, "He won the Chevy. It's the cheapest car out there. Everyone wanted to see him get the Caddy or one of the more expensive cars."

Well, I learned something about the value of automobiles that night. But I still think Pee Wee got the best car on the field.

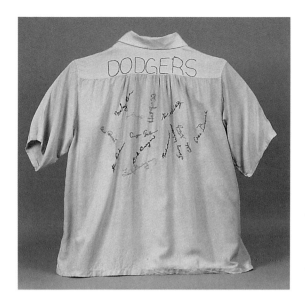

Embroidered blouse, 1940s.

The signatures Brooklynite Leslie Sachs Sherman embroidered on this shirt included such well-known players as Mickey Owen and Eddie Stanky. The shirt ultimately became a wearable testimony to the team she loved.

ther's. "A girlfriend and I (her nickname was Lucky, mine Jinx) went to all the afternoon games we could manage," she recalls. Sherman lived on East Twenty-fourth Street between Avenues N and O during the 1940s and rode the trolley to Ebbets Field. They paid for bleacher seats, then put their strategy into action. "We'd work our way down to the upper and lower grandstand by the seventh inning, [until] we were sitting in the boxes behind the Dodger dugout. The players recognized us after a while and when we asked them to sign our shirts, they were delighted. . . . Each night, we went home and embroidered the signatures and brought it with us to every game we attended." The result was a rainbow of autographs. Above the front pocket in blue is embroidered the name of Luis Olmo, the well-known Arecibo, Puerto Rico-born player; others cascade across the back.

The shirts and the intimacy of the park bestowed a few moments of fame on Sherman and her friend. "One day as Lucky and I entered Ebbets Field," she remembers, "we were told by friends listening to the radio that Red Barber and Connie Desmond, the announcers, made mention of us wearing the Dodger shirts. Were we excited when we heard about it!" A year later, in 1945, Sherman and her family moved to Los Angeles. "You can imagine the desolation I felt, leaving my beloved Bums," she said. She kept the shirt through numerous "moves, a marriage, and more houses."

While fans like Leslie Sachs Sherman proclaimed, "Win or lose, we're proud of our Bums" during those golden years, by 1953, the Dodgers had won the National League race five times and five times lost the World Series to the hated Yankees. After close matches in 1941, 1947, 1949, 1952, and 1953, Brooklyn's war cry, "Wait 'til next year!" began to take on an impotent ring.

In 1955 the Dodgers once again faced the Yankees in the Fall Classic. The Yankees won the first two games, six to five and four to two, but the Dodgers won the next three—all at home—before they lost to New York on October 3. Brooklyn held its breath as it all came down to the seventh game on October 4. In Yankee Stadium, the Dodgers' Johnny Podres was pitching shutout ball. With the Dodgers up two runs, the sixth inning began with the Yankees walking one

The Brooklyn Dodgers

Dodgers Pennant, 1955, and the 1955 Dodgers.

On October 4 in New York, when Brooklyn beat the Yankees, two to nothing, in the seventh and final game of the World Series, joyous bedlam erupted all over the borough. The 1955 Dodgers were a team of heroes.

man, followed by a single. Yogi Berra then hit a high fly ball into left field. At left center was Sandy Amoros, who desperately raced towards the ball. At the last second, he lunged for it and caught it just inside the foul line. Accompanied by some fancy work by his teammates, Podres continued to pitch shutout ball, and Brooklyn snuffed out a Yankee scoring threat to exalt in its first World Series triumph. It had been almost three quarters of a century since the Dodgers had begun their long journey in Washington Park. Now, in 1955, they had achieved baseball's highest honor.

In the locker room after the game, the players knelt, joined hands and said a prayer of thanks. Throughout Brooklyn, joyous pandemonium reigned. Fans took to the streets screaming and yelling, car caravans snaked along Flatbush Avenue and Ocean Parkway, horns blaring, tugs on the East River sounded their horns. And newspapers told the world that out in Brooklyn, the bums were bums no more. These 1955 Dodgers were heroes, a group of men who had finally shown Manhattan—and the world beyond—what Brooklyn was made of.

The Turbulent Fifties

By the 1950s the Dodgers were the major leagues' most financially prosperous team. In 1955, with their long-elusive World Series victory, the team had reached its peak. But all was not well. For some time Dodger president Walter O'Malley had been eyeing the team's future in Brooklyn with concern. A modern, state-of-the-art stadium when it opened in 1913, Ebbets Field was now old and outdated. Like others of its era—Chicago's Comiskey Park, or Pittsburgh's Forbes Field—it had been planned with the trolley and subway in mind and had only 750 spots for parking—and no room for expansion. O'Malley asked for a new stadium, even suggesting the old Long Island Railroad terminal but Robert Moses (who controlled several key government posts and wielded enormous political power) countered with Flushing, Queens, as a site. Walter O'Malley was not interested. It was not Brooklyn, and frankly, New York could not give him what he needed to make the move work. A very complicated problem, it seemed to boil down to money. Baseball was, after all was said and done, a business.

If New York City was unwilling to give Walter O'Malley what he wanted, California was making generous overtures. In Los Angeles, the Dodgers could have a virgin market, municipal support, and possibly the profits from pay TV (a mix between pay-per-view and ordinary cable that later fell through). And L.A. wanted the Dodgers badly, believing that a major-league team would boost the area's economy and enhance the city's standing in the sports world. Interestingly enough, at the same time, San Francisco was courting the New York Giants baseball team, which O'Malley supported since it would mean a built-in rival for his team. Their ballpark situation was even worse than Ebbets Field's, and they were losing money, to boot. Although each team's move was rooted in its own specific set of concerns, their situations were not that unique. Between 1953 and 1957, major-league team locations shifted more than they had in the fifty years before. In 1953 the Boston Braves franchise went to Milwaukee, and the St. Louis Browns were sold and transferred to Baltimore; in 1954 the Philadelphia Athletics were sold and transferred to Kansas City.

As word of the move became known, mail poured into New York City Mayor Robert Wagner's office, pleading with him to keep the Dodgers in New York. In

Demonstrators protesting the Dodgers' proposed move, April 22, 1957, and protest button.

On April 22 at a "Keep the Dodgers in Brooklyn" rally massed at Brooklyn Borough Hall, many wore special T-shirts and buttons. One of the ten thousand distributed by the "Keep the Dodgers in Brooklyn Committee," this button belonged to Irving Rudd, longtime Brooklyn Dodgers publicist. Young people toted signs aimed at Robert Moses, whose proposal to build a stadium in Queens outraged many Brooklynites. Demonstrators photograph courtesy of AP/Wide World Photos.

April 1957 Borough Hall, recently the site of a triumphant World Series celebration, became the target of Dodger fans intent on keeping their team in Brooklyn. Protestors toted signs with such sentiments as, "Mr. Moses Don't You Dare Take Our Dodgers Out of Brooklyn" and "3 million People of Brooklyn Say No!" Former Dodger publicist Irving Rudd years later still had his "Keep the Dodgers in Brooklyn" pin, minted to create community solidarity and displayed by those who wanted to wear their hearts on their lapels: The Dodgers must not go!

But on September 24, 1957, the Dodgers held their last game at Ebbets Field. The small crowd of 6,702 fans sang as Gladys Goodding, who Larry MacPhail had made baseball's first official organist in 1942, played "Auld Lang Syne." On October 9 Tommy Holmes, writing in the *New York Herald Tribune* sports section, announced the end:

> The Dodgers yesterday took the irrevocable step from Ebbets Field to Los Angeles. Less than twenty-four hours after the City Council of the sprawling California metropolis had approved a controversial offer for the Brooklyn baseball franchise, stockholders and directors of the ball club unanimously voted to move.
>
> Together with the formal announcement just a week ago that the Giants would quit the Polo Grounds for San Francisco, the Dodger action constitutes the abandonment of New York by the 81-year old National League.

At the end of the season the Dodgers left for Los Angeles. To a generation, their departure was more than just a franchise shift. It was the end of an era and of a way of life. Fittingly, the practice of trolley dodging that had given the team its name was coming to an end at about the same time. The phasing out of Brook-

Base from Ebbets Field, ca. 1957.

Brooklynites Irving Weissler and his wife saved three bases from Ebbets Field, given to them by family relative Marvin Kratter, the real-estate developer who bought Ebbets Field in 1956 with plans to develop middle-income housing on the site. When the B'nai Brith had a Dodgers remembrance day at Joe's Restaurant in Brooklyn, attenders signed two out of the three—this one is the unsigned third.

lyn's trolleys began in the 1930s with the introduction of buses, and they stopped running altogether in 1956. On February 23, 1960 Ebbets Field, a Brooklyn icon as powerful as the Brooklyn Bridge, fell under the wrecking ball. In April, a crowd of one hundred attended an auction at Ebbets Field and bought up bits and pieces of the one-time shrine. Officials allowed one long-time fan to smash open the stadium's cornerstone, which yielded a "1912 newspaper, scorecards, and an 1811 penny," according to the *New York Daily News*. Before long, apartment houses filled the odd-shaped square created by McKeever Place, Sullivan Place, Bedford Avenue, and Montgomery Street.

Some Dodger fans never recovered. As Marty Adler, president of the Brooklyn Dodgers Baseball Hall of Fame put it, the team had been both community backbone and a unifying, transforming force: "They took the soul out of the borough when they left. We were first generation immigrants—all our parents came from another country—and we wanted to become assimilated. This was the way we could become true Americans: by rooting for a team, and our team was the Dodgers." Other fans switched their allegiance (though perhaps never their hearts) to the New York Mets when they came on the scene in 1962. The Mets' team colors, orange and blue, seemed to unite in a comforting fashion the colors of the former New York teams: Dodger blue and Giants orange. Through the Mets, the borough continued to be connected to the city's baseball life.

Aside from memories, little remains of the shrine that stood in Flatbush. Some of the large blocks, stone, and other debris from Ebbets Field became filler for land in Mill Basin when new homes, especially those along the waterway, were built in the early 1960s. Many of the seats were auctioned off; the city bought some for use by inmates at a local correctional facility. Those objects that do survive seem not just nostalgic but poignant. Once, this brick, that seat, those bases were part of Ebbets Field. Once, a stadium stood in Brooklyn.

Epilogue
Wait 'til Next Year

Brooklynites who lived in the borough during the 1950s often look back with nostalgia on the days of the Dodgers, egg creams, the corner drugstore, and a lifetime lived in one neighborhood, on one street, even in one building, with grandparents, aunts, uncles, and cousins a few blocks away. To many, the decade was movies at the Paramount and walking along Ocean Parkway on a warm summer night with the lights of Ebbets Field in the distance and the roar of the crowd on the air like the rise and fall of surf.

But in spite of the stability many recall, the 1950s was a decade of upheaval in Brooklyn, as it was for many other older urban areas in the country, and the Dodgers' departure seemed to symbolize these changes. Much of Brooklyn's middle-class population was also moving—to new suburbs in New Jersey and Long Island—leaving behind aging buildings and an outworn urban infrastructure. The hopeful, largely Black working-class population that moved in, looking for new opportunities, often faced fear and hostility. Racial bias made it difficult for newcomers to obtain homeowners' loans and employment. As neighborhood disinvestment took place, city services declined. Urban renewal projects sometimes failed. Neighborhoods began to decay.

Industry and shipping were getting out of town as well, along with the first step up the socioeconomic ladder they had represented for earlier generations of Brooklynites. Encouraged by new government policies, companies moved to newer, cheaper facilities in New Jersey and the South, where manufacturing was less expensive. Longtime retail anchors like Namm–Loeser's shipped out too, and local shopping strips suffered as residents departed and massive highway projects like the Brooklyn-Queens Expressway cut through neighborhoods and destroyed their coherence.

For awhile it looked as if changes in social policy and the economic downturn had Brooklyn down for the count, but its residents—old and new—revived the borough and are remaking it still, finding new beauty in once obsolete housing, economic niches to fill, and a community that continues to be an exciting place to live.

Residential Rebirth

Housing stock once considered old or substandard by Brooklynites who fled to the suburbs began in the 1960s to awaken the imagination of new residents

255

entranced by high ceilings, fine woodwork, and plaster details. Vonceil Turner recalls her and her husband's decision to buy the Bedford-Stuyvesant brownstone, which they renovated themselves. "All of our friends thought we were crazy when we bought this house. I had to put in beams in the cellar and columns for support, and rewired the entire house. Aesthetically, it was beautiful, but water was coming down the side wall." The family lived on the top floors and worked their way down, refurbishing a room at a time. And then they imparted some of their own personality to it, just as previous owners had in generations before. "We found that when you came into the house, it had no ethnicity to it," Turner explained. "So we decided to get a collection of African and Haitian carvings of heads." Once completed, the restored home had new life, and became a cherished gathering place for everything from a wedding to Cub Scout meetings.

Turner and her husband, who began restoring their house in 1974, were part of a movement that began in the late 1950s and 1960s in neighborhoods like Brooklyn Heights, Cobble Hill, and Park Slope. At a time when living in rowhouses was considered unfashionable, the renovation of brownstones was a phenomenon that encouraged many professionals to choose city over suburb, contributing to Brooklyn's diversity as well as providing a boost to the city's tax base.

In Brooklyn Heights, one of the borough's earliest developed neighborhoods, local residents banded together to preserve the area's rich architectural heritage;

in 1965 the Heights was designated the first landmark district in New York City. A driving force behind the effort was the Brooklyn Heights Association, Inc., one of the oldest civic associations in the country. Founded by local residents in 1910 to preserve the character of their neighborhood, it has helped maintain the nineteenth-century fabric of the Heights. In the 1940s, for example, with the support of many Heights residents, members blocked the construction of the Brooklyn-Queens Expressway through the neighborhood. In a compromise solution, the Esplanade was built at the level of the Heights, with expressway traffic and a feeder road for the waterfront piers built below.

All across Brooklyn in the 1970s dozens of community-housing groups formed and began to work toward erasing some of the ravages of urban blight, sponsoring rehabilitation programs and new construction to serve the needs of low- and moderate-income people. In a daring political move in 1974, Williamsburg residents founded the People's Firehouse by occupying a fire station scheduled to close, a protest against the arson that was plaguing their community. From there, the group attacked arson's causes; along with a dozen other groups, they trained thousands of tenants to purchase and manage the neglected and abandoned buildings so often the target of arsonists.

Among the multitude of other community-housing groups, a standout is East Brooklyn Churches, a non-profit coalition of mostly Black churches, which has built Nehemiah Homes in Brownsville. In October 1982, Brownsville residents crowded into a local ball field to witness the groundbreaking for one thousand single-family, low-cost homes on abandoned lots. Three years later, they were finished through the efforts of a consortium of churches united with local citizens and supported by city, state, and federal sources.

People's Firehouse youth-employment program, 1985.

Their heads poking through open windows and from a dumpster below, Williamsburg youth in a program sponsored by People's Firehouse renovate one of their neighborhood's fine nineteenth-century rowhouses. Photograph by Stephen L. Senigo.

Nehemiah Homes, Brownsville, 1985.

East Brooklyn Churches, a consortium that brought together private and federal funding, built these low-cost, single-family homes in an area once thought unsalvageable. Photograph by Stephen L. Senigo.

From an area long perceived as lacking in political and economic clout, the organizers of this coup had started small, erecting street signs and boycotting price-gouging supermarkets. From there, they created an organization that in essence became its own bank. They gained the support of national church bodies impressed with their community-organizing track record, which included eight million to begin construction, and persuaded the city to pitch in with free land, modest federal subsidies, and tax breaks. From the state, they received low-interest mortgage loans. At last, East Brooklyn Churches reached its goal—affordable homes for people from nearby public-housing projects and from rental apartments around the city—nurses, mail carriers, working people who had scraped to put aside small nest eggs to help complete the deals. Where only an urban wasteland had stood a few years before, the American dream was emerging, foundation by brick by windowsill by roof: home ownership.

Commercial Renewal

From Fulton Landing to Coney Island, corporations and grass-roots organizations are energizing Brooklyn's commercial core. Faced with rising rents for cramped space, many Manhattan companies have crossed the East River to take advantage of lower rents for offices in downtown Brooklyn and other parts of the borough. In Brooklyn Heights, the first new office building built in decades rose in 1988 when Forest City Ratner built One Pierrepont Plaza. The Brooklyn Economic Development Corporation, formed in 1979, as well as local citizens groups have succeeded in preserving and revitalizing neighborhood shopping strips. Communities are banding together to effect change.

From a satisfying number of examples of commercial development by community activists in the borough to choose among, two stand out. In Bedford-Stuyvesant the grandfather of community development organizations was born in 1967 with the support of New York senators Robert F. Kennedy and Jacob K. Javits. With public funding, the corporation put members of the local community together with business and financial groups in an effort to redevelop the depressed community through a comprehensive program of redevelopment ventures. Originally based in downtown Brooklyn, in 1976 the Bedford-Stuyvesant Restoration Center opened in the old Sheffield Farms building on Fulton Street, today a 300,000-square-foot commercial center in the heart of Bedford-Stuyvesant. This active organization sponsors employment programs and residential rehabilitation and construction; its headquarters house open plazas, a health-care facility, and a center for art, dance, and theater.

A walk down Fifth Avenue in Sunset Park is another lesson in what Brooklyn's communities can do together. The old economic base of the mixed Irish, German, Italian, Polish, and Scandinavian community had begun to fall apart as jobs along the waterfront disappeared during the Depression. The Gowanus Expressway, built over Third Avenue in 1941 and widened twenty years later, separated the industrial area from the residential area to the east and devastated a once thriving commercial strip. In the 1950s the port industry began to move to New Jersey, and in the 1970s the Brooklyn Army Terminal, a military ocean-supply facility built early in the twentieth century and once a major employer, was deactivated. As jobs left, so did residents.

After World War II, Puerto Rican families began to move in, and in the 1960s Latino residents became activists in revitalizing the neighborhood's residential, cultural, and commercial landscape. UPROSE (United Puerto Rican Organization of Sunset Park-Bay Ridge, Inc.), founded by community activists in 1966, expanded

Martínez Tropical Ices, Sunset Park, 1988.

Today, Sunset Park's Fifth Avenue is a colorful commercial thoroughfare with many Latino-owned businesses. For years, the popular Martínez Tropical Ices sold natural ices made from fresh tropical fruits that arrived daily from Santo Domingo and Puerto Rico. The business was up for sale because its owners were returning to Puerto Rico. Photograph by Tony Velez.

into an umbrella service organization that worked with local residents on several fronts, including housing, youth development, adult education, and immigration. The Brooklyn brownstone movement, Latino community activists, and neighborhood-restoration organizations also came together to collaborate on solutions.

One of the most striking changes in the community since the 1960s is Fifth Avenue. The leadership of the Latino community has always included its merchants and in Sunset Park, they and non-Latino store owners founded the Fifth Avenue Merchants' Association (FAMA) to revitalize the once decaying shopping strip. Now it is the vibrant center of what is again a viable community.

Cultural Renaissance

Alone among New York's outer boroughs, Brooklyn has a history as a city and, since the nineteenth century, the highly developed cultural life and institutions of a city. The Brooklyn Academy of Music (BAM) the Brooklyn Botanic Garden, The Brooklyn Museum, The Brooklyn Children's Museum (the oldest children's museum in the world), and The Brooklyn Historical Society all have their roots in nineteenth-century Brooklyn. And all have in one way or another reinvented themselves in recent years as they reach out to new audiences through events like BAM's avante-garde Next Wave Festival or the collaborative exhibitions on Crown Heights and the 1991 riots, created by The Brooklyn Children's Museum, the Society for the Preservation of Weeksville and Bedford-Stuyvesant History, and The Brooklyn Historical Society.

The Japanese Hill-and-Pond Garden at the Brooklyn Botanic Garden.

Designed and constructed by Takeo Shiota in 1914–15 to illustrate the Japanese philosophy of peace, harmony, and serenity, this garden is one of the most tranquil spots in New York. Photograph courtesy of the Brooklyn Botanic Garden.

The Brooklyn Museum, 1994.

One of the nation's finest art museums, The Brooklyn Museum in 1994 mounted a major reinstallation of its renowned Egyptian collection. Photograph courtesy of The Brooklyn Museum.

El Puente, a center for youth and their families in Los Sures, Williamsburg, that sponsors the most comprehensive Latino art program in Brooklyn, is one of the institutions that have emerged to meet the needs of Brooklyn's changing population. There, teenagers create their own art groups to address contemporary issues like racism and AIDS. At the Society for the Preservation of Weeksville and Bedford-Stuyvesant History, a museum of African American history housed in the restored

El Puente dance ensemble, 1991.

El Puente's innovative arts program includes a dance ensemble, posed here in front of the Williamsburg Bridge, a short distance from the group's Williamsburg headquarters. El Puente has translated traditional Latino political activism into innovative educational programming that helps teens address their problems and work toward building Brooklyn's future. Photograph by Katherine McGlynn, courtesy of El Puente.

nineteenth-century homes of free African Americans, children learn the art of storytelling and how to document their families' histories. The Brooklyn Bridge anchorage becomes an art gallery in summer months, and under the bridge, "Bargemusic" offers classical concerts to audiences gently rocked by the wakes of passing ships. At the bandshell in Prospect Park, summer audiences enjoy music and theater, Brooklyn's burgeoning art scene in Williamsburg and Red Hook includes numerous artists' studios, and Fort Greene has become a center for a growing number of African American musicians and artists.

Community spirit, Brooklynites have learned, does not depend on a baseball team after all, but springs from a quality that belongs to Brooklynites themselves. This spirit, fed by the creative union of the city's rich heritage, the cultural diversity brought by wave after wave of new residents, and the energy of its people portends well for the borough's future. For the powerful stories that come out of this dynamic mix—tales of human hopes and hard work, of community building, of cooperation and mutuality of interest—rarely make the evening news or the front page. Yet they give heart and soul and life to the borough's brownstones and bridges, to Coney Island and Brooklyn Heights, to every block in every neighborhood that is Brooklyn.

Bibliographical Essay

Brooklyn! An Illustrated History draws upon diverse materials and literature, much of which can be found at The Brooklyn Historical Society, whose library and museum collections constitute the single greatest collection of Brooklyn-related materials. Among the primary sources are newspapers, including the *Long Island Star*, the *Brooklyn Daily Eagle*, and the *Brooklyn Citizen* (as well as such contemporary newspapers as the *New York Times*, the *New York Daily News*, and *New York Newsday*); nineteenth-century illustrated magazines such as *Harper's Weekly* and *Frank Leslie's Illustrated Newspaper*; the U.S. census; city directories; city guidebooks; newspaper-clippings files; company and personal records; diaries; and a variety of manuscript and archival resources. In addition, such visual resources as maps, photographs, paintings, prints, broadsides, and advertisements were heavily used.

Several general Brooklyn-related secondary works proved indispensable. Nineteenth-century compiler Henry Stiles's massive histories of the City of Brooklyn (published by subscription, 1867–70) and Kings County (1884) are incomparable resources for the period through the late nineteenth century. The group of pamphlets and books published by Brooklyn Rediscovery in the late 1970s and early 1980s is invaluable, in particular David Ment's *Shaping of a City: A Brief History of Brooklyn*, Joshua Brown's and David Ment's *Factories, Foundries, and Refineries: A History of Five Brooklyn Industries*, and the *Brooklyn Almanac*. The complete series is listed under suggested reading for Brooklyn and New York City history in general. The *Brooklyn Neighborhood Book*, published by the Fund for the Borough of Brooklyn, Inc. in 1985 was invaluable for the study of neighborhood development, as were the neighborhood profiles published by the Brooklyn In Touch Information Center. Brooklyn College's volume, edited by Rita Seiden Miller, titled *Brooklyn U.S.A.: The Fourth Largest City in America*, contains numerous brief articles on various aspects of Brooklyn history. The New Muse Museum's *Introduction to the Black Contribution to the Development of Brooklyn* (1977) is a helpful source on African American history in Brooklyn, particularly for the nineteenth century. *The Encyclopedia of New York City*, edited by Kenneth T. Jackson (New Haven: Yale University Press, 1995) is a comprehensive compilation with extensive coverage of Brooklyn topics. *The Journal of Long Island History*, published by The Brooklyn (then Long Island) Historical Society until 1982, contains many useful articles on Brooklyn history.

For books that focus on visual depictions of Brooklyn, standouts are: *Brooklyn Before the Bridge: American Paintings from The Long Island Historical Society* (Brooklyn Museum, 1982); William Lee Younger's *Old Brooklyn in Early Pho-*

tographs, 1865–1929 (New York: Dover, 1978); John A. Kouwenhoven's *Columbia Historical Portrait of New York* (Garden City, N.Y.: Doubleday, 1953); and I. N. Phelps Stokes's *Iconography of Manhattan Island, 1498–1909* (New York: R. H. Dodd, 1915–1928). Norval White and Elliot Willensky's *AIA Guide to New York City* (New York: Macmillan, 1978), and Andrew S. Dolkart's book with photographs by Tony Velez, *This is Brooklyn: A Guide to the Borough's Historic Districts and Landmarks* (New York: The Fund for the Borough of Brooklyn, 1990) offer extensive information about Brooklyn neighborhoods, architecture, and landmarks, accompanied by contemporary photographs.

Published firsthand accounts provided additional helpful insight: Jasper Danckaerts and Peter Sluyter's *Journal of a Voyage to New York,* first published in Brooklyn (with the spelling Dankars) in 1867; Moreau de St. Méry's *American Journey (1793–1798)*; Gabriel Furman's diary of life in Brooklyn in the early nineteenth century; Timothy Dwight's *Travels; In New-England and New-York,* 1821; and Frederika Bremer's *Homes of the New World,* 1853. Complete citations can be found in the list of suggested reading.

This book would not have been possible without the numerous documentation, exhibition, and oral-history projects that The Brooklyn Historical Society has undertaken over the years. Many of the exhibitions' interpretive brochures can be found in the Society's library. The exhibitions, with their curators in parentheses, include: "AIDS/BROOKLYN" (Robert Rosenberg); "Another Side of Brooklyn's Renaissance: The Community Housing Movement" (Jim Sleeper, photographs by Stephen L. Senigo); "Art & Nature: Views of Prospect Park 1870–1915" (Ellen M. Snyder-Grenier); "At Home in Brooklyn" (Mary Childs Black, photographs by Dinanda Nooney); "Black Churches & Brooklyn" (Ruth Ann Stewart); "Black Women of Brooklyn," cosponsored with the Society for the Preservation of Weeksville and Bedford-Stuyvesant History (Floris Barnett Cash); "Brooklyn Baseball and the Dodgers" (Elizabeth Reich Rawson); "Brooklyn Neighborhoods and How they Grew" (Elizabeth Reich Rawson); "Brooklyn's History Museum" (Ellen M. Snyder-Grenier); "Crown Heights: Perceptions and Realities," part of "The Crown Heights History Project" (Jill Vexler and Craig Wilder, codirectors); "The Giglio: Brooklyn's Dancing Tower" (I. Sheldon Posen and Joseph Sciorra); "The Great Divine: Brooklyn's Henry Ward Beecher" (Elizabeth Reich Rawson); "In Transit: Two Centuries of Commuting in Brooklyn" (researched by Allen Steinberg); "New World Encounters: Jasper Danckaerts' View of Indian Life in 17th-Century Brooklyn" (Robert S. Grumet); "Volunteer Firefighting in 19th Century Brooklyn" (Judith M. Giuriceo, Daniel Barron, and Rose Garvin; researched by Stephen J. Sullivan); "The Old Dutch Homesteads of Brooklyn" (Eric Nooter); "¿Por Qué Brooklyn? Our Borough's Latino Voices" (Ellen M. Snyder-Grenier and Jill Vexler); "Rediscovering Green-Wood Cemetery" (Ellen M. Snyder-Grenier).

Oral histories and photodocumentation are available in the library of the Society for many of the documentation and oral-history projects, which include: Brooklyn's Hispanic Communities Documentation Project, by Morton Marks with photographs by Tony Velez, and the earlier pioneer Puerto Rican community oral-history project; Stephen J. Sullivan's work on firefighting in Brooklyn; Susan Lindee's work on Pfizer and penicillin, documented in *Yellow Magic: The Story of Penicillin, Teacher's Curriculum Guide* (New York: The Brooklyn Historical Society, 1992); the Chinese community of Sunset Park in collaboration with Manhattan's Museum of the Chinese in the Americas, Gregory A. Ruf, project director; Brooklyn's West Indian Carnival, Dwandalyn Reece King, curator and project director.

Suggested Reading

Brooklyn and New York City History in General

"A New Day Dawns in Brooklyn." *New York.* Special issue. April 21, 1986.

Bookbinder, Bernie. *City of the World: New York and Its People.* New York: Abrams, 1989.

Brooklyn Daily Eagle. Series on Brooklyn's six original townships: *Brooklyn (Breukelen), New Utrecht, Bushwick, Flatbush, Flatlands, Gravesend.* Brooklyn: Brooklyn Eagle Press, no date.

Brooklyn Museum. *Brooklyn Before the Bridge: American Paintings from The Long Island Historical Society.* Brooklyn: Brooklyn Museum, 1982.

Brown, Joshua, and David Ment. *Factories, Foundries, and Refineries: A History of Five Brooklyn Industries.* New York: Brooklyn Educational & Cultural Alliance, 1980.

Christman, Henry M., ed. *Walt Whitman's New York: From Manhattan to Montauk.* New York: Macmillan, 1963.

Dankars, Jaspar, and Peter Sluyter. *Journal of a Voyage to New York.* Ann Arbor, Mich.: University Microfilms, 1966. Reprint of *Journal of a Voyage to New York and a Tour in Several of the American Colonies in 1679–1680,* 1867.

Frommer, Myrna Katz, and Harvey Frommer. *It Happened in Brooklyn: An Oral History of Growing Up in the Borough in the 1940s, '50s, and '60s.* New York: Harcourt Brace, 1993.

Glueck, Grace, and Paul Gardner. *Brooklyn: People and Places, Past and Present.* New York: Abrams, 1991.

Hamill, Pete. "Brooklyn: The Sane Alternative." *New York.* July 14, 1969, pp. 24–33.

Jackson, Kenneth T., ed. *The Encyclopedia of New York City.* New Haven: Yale University Press, 1995.

Kouwenhoven, John A. *Columbia Historical Portrait of New York.* Garden City, N.Y.: Doubleday, 1953.

Latimer, Margaret. *Two Cities: New York and Brooklyn the Year the Great Bridge Opened.* New York: Brooklyn Educational & Cultural Alliance, 1983.

———, ed. *Brooklyn Almanac.* New York: Brooklyn Educational & Cultural Alliance, 1984.

Leisner, Marcia. *Literary Neighborhoods of New York*. Washington, D.C.: Starrhill, 1989.

Lopate, Carol. *Education and Culture in Brooklyn: A History of Ten Institutions*. New York: Brooklyn Educational & Cultural Alliance, 1979.

McCullough, David W. *Brooklyn . . . and How It Got That Way*. New York: Dial, 1983.

Ment, David, and Mary S. Donovan. *The People of Brooklyn: A History of Two Neighborhoods*. New York: Brooklyn Educational & Cultural Alliance, 1980.

Ment, David, Anthony Robins, and David Framberger. *Building Blocks of Brooklyn: A Study of Urban Growth*. New York: Brooklyn Educational & Cultural Alliance, 1979.

Miller, Rita Seiden, ed. *Brooklyn U.S.A.: The Fourth Largest City in America*. Brooklyn: Brooklyn College Press, 1979.

Mills, Thomas. *Rediscovering Brooklyn History: A Guide to Research Collections*. New York: Brooklyn Educational & Cultural Alliance, 1978.

Miska, Maxine, and I. Sheldon Posen. *Tradition and Community in the Urban Neighborhood: Making Brooklyn Home*. New York: Brooklyn Educational & Cultural Alliance, 1983.

New Muse Community Museum of Brooklyn. *An Introduction to the Black Contribution to the Development of Brooklyn*. Brooklyn: New Muse Community Museum of Brooklyn, 1977.

Roberts, Kenneth, and Anna M. Roberts, ed. and trans. *Moreau de St. Méry's American Journey (1793–1798)*. Garden City, N.Y.: Doubleday, 1947.

Ross, Peter. *A History of Long Island, from Its Earliest Settlement to the Present Time*. New York: Lewis, 1902.

Schroth, Raymond A. *The Eagle and Brooklyn: A Community Newspaper 1841–1953*. Westport, Conn.: Greenwood, 1974.

Small, Linda Lee, Deborah Romano, Diane Moogan, Lenore Jenkins-Abramson, with research by Joseph Sciorra, Nanette Rainone, ed. *The Brooklyn Neighborhood Book*. New York: Fund for the Borough of Brooklyn, Inc., 1985.

Spann, Edward K. *The New Metropolis: New York City, 1840–1857*. New York: Columbia University Press, 1981.

Stiles, Henry R. *History of the City of Brooklyn*. 3 vols. Brooklyn: Published by subscription, 1867–70.

———, ed. *The Civil, Political, Professional, and Ecclesiastical History and Commercial and Industrial Record of the County of Kings and the City of Brooklyn, New York, from 1683–1884*. 2 vols. New York: W. W. Munsell, 1884.

Stokes, I. N. Phelps. *The Iconography of Manhattan Island, 1498–1909*. New York: R. H. Dodd, 1915–1928.

Weld, Ralph Foster. *Brooklyn Is America*. New York: Columbia University Press, 1950.

———. *Brooklyn Village, 1816–1834*. New York: Columbia University Press, 1938.

White, Norval, and Elliot Willensky. *The A.I.A. Guide to New York City*. New York: Macmillan, 1978.

Willensky, Elliot. *When Brooklyn Was the World, 1920–1957*. New York: Harmony, 1986.

Wolfe, Thomas. "Only the Dead Know Brooklyn." In *From Death to Morning*. New York: Scribner, 1935.

Younger, William Lee. *Old Brooklyn in Early Photographs, 1865–1929.* New York: Dover, 1978.

Brooklynites

Brooklynites on Film and Television

Brooklyn Rediscovery. *Brooklyn on Film.* Working Paper No. 1. New York: Brooklyn Educational & Cultural Alliance, 1979.

McCrohan, Donna. *The Honeymooner's Companion: The Kramdens and the Nortons Revisited.* New York: Workman, 1978.

Immigration, Migration, Cultural Groups

Blackburn, Roderic. *Remembrance of Patria: Dutch Arts and Culture in Colonial America 1609–1776.* Albany, New York: Albany Institute of History and Art, 1988.

Brooklyn Historical Society. *Brooklyn's Hispanic Communities.* Brooklyn: The Brooklyn Historical Society, 1989. Text by Morton Marks with photographs by Tony Velez.

Cohen, David Steven. *The Dutch–American Farm.* New York: New York University Press, 1992.

Colón, Jesús. *A Puerto Rican in New York and Other Sketches.* New York: International, 1982.

Connolly, Harold X. *A Ghetto Grows in Brooklyn.* New York: New York University Press, 1977.

Crew, Spencer R. *Field to Factory: Afro-American Migration 1915 -1940.* Washington, D.C.: Smithsonian Institution, 1987.

Diffin, Debra. "A Demographic Study of the Irish in Brooklyn for Wards 1, 2, and 10." Brooklyn Historical Society, Brooklyn, 1976. Manuscript.

Foner, Nancy, ed. *New Immigrants in New York.* New York: Columbia University Press, 1987.

Graydon, Alexander. *Memoirs of His Own Time. With Reminiscences of the Men and Events of the Revolution.* Ed. John Stockton Littell. Philadelphia: Lindsay & Blakiston, 1846.

Green, Albert. *Recollections of the Jersey Prison-Ship; Taken, and Prepared for Publication, from the Original Manuscript of the Late Captain Thomas Dring . . .* Providence, R.I.: H. H. Brown, 1829.

Grumet, Robert S. *The Lenapes.* New York: Chelsea House, 1989.

History of the Brooklyn and Long Island [Sanitary] Fair, February 22, 1864. Brooklyn, New York: "The Union," Steam Presses, 1864.

Horne, Lena, and Richard Schickel. *Lena.* Garden City, N.Y.: Doubleday, 1965.

Howe, Irving. *World of Our Fathers: The Journey of the East European Jews to America and the Life They Found and Made.* New York: Harcourt Brace Jovanovich, 1976.

Iglesias, César Andreu, ed. *Memoirs of Bernardo Vega: A Contribution to the History of the Puerto Rican Community in New York.* Trans. Juan Flores. New York: Monthly Review Press, 1984.

Judd, Jacob. "Brooklyn's Changing Population in the Pre-Civil War Era." *Journal of Long Island History* 4, no. 2 (Spring 1964): 9–18.

———. "The History of Brooklyn, 1834–1855: Political and Administrative Aspects." Ph.D. diss., New York University, 1959.

Kasinitz, Philip. *Caribbean New York: Black Immigrants and the Politics of Race.* Ithaca, N.Y.: Cornell University Press, 1992.

Kessner, Thomas. *The Golden Door: Italian and Jewish Immigrant Mobility in New York City 1880–1915.* New York: Oxford University Press, 1977.

Kiser, Clyde Vernon. *Sea Island to City: A Study of St. Helena Islanders in Harlem and Other Urban Centers.* New York: Columbia University Press, 1932.

Klingle, Philip. "Kings County during the American Revolution." In *Brooklyn U.S.A.: The Fourth Largest City in America,* ed. Rita Seiden Miller, Brooklyn: Brooklyn College Press, 1979.

Korrol, Virginia Sánchez. *From Colonia to Community: The History of Puerto Ricans in New York City, 1917–1948.* Westport, Conn.: Greenwood, 1983.

Kwong, Peter. *The New Chinatown.* New York: Noonday, 1987.

Landesman, Alter F. *Brownsville: the Birth, Development, and Passing of a Jewish Community in New York.* New York: Bloch, 1969.

———. *A History of New Lots, Brooklyn to 1887, including the Villages of East New York, Cypress Hills, and Brownsville.* Port Washington, New York: Kennekat 1977.

Leed, Mark. *Passport's Guide to Ethnic New York: A Complete Guide to the Many Faces and Cultures of New York.* Chicago: NTC, 1991.

Marshall, Paule. "The Rising Islanders of Bed-Stuy." *New York Times Magazine,* 3 November, 1985.

Moore, Deborah Dash. *At Home in America: Second Generation New York Jews.* New York: Columbia University Press, 1981.

Palone, Anne Marie Barba. *East Flatbush: a Neighborhood History.* Brooklyn: Neighborhood Housing Services of East Flatbush, 1994.

Posen, I. Sheldon, and Joseph Sciorra. "Brooklyn's Dancing Tower." *Natural History,* (June 1983): 31–37.

Ridge, John T. *The Flatbush Irish.* Brooklyn, New York: The Ancient Order of Hibernians, 1983.

Rosenwaike, Ira. *The Population History of New York City.* Syracuse: Syracuse University Press, 1972.

Sharp, John Kean. *History of the Diocese of Brooklyn, 1853–1953.* 2 vols. New York: Fordham University Press, 1954.

Skemer, Don C. "New Evidence on Black Unrest in Colonial Brooklyn." *Journal of Long Island History* 12 (Fall 1975): 46–49.

Stayton, Kevin L. *Dutch by Design: Tradition and Change in Two Historic Brooklyn Houses: The Schenck Houses at the Brooklyn Museum.* New York: Brooklyn Museum/Phaidon Universe, 1990.

Sunset Park: A Time Remembered. Brooklyn: Sunset Park Restoration Committee, no date.

Sutton, Constance R., and Elsa M. Chaney, eds. *Caribbean Life in New York City: Social and Cultural Dimensions.* New York: Center for Migration Studies, 1987.

Swan, Robert J. "The Black Presence in Seventeenth-Century Brooklyn." *De Halve Maen* 63, 4 (December 1990):1–6.

Syrett, Harold Coffin. *The City of Brooklyn, 1865–1898: A Political History.* New York: AMS Press, 1968.

Taylor, Clarence. *The Black Churches of Brooklyn.* New York: Columbia University Press, 1994.

The Brooklyn Bridge

Building the Bridge

Brooklyn Museum. *The Great East River Bridge, 1883–1983.* New York: Brooklyn Museum, 1983.

McCullough, David. *The Great Bridge: The Epic Story of the Building of the Brooklyn Bridge.* New York: Simon & Schuster, 1972.

Trachtenberg, Alan. *Brooklyn Bridge: Fact and Symbol.* Chicago: University of Chicago Press, 1965.

Brooklyn and New York

Hammack, David C. *Power and Society: Greater New York at the Turn of the Century.* New York: Russell Sage, 1982.

Morley, Christopher. *Parnassus on Wheels.* New York: Grosset & Dunlap, 1917. Reprint, Philadelphia: Lippincott, 1955.

Neighborhood and Transportation Development

Bremer, Frederika. *The Homes of the New World.* 2 vols. New York: Harper, 1853.

Connolly, Harold X. *A Ghetto Grows in Brooklyn.* New York: New York University Press, 1977.

Dolkart, Andrew, with photographs by Tony Velez. *This is Brooklyn: A Guide to the Borough's Historic Districts and Landmarks.* New York: The Fund for the Borough of Brooklyn, 1990.

Hood, Clifton. *722 Miles: The Building of the Subways and How They Transformed New York.* New York: Simon & Schuster, 1993.

Jackson, Kenneth T. *Crabgrass Frontier: The Suburbanization of the United States.* New York: Oxford University Press, 1985.

Lancaster, Clay. *Old Brooklyn Heights: New York's First Suburb.* 2d ed. New York: Dover, 1979.

Marshall, Paule. *Brown Girl, Brownstone.* New York: Random House, 1959.

Pierrepont, Henry E. *Historical Sketch of the Fulton Ferry, and its Associated Ferries.* Brooklyn: printed for the private use of the [Union Ferry] Company, 1879.

The Brooklyn Navy Yard

The Brooklyn Navy Yard

Miller, Nathan. *The U.S. Navy: An Illustrated History.* New York: American Heritage; Annapolis: U.S. Naval Institute, 1977.

Palisi, Joseph. "The Brooklyn Navy Yard." In *Brooklyn U.S.A.: The Fourth Largest City in America,* ed. Rita Seiden Miller. Brooklyn: Brooklyn College Press, 1979.

The Shipworker (house organ of the Brooklyn Navy Yard). Microfilm at The Brooklyn Historical Society, 1941–1966.

West, James H. *A Short History of the New York Navy Yard.* Typescript pamphlet at The Brooklyn Historical Society. Brooklyn, 1941.

Witteman, Adolph. *U.S. Navy Yard, Brooklyn.* New York: Albertype, 1904.

Port of New York, Industry, Commerce, Workers

Albion, Robert Greenhalgh, with Jennie Barnes Pope. *The Rise of New York Port (1815–1860).* New York: Scribner's, 1939.

Anderson, Will. *The Breweries of Brooklyn, New York.* Published by the author, 1976.

Bendersky, Jay. *Brooklyn's Waterfront Railways: A Pictorial Journey.* East Meadows, N.Y.: Meatball Productions, 1988.

Chafe, William H. *The American Woman: Her Changing Social, Economic, and Political Roles, 1920–1970.* New York: Oxford University Press, 1972.

Daly, Robert W., ed. *Aboard the U.S.S. Monitor, 1862.* Annapolis: U.S. Naval Institute, 1964.

DiFazio, William. *Longshoremen: Community and Resistance on the Brooklyn Waterfront.* South Hadley, Mass.: Bergin & Garvy, 1985.

Dreiser, Theodore. *Sister Carrie, a Novel.* New York: Boni & Liveright, 1917.

Dwight, Timothy. *Travels; In New-England and New York . . . in Four Volumes.* New Haven, Conn.: Timothy Dwight, 1821.

Hill, Isabel. "Made in Brooklyn." Brooklyn: Isabel Hill Productions, 1993. Video.

Hillier, Bevis. *Pottery and Porcelain, 1700–1914: England, Europe, and North America.* New York: Meredity Press, 1968.

Landmarks Preservation Commission. *Greenpoint Historic District Designation Report, City of New York.* New York: Landmarks Preservation Commission, 1982.

McCullers, Carson. *The Mortgaged Heart.* Boston: Houghton Mifflin, 1956.

Randolph, A. Philip. "Keynote Address to the March on Washington Movement." In *Documentary History of the Modern Civil Rights Movement,* ed. Peter B. Levy. Westport, Conn.: Greenwood, 1992.

Tax, Meredith. *The Rising of the Women: Feminist Solidarity and Class Conflict, 1880–1917.* New York: Monthly Review Press, 1980.

Coney Island

Coney Island

Bogart, Michele H. "Barking Architecture: The Sculpture of Coney Island." *Smithsonian Studies in American Art* 2 no. 1 (Winter 1988): 3–17.

Dreiser, Theodore. *The Color of a Great City.* New York: Boni and Liveright, 1923.

Fried, Frederick, and Mary Fried. *America's Forgotten Folk Arts.* New York: Pantheon, 1978.

Fried, Frederick. *A Pictorial History of the Carousel.* New York: Barnes, 1964.

Ierardi, Eric J. *Gravesend: The Home of Coney Island.* New York: Vantage Press, 1975.

Kasson, John F. *Amusing the Million: Coney Island at the Turn of the Century.* New York: Hill and Wang, 1978.

Mangels, William F. *The Outdoor Amusement Industry*. New York: Vantage Press, 1952.

McCullough, Edo. *Good Old Coney Island: A Sentimental Journey into the Past*. New York: Scribner, 1957.

Peiss, Kathy. *Cheap Amusements: Working Women and Leisure in Turn-of-the-Century New York*. Philadelphia: Temple University Press, 1986.

Pilot, Oliver, and Jo Ranson. *Sodom by the Sea: An Affectionate History of Coney Island*. Garden City, N.Y.: Doubleday, 1941.

Snow, Richard. *Coney Island: A Postcard Journey to the City of Fire*. New York: Brightwaters, 1984.

Stevenson, Beatrice L. "Working Girls' Life at Coney Island." *Yearbook of the Women's Municipal League,* November 1911.

Weinstein, Stephen F. "The Nickel Empire: Coney Island and the Creation of Urban Seaside Resorts in the United States." Ph.D. diss., Columbia University, 1984.

Public Parks Movement, Cemeteries

Beveridge, Charles E., and David Schuyler, eds. *FLO: Creating Central Park, 1857–1861*. Baltimore: Johns Hopkins University Press, 1983.

Cubertson, Judi and Tom Randell. *Permanent New Yorkers: A Biographical Guide to the Cemeteries of New York*. Chelsea, Vt.: Chelsea Green Publishing Co., 1987.

Kelly, Bruce, Gail Travis Guillet, Mary Ellen W. Hern. *Art of the Olmsted Landscape*. New York: New York City Landmarks Preservation Commission, Arts Publisher, 1981.

Schuyler, David. *The New Urban Landscape: The Redefinition of City Form in Nineteenth-Century America*. Baltimore: Johns Hopkins University Press, 1986.

Schuyler, David, and Jane Turne Censer, eds. *The Papers of Frederick Law Olmsted/Volume VI/The Years of Olmsted, Vaux & Company, 1865–1874*. Baltimore: Johns Hopkins University Press, 1992.

Simon, Donald E. "The Public Park Movement in Brooklyn, 1824–1873." Ph.D. diss., New York University, 1972.

Vaudeville, Theater, and General Leisure

Butterby, Michael and Ariane Butterby. *On the Town in New York from 1776 to the Present*. New York: Charles Scribner's Sons, 1973.

Culin, Stewart, "Street Games of Boys in Brooklyn, N.Y." *Journal of American Folklore* 4, no. 13 (April–June 1891), 221–237.

Dargan, Amanda, and Steven Zeitlin. *City Play*. New Brunswick: Rutgers University Press, 1990.

Flatbush: Architecture and Urban Development from Dutch Settlement to Commercial Strip. Preservation Working Paper No. 1. New York: Graduate School of Architecture, Planning, and Preservation, Columbia University, 1990.

Furman, Gabriel. *Antiquities of Long Island*. New York: J. W. Bouton, 1875.

———. "Extracts from His Diary 1822–1823." Typeset manuscript at The Brooklyn Historical Society.

Smith, Robert P. "Brooklyn at Play: The Illusion and the Reality, 1890–1898." Ph.D. diss., Indiana University, 1973.

Snyder, Robert W. *Voice of the City: Vaudeville and Popular Culture in New York.* New York: Oxford University Press, 1989.

Williams-Myers, A. J. *Long Hammering: Essays on the Forging of an African American Presence in the Hudson River Valley to the Early Twentieth Century.* Trenton: Africa World Press, 1994.

The Brooklyn Dodgers

Baseball in General

Adelman, Melvin L. *A Sporting Time: New York City and the Rise of Modern Athletics, 1820–70.* Urbana: University of Illinois Press, 1990.

Kirsch, George B. *The Creation of American Team Sports: Baseball and Cricket, 1838–1872.* Urbana: University of Illinois Press, 1989.

Lowry, Philip J. *Green Cathedrals.* Cooperstown, N.Y.: Society for American Baseball Research, 1986.

Riess, Steven A. *Touching Base: Professional Baseball and American Culture in the Progressive Era.* Westport, Conn.: Greenwood, 1980.

Seymour, Harold. *Baseball: The Early Years.* New York: Oxford University Press, 1960.

———. *Baseball: The Golden Age.* New York: Oxford University Press, 1971.

Smith, Robert. *World Series: The Games and the Players.* Garden City, N.Y.: Doubleday, 1967.

Voigt, David. *America through Baseball.* Chicago: Nelson-Hall, 1976.

The Dodgers

Barber, Red. *1947–When All Hell Broke Loose in Baseball.* Garden City, N.Y.: Doubleday, 1982.

Goldstein, Richard. *Superstars and Screwballs: One Hundred Years of Brooklyn Baseball.* New York: Dutton, 1991.

Golenbock, Peter. *Bums: An Oral History of the Brooklyn Dodgers.* New York: Putnam, 1984.

Graham, Frank. *The Brooklyn Dodgers: An Informal History.* New York: Putnam, 1945.

Honig, Donald. *The Brooklyn Dodgers: An Illustrated Tribute.* New York: St. Martin's Press, 1981.

Kahn, Roger. *The Boys of Summer.* New York: Perennial Library, 1987.

———. *The Era, 1947–1957: When the Yankees, the Giants, and the Dodgers Ruled the World.* New York: Ticknor and Fields, 1993.

Robinson, Jackie. *I Never Had It Made: An Autobiography.* New York: Putnam, 1972.

Sullivan, Neil J. *The Dodgers Move West.* New York: Oxford University Press, 1987.

Tygiel, Jules. *Baseball's Great Experiment: Jackie Robinson and His Legacy.* New York: Oxford University Press, 1983.

The Negro Leagues

Ashe, Arthur R., Jr. *A Hard Road to Glory: Baseball.* New York: Armistad, 1993.

Bruce, Janet. *The Kansas City Monarchs: Champions of Black Baseball.* Lawrence: University of Kansas Press, 1985.

Chadwick, Bruce. *When the Game was Black and White: The Illustrated History of Baseball's Negro Leagues.* New York: Abbeville, 1992.

Holway, John B. *Blackball Stars: Negro League Pioneers.* Westport, Conn.: Meckler, 1988.

Timeline

1636: Dutch make initial purchases in what is today Brooklyn of land until then Native American, with a history of 11,000 years of cultural development

1645: Gravesend town patent issued for the only one of the six original towns not settled by the Dutch

1646: Town of Breuckelen (Brooklyn) chartered by the Dutch West India Company

1647: Town of New Amersfoort (Flatlands) chartered

1652: Town of Midwout (Flatbush) chartered

1657: Town of New Utrecht chartered

1661: Town of Boswick (Bushwick) chartered

1664: New Netherland taken over by the English and renamed New York

1673: New York recaptured by the Dutch

1674: English rule reestablished by treaty

1683: Kings County established, comprised of six agricultural towns: Brooklyn, Bushwick, Flatbush, Flatlands, Gravesend, and New Utrecht

1684: All Brooklyn lands transferred to Europeans by Native American sachems, or chiefs, in almost two dozen deeds (1636–84)

1698: Kings County population is 2,017: 1,721 white, 296 Black

1776: Battle of Long Island, first major contest of the Revolutionary War fought on Brooklyn soil; George Washington's troops retreat across the East River to Manhattan

1783: End of British occupation with Britain's recognition of U.S. independence

1799: System of gradual emancipation of slaves begun in New York State; Brooklyn's first newspaper, the *Long Island Courier,* published

1801: Brooklyn Navy Yard established by U.S. Navy on Wallabout Bay

1812: Fortifications built at Fort Greene during War of 1812

1814: Steam-ferry service inaugurated between Brooklyn and Manhattan

1816: Village of Brooklyn incorporated within the Town of Brooklyn

1818: Brooklyn's oldest Black church, Bridge Street A.W.M.E. Church, founded

1823: Brooklyn Apprentices Library forms, forerunner of The Brooklyn Museum

1827: Village of Williamsburgh incorporated within Town of Bushwick

1827: Slavery abolished in New York State

1832: Jim de Wilt, reputed to be the last "full-blood" Native American of Brooklyn, dies at Canarsie

1834: City of Brooklyn (former Town of Brooklyn) incorporated

1838: Green-Wood Cemetery incorporated

1839: Brooklyn city plan adopted; street grid mapped

1840s–1850s: First great wave of European immigration begins around midcentury, largely northern and western Europeans

1847: Atlantic Basin completed

1849: Brooklyn City (now Brooklyn Borough) Hall completed

1851:	City of Williamsburgh chartered
1852:	Town of New Lots, formerly part of the Town of Flatbush, organized
1855:	Consolidated City of Brooklyn established, merging former City of Brooklyn with City of Williamsburgh and Town of Bushwick
1855:	47 percent of Brooklyn's population is foreign-born (compared to 51 percent of Manhattan's)
1858:	National Association of Base Ball Players (NABBP), baseball's first centralized organization, formed by delegates from New York and Brooklyn; 71 teams in Brooklyn
1860:	Brooklyn is third-largest U.S. city, with a population of almost 267,000
1861:	U.S. Civil War begins
1863:	The Brooklyn Historical Society founded as The Long Island Historical Society in Brooklyn Heights; New York City draft riots break out and violence spreads to Brooklyn
1864:	Brooklyn Long Island Sanitary Fair held at new Brooklyn Academy of Music to raise money for wives and children of impoverished Civil War draftees
1874:	Prospect Park completed; street grids mapped for Towns of Flatbush, Flatlands, New Utrecht, and Gravesend
1880s:	Second great wave of European immigration lasts into early twentieth century, largely eastern and southern Europeans
1880:	Brooklyn is fourth-largest producer of manufactured goods in nation
1881:	The Brooklyn Historical Society opens new building on Pierrepont Street in Brooklyn Heights, still its home today
1882:	Chinese Exclusion Act; repealed in 1943
1883:	Brooklyn Bridge completed; Dodgers organized as minor-league team in Brooklyn
1886:	Town of New Lots annexed to Brooklyn
1894:	Towns of Flatbush, Gravesend, and New Utrecht annexed to the City of Brooklyn

1896:	Town of Flatlands annexed to the City of Brooklyn
1897:	Brooklyn Public Library formed; Steeplechase Park opens in Coney Island
1898:	City of Brooklyn (Kings County) consolidated into Greater New York
1902:	Bush Terminal erects new buildings
1903:	Williamsburg Bridge opens; Luna Park opens in Coney Island
1904:	Dreamland opens in Coney Island
1908:	The IRT, New York's first subway, connected to Brooklyn via the Joralemon Street tunnel
1909:	Manhattan Bridge opens
1913:	Ebbets Field, home to the Brooklyn Dodgers, opens
1915:	Brooklyn Navy Yard builds *Arizona, New Mexico*, and other battleships
1915:	"Great Migration" of African Americans from America's rural South, continues through 1930s and is followed by renewed migration from the South during and after World War II
1917:	United States gives citizenship to Puerto Ricans; beginning of large migration to Brooklyn and New York area
1919:	Brooklyn Army Terminal completed
1920:	Subway arrives at Coney Island
1924:	Immigration Act of 1924; United States enacts restrictive legislation, aimed largely at southern and eastern Europeans, which sharply reduces immigration for next forty years
1930:	Brooklyn is New York City's most populous borough, population 2,560,401
1936:	IND (Independent) subway opens in Brooklyn
1941:	Attack on U.S. naval base at Pearl Harbor triggers U.S. entry into World War II
1942:	*Iowa* launched in record time at Brooklyn Navy Yard; U.S. Navy transforms Floyd Bennett Field, New York City's first airport, into naval air training station

1947: Jackie Robinson joins the Dodgers as the first African American player in the major leagues

1950: Brooklyn's population peaks at 2,738,175

1955: *The Honeymooners* appears as a weekly thirty-minute series on CBS

1955: Brooklyn Dodgers win World Series against longtime rival New York Yankees

1955: *Brooklyn Eagle* folds after 114-year run

1957: Dodgers play their last game at Ebbets Field; leave for California and become L.A. Dodgers

1964: Verrazano Narrows Bridge completed, the longest suspension bridge in the world

1965: U.S. immigration laws ease; new immigrants mainly of Caribbean, Latin American, and Asian origin

1966: Brooklyn Navy Yard closes; in early 1970s City of New York and local nonprofit groups begin to transform into an industrial park

1966: Brooklyn Heights designated New York's first historic district

1969: West Indian/American Day Carnival parades along Brooklyn's Eastern Parkway for the first time; for many years had been held in Harlem

1977: Fulton Mall built in downtown Brooklyn

1983: Centennial of Brooklyn Bridge celebrated

1990: Brooklyn remains New York City's most populous borough; population of 2,300,664 the equivalent of the fourth-largest city in the nation after New York City, Los Angeles, and Chicago

1995: World Series banner won by Brooklyn Dodgers in 1955 donated to The Brooklyn Historical Society by the L.A. Dodgers

Index

Brooklyn City Water Works, *9*
Brooklyn College, 12, 108
Brooklyn Daily Eagle, 10
   on African Americans in Brooklyn, 43
   on automobiles in Brooklyn, 113
   baseball coverage in, 221, 222–25,
     227–30, 233, 238, 245
   on Brooklyn Navy Yard, 33, 118, 126,
     134, 157, 159, 161
   on Coney Island, 182, 206, 209–10,
     214
   on rapid transit in Brooklyn, 100,
     103–4, 109, 111
   on Manhattan, 81
Brooklyn Daily Times, 39–40, 99–100,
   147, 149, 206–7
Brooklyn Dodgers, 2, 218–53
   departure for Los Angeles of, 12
   golden age of, 240–51
   as minor-league team, 232–36
   move to Ebbets Field, 237–39
   origin of team name, 104
   as pennant winners (1899–1900), 234
   relocation to Los Angeles, 251–53
   World Series of 1947, 218–19
   World Series winners in 1955, 249–51
Brooklyn Dodgers Baseball Hall of Fame,
   253
Brooklyn Eagles, 235
Brooklyn Economic Development Cor-
   poration, 258
Brooklyn Evening Star, 225, 226
Brooklyn Female Academy, 36
Brooklyn Flint Glass, 147
Brooklyn Gas Light Company, 28
Brooklyn Gazette, 106
Brooklyn Heights, 83, 89–91
   origins of, 6, 86–88
   residential restoration in, 256–57
   waterfront development in, 142
Brooklyn Heights Association, Inc., 257
Brooklyn Historical Society, 8, 36,
   74–76, 83, 138, 260
Brooklyn Hospital, 55
Brooklyn Jewish Hospital, 135
Brooklyn Jockey Club, 181
Brooklyn Long Island Sanitary Fair, 39
Brooklyn Lyceum of Natural History, 28
Brooklyn Metal Trades Council, 161
Brooklyn Museum, 10, 28, *99,* 260–61
Brooklyn Navy Yard, 2, 27, 33–34,
   45–46, 118–65, 219
   asbestosis in workers from, 130
   closing of, 159–62

early history of, 122–26, 223
   security at, 130–31
   women workers at, 128–33
   World War II wartime production in,
     119, 126–36
Brooklyn Public Library, 10, *99*
Brooklyn Rapid Transit (BRT), 100
Brooklyn Royal Giants (baseball team),
   231, 235–36
Brooklyn Standard Union, 231
Brooklyn Temperance Society for Free
   People of Color, 140
Brooklyn Times, 159–60, 175–76, 194
Brooklyn Trust Company, 239
Brooklyn Wharf and Warehouse Com-
   pany, 153
Brooklyn-Battery Tunnel, 67
Brooklyn-Queens Expressway, 67, 88,
   116, 159, 254, 257
Brotherhood League, 232
Brotherhood of Sleeping Car Porters,
   133
Brown, Charles S., *99*
Brownsville, 48, 83, 99–103, *232–33,*
   257
Buffalo Bill's Wild West Show, 11
Burns, Mary, 32
Bush, Irving T., 156
Bush Terminal, 155–58
Bushwick, 7, 80
Bushwicks (baseball team), 231
Byrne, Charles, 232, 235

Cagney, Michael, 32
Caiafo, Jennie, 44
Caiafo, Louisa and Michael, 43
caisson disease, 72–74
Calhoun, John C., 171
Camilli, Dolph, 241, 243
Cammeyer, William, 225
Campanella, Roy, 219, 241, 245
Canarsies (Native Americans), 18
Canarsie neighborhood, 112
Capitoline Skating Grounds, 225–26
Capote, Truman, 90–91
Carey, Max, 239
Caribbean immigrants in Brooklyn,
   55–57, 64, 108–9, 132
Carnival festival, 56–57
Carroll Gardens, 15, 67
Carrville, 41–42, 91–94
Casano, Angelo P., 135
Casey, Hugh, 242
Cashmore, John, 245